Her Story

Kelly's Ordinary Life in Extraordinary Times: 2020

Her Story

Kelly's Ordinary Life in Extraordinary Times: 2020

By Kelly M. Hackman

Copyright © 2024 Kelly M. Hackman

All rights reserved. This book or any portion thereof may not be reproduced or used in any manner without the express written permission of the publisher except for the use of brief quotations in a book review.

ISBN: 979-8-9912431-0-0

Library of Congress Control Number: 2024916520

This work depicts actual events in the life of the author as truthfully as recollection permits. While all persons within are actual individuals, full names and identifying characteristics have been changed or removed to respect their privacy.

Self-published by: Kelly M. Hackman, New Port Richey, Florida 34653

www.kellymhackman.com

*For my mom, who embraces every idea I have, practical or not.
I love you so much and appreciate how much you support me in everything I do!*

Acknowledgments

I have been so blessed in my life, to have so many people encouraging me, no matter what I'm doing.

First and foremost, I want to thank my husband, Bryan, who stands beside me, in front of me, and behind me, to give me whatever support I need to be successful. I don't know how I ever got so lucky to find the love of my life, and someone who never questions my ideas, but steps up and askes what he can do to support me.

Equally as encouraging, my mom, Debra, has been my number one and biggest cheerleader my entire life. Whenever I say I want to do something, including finishing this book, she is the first to offer her support and help to make it happen. I don't know how I ever got so lucky to have such a great and loving mom.

Thank you my amazing friend, and editor, Courtney Boettcher, for reading my very rough manuscript and helping me make sense of it all. I know it wasn't easy but I appreciate you taking your time to help me make this dream of mine come true.

Thank you to my friend Jennifer O'Conner, for helping me pick up the pieces of a shattered cover design, and putting together something that is simple, but cute, and totally what I envisioned for my cover to be. You are such an amazing talent and I hope this is the first of many covers and design projects we get to work on.

Thank you to my cousin-in-law, Mark and my cousin Kim. Both of them have been so supportive of my writing. In fact, it was at Mark's encouragement that I even put this book together. I appreciate that he sees my passion for the written word and encouraged me to take this step.

In addition to these to amazing people, I would not be where I am today without so many countless others. It would be nearly impossible to thank everyone so please know that if you are in my life in any way, I am forever thankful for you and appreciate you and all of the love and support you have given me and continue to give me every day.

Thank you!

Introduction

I think I've always been a writer. I don't remember exactly when I started writing or when I actually started enjoying it, but I know I was young.

My first recollection of writing something for fun was a contest put on by local churches in the area. I was in fifth grade when my mom showed me our local bulletin, calling for entries into an essay contest for the local Knights of Columbus chapter. Being the ever-creative type, I thought why not give it a try. Apparently, it must have been pretty good, even at that early age, because I took second place in the contest.

I continued my daily writing practice the way most young girls did—by keeping a diary. Looking back, it was filled with silly kid stuff, but it was writing practice none the less.

In my youth, I explored other creative avenues, mainly music. Music, like writing, has always been in my soul. I don't know what it is, but there is something that hits my very core when I hear violin, cello, and brass—not that I don't love woodwinds, I started on clarinet. My family can tell you; music lives in my soul; I feel it and am moved by it. As I progressed through school, music played a critical role in the person I was to become. I participated in the band program from fifth grade until I graduated. Now, some twenty years later, not a day goes by that I'm not thankful for each and every musical experience.

Being involved in music helped keep my creative curiosity alive, and it wasn't until I was a senior in high school that I took my first creative writing class. I became hooked on writing again. Gosh, that class was great! We would walk in each day and there would be a writing prompt on the board, which we had ten to fifteen minutes to just write. Whatever came to mind, wherever our minds took us—we were free to express ourselves and do what came naturally.

I chose not to pursue a career in writing for two reasons.

First, I did not pursue a career as a writer because, back at that time, most writing was done for journalism. It's not that I can't write newspaper articles or interview someone, but writing for news and magazines is much different than using your creative voice to write what you want. I only saw the potential for writing for a newspaper, not to pursue my creative desire, and so I chose not to pursue writing as a career or to go to school for it.

Second, as much as my mom loved my desire to be creative, she had concerns over the ability to actually make a living as a writer. She and I often talk about her advice, and while many people would be upset at their family member for discouraging them to follow their heart, her advice actually saved me a lot of heartache. It also allowed me a chance to follow different avenues, such as being involved in my community, running events, getting a degree in Political Science (which I don't use) with a minor in American History (which I got to research and write a lot about), and to finally becoming a small business owner. Had I pursued and struggled in my search to be a writer, I doubt I would have the amount of content that now crowds my brain and leaves me with an endless array of topics to explore and write about.

Becoming involved in my community and working to make it a better place became my life goal. I am fortunate to live in a smaller community surrounded by bigger communities. Consequently, I wanted to help preserve our small-town way of life, while at the same time working to make our community a well-rounded place for all ages. With a sense of purpose to do all I could for my community, I adjusted my role and focus to do just that. That also meant that writing often fell to second or even tenth priority. I continued to write in my journal when I found the time, but that was often few and far between. If I looked back in my latest journal, I believe there would be several years where I didn't take the time to write. What a bummer.

All of that changed when our world changed in 2020.

It was never my intention to create a blog or become a voice for others, to encourage and provide a light spot in a world that seemed to have gone dark. However, I, like so many other people, returned to things that made them happy as a way to escape the day-to-day trials of dealing with a world-wide pandemic.

I will never forget the days leading up to our business's closing in March 2020. I was sitting in my tiny closet office at my tea shop, The White Heron Tea & Gifts, watching news conference after news conference, anxiety building, until we finally heard that our businesses were too close to the public for several weeks. Owning several businesses and having staff that rely on you for their livelihood and survival, it became abundantly clear that I had to remain positive and utilize my creative abilities for all of us to come out of this as unscathed as possible. We were lucky. But what about the rest of our community?

So many were people were secluded during this time. I have so many friends that didn't leave their house for weeks on end. Seclusion is a very scary thing. It often leads to anxiety and depression, which can then lead to sickness, which is the last thing we wanted. We are naturally social creatures. We thrive in social environments, and then all at once we found ourselves cut off.

In this dark time, I did the only thing that I knew how to do…I wrote. I took to my social media page to write about my day, one of the first days of the lockdown. I decided to share what I was going through and what I was doing—to share about my businesses, my team and my family. I started with one day. I had a few friends comment on how they enjoyed seeing something positive. So, I wrote a second day, and a third, and I just kept writing. Even on days that I didn't have much going on—I just kept writing.

I wrote so much that when businesses started reopening, I would run into friends and they would tell me how refreshing it was to read about my day, that they enjoyed reading about my adventures, my trials, my successes and my stresses. I made them feel...like they were not alone. I just chose to publicly share my time with my friends on social media.

I never wrote my blogs on social media with the intention of turning them into a book, but after the encouragement of my cousin Mark, I decided to take a swing at it. Mark read my daily postings all through Covid and enjoyed my writing so much that he continuously told me I needed to write a book. At each of his suggestions, I told him that I didn't know what to write about. What type of book could I possibly write? Then, one day, he replied with, "you have already written so much with your blog, why don't you use that as your book." That was my 'a-ha' moment. That moment that I realized, through all this trial and tribulation, through good and bad, I had been creating my book without realizing it.

As I started copying all of my posts, I realized just how much I had written. After copying just my entries from 2020, my document stood at two hundred and twenty-four pages. That's a decent size book, so I decided to stop right there, for now.

This book, the first of several (I have lots of content from 2021, 2022, and 2023 for future books) is a culmination of my writings on my social media, beginning in March of 2020 and ending on December 30, 2020. As you read through the posts, you may notice multiple entries have the same date stamp. I often found myself writing late into the evening and when I posted, it was submitted on the next calendar day—think posting something at 12:15 a.m.

In order to keep the integrity of the posts, I kept the actual date the post was published.

I hope by sharing my journey with you, it serves as a reminder that even when going through difficult times, we have the option to approach situations with a positive mindset. How we look at and handle events in our lives can directly impact how we come out of them. I chose to handle mine with patience and grace whenever possible, and I hope after enjoying my book, you can too.

-Kelly

March 2020

March 25, 2020

Today is the second day my shop has been closed since this crazy fiasco started. I'm lucky I've only been closed two days when other businesses have been closed longer... but I'm using the time to get caught up on house and shop stuff.

In the last two days I've done more laundry and dishes than I have in months. I guess you could say I've neglected my house. Not that I'm looking forward to more time off, but I am looking forward to making the house livable again! LOL. But I'll also admit that housework makes me bored. Zzzz!

I'll keep you posted as to how this domestic thing goes!!

March 26, 2020

I had to run to Clearwater to get wine for our brewery (Cotee River Brewing Company), stop at Office Depot to get more envelopes to send out tea that was ordered online, and make a quick stop to fill up the truck with gas.

While at home, I had the pleasure of trying to open one of our pretty patio umbrellas that we haven't used in two years. It only took fifteen minutes in the blazing sun, and every ounce of strength I had to get it fully open! A small but very sweaty win! The rest of the day was a bore, but I did manage to watch the Swiss Family Robinson on Disney+. I love old movies.

Hoping tomorrow is a little more productive!

March 27, 2020

I wasn't home at all. I practiced social distancing by staying in my truck with my mom and driving all the way to St Augustine and back. The only interaction we had was with 1 person when we picked up our growlers for the brewery.

Being isolated in a car is much different than in a house, because at home you can get up and walk around. And even though the scenery changes, it can still get boring in a car.

All I can say is that it's only been six days since my tearoom closed for this pandemic and it feels like a month. I can't wait for a real month to go by.

March 28, 2020

Today consisted of getting an online tea order to the post office. Did you know they put up plastic to protect their staff? Yes, they took clear sheet curtains (like shower curtains), cut them, and hung them from the ceiling. You can still pass items under it, but there is no chance of passing germs to our post office staff. Hey, if it works, use it!

The trip to Publix was interesting...I haven't been to a grocery store since this whole thing started. A lady checking out in the next lane was trying to buy five rolls of paper towels and two Lysol wipes. The cashier politely took them away from her because they have a maximum of these items you can purchase. Another cashier told me that things have calmed down quite a bit compared to the previous week.

My work at the brewery was light since the staff is back for a few shifts. Still, we stayed busy, and broke a record. Today we blew through a 5.5-gallon keg of our homemade apple pie sangria in three and a half hours!! That's the fastest we have gone through it, and we had to make a second keg quick. If today is any indication, we will have to make another one tomorrow!

Tonight was dinner at home, burgers and corn on the cob in the grill. We had my mom, sister, and mom-in-law over. We sat out on the deck and enjoyed dinner for the first time in two years. It was a great day and an even better evening!

March 29, 2020

Today was a good day. I got some great sleep last night, so getting up wasn't too hard today. That and my weekly Vitamin D is kicking in, so I'm pretty motivated to move for the next few days (wish I had an IV drip of that stuff since my body is completely deficient in it).

Bryan and I got to the brewery early this morning, and after enjoying a delicious take-out breakfast from Rose's Bistro, Bryan got the long-anticipated Chocolate Covered Strawberry Porter in the keg. Good thing because it was a big hit today with growler refills.

The brewery stayed steady today, and every day we are open is a day that I am more and more grateful to the amazing people in our community who continue to support us. It's truly overwhelming at times. Today and yesterday, we had staff with us, so we were happy to be able to provide some employment for them. After all, we are in this whole thing together and we must take care of our amazing team, so they are ready when we can come back (and let me tell you, it's going to be crazy when we come back!).

After the brewery closed and we cleaned up, Bryan and I came home for a quiet evening. It's not what we are used to, but we are really enjoying this time together. I am enjoying it so much that I am dreading the days that we are so busy that we won't see each other. It's time to come up with a plan for a happy medium in our lives.

    I hope you all are doing well. I miss my friends and I can't wait to see everyone again. For now, I will continue to post my daily stories on here. Not that it's interesting at all, but it helps me keep track of my days. And who knows if it gets interesting, it may make for a good book someday, LOL. Stay safe and love you all!

March 30, 2020

    Today, I went into my tea shop and worked on getting tea orders sent out and delivered. In one day, we received orders for over $180 in tea! While it's not anywhere near where we are on a normal daily basis, I am so thankful for every order we get in. If we can keep the tea sales going, it will help as we try to sustain this closure for longer than we had hoped.

    This afternoon consisted of enjoying some leftovers for lunch and watching my friend Gene from Celtic Conundrum test their online show as they are going to do a "behind closed doors concert" at our brewery this coming Saturday night. While we won't have anyone there to watch it, I love that they are doing their show online so everyone can watch from a safe distance at home.

    This afternoon I took a nap in my comfy side chair in my home office (it's pretty comfortable). I blame the nap on the mac and cheese I had for lunch and the half container of sweet and crunchy peanuts I had for a snack. That many carbs and sugar, plus a soda, can only ever lead to a sugar crash. Hello quarantine binge!

    Tonight, we ran to Walgreens where my husband was so thoughtful and got me a bottle of my favorite perfume. My grandfather always bought it for me, and I haven't had it in years, since he passed away. It was so sweet of my hubby!

Tonight, we had take-out because, let's face it, having such a crazy busy afternoon napping (LOL, just kidding), I didn't feel like cooking. We spent the evening watching the final shows of "Tiger King." I tell you—you truly couldn't make up the stuff in that show! Then again, the truth is often much more unbelievable than fiction.

Tomorrow, my team is coming into the tearoom to do some work, and it's Bryan's first day working from home. Then the brewery is open in the afternoon for growler refills.

I know this downtime wasn't supposed to be a vacation, but when did it become so busy? I haven't even gotten to do anything at home…other than take a few good naps! Boy, I hope I have some time in the next four to six weeks to clean my house, paint the outside, do some gardening, and enjoy my back deck. Only time will tell.

March 31, 2020

Today was pretty typical. I went into my shop and my team came in to help with some things. We were able to clean out the inventory closet and get lots of tea bagged up. It felt good to get some things done because to be honest, it's not always so easy to stay motivated.

After lunch, I joined twenty-five other tea professionals on a zoom meeting. Now, keep in mind that I have been using Zoom as a part of a tea mastermind group that I've been a part of for the last two plus years. It's amazing how many people do not know virtual etiquette! People, if you aren't talking, then mute your microphone. No one wants to hear your conversation with your kids or listen while your house phone rings, and you answer! It's not hard. Mute the mic when you aren't talking, unmute when you want to talk. It's one button!

This afternoon I opened the brewery and we filled quite a few growlers. It was good for a Tuesday! Now I don't have to be back there again until Friday, though I'm sure I will get "conned" into helping keg the rest of the chocolate covered strawberry porter tomorrow...

Tonight, I joined my weekly Tea Mastermind group. This amazing group of about ten ladies in the tea industry meets every week to learn how to make our tea businesses better, discuss ideas, and offer support for one another. It's truly wonderful to have them, as they are helping to keep me motivated and positive during this crazy time.

Now it's time for bed. Hoping I get some rest tonight and that the crazy dreams I've had the past few nights take a break. I would love one good night's sleep.

Tomorrow is a new day, a new month, and a new beginning. And, if anyone even thinks of playing an April Fools' joke, well, let's just say they better not...night all!

April 2020

April 1, 2020

A pretty good start to April, another month that I feel will never end!

Today was a pretty average day! I actually slept a little last night and got up later than normal. I spent a few hours at my shop, working on social media and answering emails. Then I took tea shipments to UPS and the post office. I'm glad we are staying busy sending tea orders out!

This afternoon Bryan and I ventured over to Astro Cycles while Bryan took a lunch break. Yes, working from home, he has been very strict about his work time. I'm so proud of him, as I don't think I would have the same discipline. Brad was awesome and filled my bicycle tires with air. Bryan traded in several of his bikes and put them toward getting a new cruiser. Apparently, he wants to cruise around town by bike…and since I had mine already, I couldn't deny him his. Hopefully, he will have it in a few days.

Also, this afternoon, the governor issued an order for everyone to stay at home. After checking with the Florida Brewers Guild attorney for clarification, we have learned that the Department of Homeland Security has outlined what is deemed essential and manufactures of beverages are considered essential, thus meaning breweries fall under the essential category. So, not a lot of rest for us as our brewery will be where I am this weekend. I'm very happy about that because being open there helps alleviate the pressure and financial fallout of having two businesses shut down. Though, the tearoom will open to a limited schedule on the fifteenth of this month…still, we are so fortunate and every day I pray that we can continue, and I pray for those businesses that can't.

Tonight was relatively quiet. I did some more work on my tea website and cart, and Bryan finished up his work. We enjoyed leftovers and watched a little TV.

Now I'm exhausted and heading to bed. I have to be ready because tomorrow is going to be a full day.

I hope all my friends are staying well out there. I love you all and can't wait until we can see each other again!

April 2, 2020

My morning was really nice. It started with making delicious bagel sandwiches for Bryan and me. Then, I journeyed to my shop to meet up with my team. My team is amazing! They are working so hard to get us reorganized and ready for when we can reopen. One of the things I couldn't do is furlough my team so they are helping us to be ready so we can hit the ground running when this closure ends.

This afternoon I spent some time at the brewery, working on our public comment about our brewery staying open on a limited basis. Bryan also got the rest of the Chocolate Covered Strawberry Porter kegged for this weekend. I also got a few things done for my shop, including a new landing page for my tearoom website that has a link to order tea, and a teacup coloring sheet.

Tonight, I made dinner...sloppy joes! It has been years since I made them. They were really good! Now I'm wondering why I haven't made them sooner. I guess this is something that I have enjoyed being home more, discovering old foods that I enjoy.

On another note, today, after ten years, our fridge at home decided it no longer wants to make ice or provide water. It worked great this afternoon when Bryan used it, but when I got home...bone dry! You know it's like the old Paula Abdul song... "I take one step forward; I take two steps back." I don't usually feel that way, but for some reason this song came right into my head when this happened, LOL!

My days certainly aren't very entertaining, but at least I get out of bed and do something...it's been hard staying motivated. I know everyone says it's important to slow down, but I really do not do well without deadlines. I know the governor said April 30th, but at this point I'm not convinced that will be the end, so it's hard.

I hope everyone else is doing well and that you are getting to have some kind of unique adventure. I'm hoping my next adventure is just a day away!

April 3, 2020

My day started at 6:30 a.m. I don't know why, but for some reason I was wide awake early today. Anyone who knows me knows how much I love my sleep and that I'm never up before 8 a.m. The worst part is that I didn't have to get up, but I was. I blame it on my friend, Chris, who said to wake up before the sun...or something like that. LOL! And I did.

I spent the morning at my tea shop fulfilling nine tea orders that came in overnight. Talk about crazy! I've never had so many in one today and I was truly feeling the warmth and fuzzies! I got all of them out in the mail and picked up by local friends that ordered...and then when I was at the brewery this evening another one came in. I love it! I mean, tea is the number one anti-viral so why not?!?

The brewery was busy today and I am feeling so blessed that we can keep doing what we are doing, and that our guests continue to bless us by continuing to come and get beer and wine. Bryan puts his heart and soul into the beer he makes, and I love it when people come in and tell us how much they enjoy it.

I had an interesting trip to the post office today. Well, actually two trips. The first time I went in there must have been no less than twelve people waiting in line, and the woman two in front of me was coughing like crazy. Um, no!! So, of course, I left. I went back thirty minutes before closing to five people in front of me. The supervisor came running out and said they could only have five total in the lobby, and we needed to wait in the entrance. So, we waited and waited and about ten minutes later I finally got into the lobby and to a clerk. Funny that one of the clerks saw me there earlier and asked why I left...I love that they recognize me and are friendly especially with all they are dealing with.

I was shocked to see so many people out today. Truly, in my few errands for my shop and picking up some delicious cupcakes from a friend's shop, MMMM Delicious Cupcakes. I wanted to help support her local business. While out, I saw more people driving and shopping than I have in weeks. Granted I was out, but with a very specific purpose in mind. When I was done, right back to my business I went, then home. There's no lollygagging here. Man, I hope people were just out doing their essential shopping and heading back home otherwise this thing will never end!

The highlight of my night was video chatting with Ava and Deidra. Anyone who knows me knows how much I love them, and I miss them. Ava was telling me stories, and about school, and I told her a joke, that maybe I shouldn't have but it was cute...she laughed and laughed. If I'm lucky, I will get to see her tomorrow. I told her I got a treat for her and if she was good, that mommy would bring her by to get it. Gosh I hope she's good. I just want to pick her up and kiss her cheeks!

Well off to bed I go. Hopefully, I will not be up before sunrise tomorrow (though I did take my vitamin D today so I will feel pretty good the next few days so I may just get up early...). I'm looking forward to a good weekend, though I am a little bummed that I've had off the last three weekends from the tearoom and haven't gone anywhere... oh wait, we can't. Look at that, finally time off for that vacation and everything is closed, LOL.

Wishing you all sweet dreams and a great whatever day of the week it is tomorrow.

April 4, 2020

Is it sad that the only way I know the actual day is to look at what pill I'm on for my birth control? LOL (full disclosure—I only take it for hormones which my body no longer produces) ...

Today was a great day! Not for any particular reason, just that I feel really good. But then, that's what 50,000 IUs of Vitamin D can do for you. I take it once a week on Friday (since I'm completely deficient in it) and by Saturday I'm feeling really good. It's a feeling that lasts until Tuesday when I start dragging again.

I spent time at the brewery today, after I mailed out more tea orders. No sooner did I drop off the packages in the mail and more orders came in. It was only two, but man, I am thankful for every order we get, no matter the size! We are definitely becoming a shipping machine.

The brewery did well today thanks to our awesome guests! It's been kind of fun for me to be at the brewery each weekend, and to see our guests over and over again. I feel like I'm getting to know them. We truly are blessed.

Tonight, we had dinner with the family. We had some delicious steaks on the charcoal grill, mashed potatoes, and corn bake. Man, I'm really getting used to cooking and eating at home. I mean, I miss going out, but we haven't cooked at home so much since before we opened our shop and brewery. It's actually delicious! Tomorrow night we are going to have boneless BBQ ribs with the family.

I know our moms live in different houses but if we aren't home, we are all together. We only go to the same places together, and it helps our morale. Mental health is just as important as physical health, and having my mom and mother-in-law around has been nice. I'm so glad they live close, and we have a great relationship. It makes this so much easier to get through.

Tomorrow, I have some work to do! I have to get ready for next week. Hopefully we will have lots of tea orders and scones to go, and I can really start focusing on our future. It's been hard to focus with so much unknown, but I'm starting to feel a little better now, and hoping I can continue to move forward.

I pray all my friends are doing ok. I miss you all and can't wait until we can visit again. But, until then you have to deal with my daily reports, LOL.

April 5, 2020

The morning started off nice. My mom picked us up breakfast and we enjoyed it sitting in my tearoom parlor. It was nice to relax in there for a little bit.

Before opening the brewery, we ran to Publix to grab a few things for the house. Not too much, just a few things we are running low on, like sliced cheese, chips, pound cake, etc. You know, the food you never buy but now that there's a pandemic, you crave—like BBQ twist Fritos and mini cakes. No?? Maybe it's just me, LOL.

The brewery was interesting today. Before we opened, some guy rammed his bicycle into our front door. I yelled at him from the inside. He said it was an accident and I brushed it off. About an hour and a half later the same guy was riding down the sidewalk and ran into our open door. He proceeded to be profane and showcased some not so classy hand gestures when confronted. Of course, I had just stepped out but when I got back, I hopped in my truck and tried to find him. We called the police, and they were going to keep an eye out for him. Seriously, it's good that our door is impact resistant. If it was an older door, he would have come right through it. I mean, is this what people are really doing today?!?

Tonight, we were home early. We had planned to BBQ out with family but with the bad weather, we decided to cook in. I had some of my niece's favorites: chicken nuggets and mac and cheese.

We watched a movie when we got home. Of course, I fell asleep. Bryan woke me up and told me it was only 6:30 and too early to go to bed. I told him that this is what happens when I'm bored. Everyone tells me to take a break but when I stop, I sleep. I can't help it. When I'm bored my brain shuts down and I hate it so that's why I stay so busy, it keeps my mind going, keeps me active, and keeps my mind fresh and young. Too much downtime is not good for me. So now it's time to come up with some good creative project. Hmm?

Well, another weekend has passed and if you ask me, it felt just like mid-week. Now that I've got a way to track the day, I must figure out how to remember the date. Boy, such simple things I never had to think about before.

I hope everyone has enjoyed their extended April weekend. By the way, tomorrow is Monday and the start of another amazing (albeit slower) week. Love you all!

April 6, 2020

My day started like all the others. I went to my shop and got to work on some orders that came in. Every day I have been blessed to at least have an order or two. That helps pay a bill here and there.

I tried to take my orders to the post office and holy cow, it was packed. There must have been twenty people in line, all evenly spaced, waiting to ship something.

Obviously, I turned right around and left. I did go back at 3:50 and walked right in. I got my favorite clerk, Ann Marie. She's so awesome; she knows exactly how I ship now so it goes quick. So, the packages go off...with three here in Florida, one to Maryland, and one to New York. Yes, New York! Did you know that officials in northern states are telling their residents to drink warm liquid because of helps reduce phlegm? And that they are telling them to drink tea, coffee and soup! I mean, I already knew tea was good for you, but how awesome!

This afternoon my mom and I went up to Canterbury Farms in Hudson. Wow, that place is awesome. And now that it's not easy to get into the garden section of Home Depot, it's the perfect place to go for outdoor plants. They had the most beautiful hydrangeas and I kind of kicked myself for not getting some. They were gorgeous. Oh well, just another reason to take another trip up there!

Tonight, we had dinner with "the moms" and my sister Wendy. We enjoyed some delicious boneless pork ribs that we picked up from Acropolis market in Hudson (supporting local!). I haven't had them on the wood fired grill in so long. Yum!! We laughed and had a nice time. It was a good escape from the world around us...

Tomorrow my team is coming into the tearoom to do some work. I have some ideas in mind for some changes to make our place even better. And we are getting ready for when we open Wednesday and Thursday for scone pickups (two minutes after I posted about 'scones to go' our phone rang with an order. I guess people miss us!).

Tomorrow, I start to work on a fun project—a t-shirt for the brewery. I was thinking something like #coteeriverbrewing on the front. And on the back, writing something like: Helping you survive the 2020 pandemic with the freshest beer in New Port Richey. Or something like that. Ideas? Anyone got any ideas? If you do, let me know. I'm sending something off to the printer tomorrow!

Now I'm turning into bed, not hopeful about anything for tomorrow. I have no expectations anymore because everything is constantly changing. It's hard to be motivated to do anything without knowing when you will be able to start your business back up. As a person who needs deadlines, this is brutal, unnerving, disheartening, depressing and just plain sad. I know quite a few people feeling the same way and it's hard to fight through it. I know we will, but right now I don't know how...I'm just hoping this is a case of the Monday blues.

Good night, all! See you tomorrow!

April 7, 2020

This morning, I woke up like any other morning. I got up and did my normal morning routine. Then, as I was finishing up my hair, my husband had to get into the bathroom to blow his nose (he has severe allergies). Normally, I don't mind, but today I was trying to get out of my house and to my shop to be with my team, so it threw my routine off ever so slightly. For some reason it put me on edge and made me very short with people. It's funny how one little shift in your normal routine can throw everything into disarray.

I got to my shop at a good hour and for some reason I was extremely irritated, not at anyone or anything in particular, just irritated. Do you ever have those moments where you could just bite someone's head off? Yea, that was me today. I did the best I could at controlling it and I didn't make anyone upset or cry...a win!

My team was working hard, so I kept to myself and got some of my own work done. All I can say is that my team is amazing. I chose not to furlough them and to keep them on their somewhat normal schedules so I could continue to pay them. It's important to me that we keep moving forward even during this time of uncertainty. Next week we have some plans to do some really cool offerings through our restaurant side and I'm excited to see how they turn out. One thing I love about my team is that no matter how crazy an idea, they hear me out and are genuinely supportive.

This afternoon I spent a little bit of time at the brewery. It opened to help support our neighbor at Juan-a-Taco for their weekly Taco Tuesday. After all, what goes better with tacos than beer? It's a match made in heaven to enjoy at home!

I'm also excited that the brewery is offering engraving on pint glasses. What a cool Easter gift idea! We had quite a few takers already and I know more will come in this weekend! I love this because it's a way for us to support another local business and a friend! Yeah!!

Tonight, I had a meeting with my Tea Mastermind group. I have come to really enjoy my Tuesday evening meet-up with other tea professionals. They are part of my solace and motivation. As much as it's hard for me to keep going during this uncertain time, this amazing group of women encourages me and offers great support. This situation is hard enough to deal with but having 'tea friends' has been so important for my sanity. I'm hoping their motivation can keep me going because it's been hard to focus and keep moving forward.

My days are starting to run together. I'm hoping tomorrow is a standout day. We have lots of 'scones to go' orders at the tearoom and it feels good to be able to offer something unique and different during this time. Hopefully, I will have some fun stories for y'all tomorrow!

Wishing you all a great night!

April 8, 2020

Today started off great and I'm ending it in a good place. It's been a while since I have been able to say that, but some things happened today that happen every day during normal times, that just raised morale a little.

This morning, I arrived at my tearoom and worked to get our 'scones to go' that were ordered into their boxes. I wanted to make them pretty for our guests, with doilies and such, so they felt special when they opened them. I packaged them all up and was excited to see that we sold through almost every one of them (tomorrow is also 'scone day' so my team will be busy making more).

We opened the shop today at 11 a.m. for guests to come in and pick up their orders. Everyone was so nice, respectful and happy to see us. I wasn't sure how it would go, but just being open for those three hours, getting to talk to our amazing guests, and feeling like we were providing some joy to people was so worth it. After all that we have been through, the ups and downs and having to close certain parts of our business, it was so nice to be able to feel good about what I do every day. It makes me realize that no matter how small my tearoom is in the grand scheme of things, my tearoom has meaning and that gives me meaning.

After getting all our scones out, we received some more online orders, so I went to the post office. It wasn't as packed as Monday, but I still had to wait in the first lobby area (they only let five people in the main lobby at one time). While I was standing there, a supervisor brought another woman out to stand and wait (apparently, she was #6, LOL). She had a mask on, and we started talking. She told me she works at Trinity Hospital but that she doesn't interact with patients, and she sits in a negative pressure room. She had cancer last year and so she was being cautious. She asked what I was shipping, and I told her about my tea and my tearoom. Then it was her turn to go in, and I joined her quickly...as I walked in the door she said, "There's my new friend," and I said, "Hi neighbor, it's so good to see you again," and we both started laughing. The lady in front of her looked at both of us and smiled, and said, "that's what I miss, hearing people laugh." That got me thinking, how sad is it that this virus has driven us to the point where we don't laugh—that we are too depressed or sad and can't even laugh.

Today was an eye-opener for me. This virus, the news, the concern and being scared has zapped the happiness of life right out of us. We are sad to stay at home, sad we can't see friends or visit our favorite places, sad at everything. So, how do we fix that? How do we enjoy life during this difficult time? For me, I'm going to start smiling at strangers. If I'm wearing a mask, which I have yet to do, I'm going to tell them that under my mask I'm smiling like the lady that came into the brewery to get a growler refill did. Her telling us she was smiling made us all smile too. Anything that I can do to make the world a little brighter in this crazy time, I'm going to do. It goes a long way for the people around us, and I hope they will carry that little bit of joy on too.

So, what are you going to do to have a little laugh today? Trust me, it makes a huge difference. And just know, if I see you out, I'm going to smile at you because, despite all we are going through and how hard it is to stay put, my life is really good, and I have so much to be thankful for. How about you?

April 9, 2020

Today was a great day. Not for any other reason than I am just going to make every day that way—as long as I can.

My shop was open again today, and we sold over seven dozen scones and lots of tea. Tea orders continue to come in online daily, which is awesome, and it's keeping me and my tea team busy.

I have to tell you; I love our tea guests. They are awesome! I don't think I've smiled or laughed so much in the last two weeks as I have in the last two days. Something happened today that was funny, and I laughed about it and thought how good it felt. Oh, I remember...I saw a photo that Lou from Boulevard Beef & Ale posted of two horses that went to Pete's Grand Central today. I immediately grabbed my mom and went running down to the corner of our building to see if it was true, and it was! Two horses bellied up to the bar, lol.

On the way back, Lou came out to make sure we saw them. She told us that when she went over to take a picture of them, one of the horses pooped. We all laughed and then laughed more. She regaled us with a story about the horses in a parade and the inmate following behind them, cleaning up after them. We all laughed some more, and I remember stopping for just a second to watch Lou and my mom laugh. I made a point to remember their faces and how good it felt to have some joy. It was truly like old times before we were all stuck in what feels like an alternate universe. The rest of my day just didn't compare to that moment.

Bryan and I ran to Clearwater to pick up more Lazy Days wine that we use for our apple pie sangria at the brewery. It was good seeing Bill at Aspirations Winery. He gave me a chuckle when we talked about bringing on some more of his wines...he said he knows we will do well because of how well we do with his lowest volume wine...you guessed it, Lazy Days. It made me feel good that we can promote and sell his wine. I can't wait until we can bring more of his wine in, hopefully in the next few weeks so we will be ready when we reopen the brewery.

Tonight, we laid low at home. I worked in the home office and got some things done. Bryan got his application completed and all documentation submitted for the PPP (Paycheck Protection Program). This afternoon I received an email telling me that my PPP was waiting for final approval from SBA (Small Business Administration), but that the bank said it was good to go. Keep your fingers crossed that we get final approval soon!

To provide me with a little grounding during this Holy Week, I took time to watch Holy Thursday services online from my church. I just love Father Sebastian and am so grateful that he and the other priests and staff at Our Lady Queen of Peace can offer us some solace and love even though we can't celebrate this sacred time together in person. I look forward to watching the rest of their services this week and weekend.

Now it's time to turn in. I've got lots to do tomorrow to keep my tea train moving forward! It feels good and I know it's going to keep the momentum. At least I'm going to try, though I'm sure there are still hard days ahead.

I wish you all a great night. Here's to turning the corner soon, and to better days filled with more smiles and laughter together.

April 10, 2020

Ok, seriously people, the first time you called the police on my brewery when we were open and were allowed to be, it was funny. But, to call and blatantly lie that we are serving people and letting them sit at our bar is enough!

If you think we wouldn't find out who was calling, you were wrong, and I'm seriously disappointed in you. When people go after good businesses that follow the rules, it makes me question your ethics and how you run things.

Karma wins every time, and I can go to sleep every night with a clear conscious, knowing I have never called the police on you or any other person/business, even though I may have wanted to. I'm not sure what you are trying to prove, other than wasting our police department's time and resources. Smart!

April 10, 2020

Happy Friday?? Is it Friday yet?? The days are running all together, so I have a hard time keeping track. I forgot it was Friday and I forgot I was supposed to take my vitamin D! No wonder why I'm dragging...I'm hoping tomorrow's dose will give me the jump I need. It's crazy but my body is so low in vitamin D, completely deficient in it. In fact, I look forward to the day each week where I take a pill to help with a little energy boost. It doesn't last long, maybe two to three days, but I'll take it. Just image what I could do if I had normal vitamin D and normal energy? Oh, the possibilities!

Today my team came into the tearoom to do some tea and general maintenance stuff. I always look forward to the days when I get to see them because during normal times, we see each other almost every day.

This morning, I decided that instead of just rushing in and getting to work that our team would spend some quality time together. I asked one of my team to make some cinnamon rolls for us to enjoy and when we were ready, we all sat down to our own pot of tea and enjoyed them. It was nice to have all of us sit down over a pot of tea and relax and just be ourselves. We have all been so stressed that I felt we just needed some downtime. We talked and caught up with what each other were doing. We laughed so hard at one of our team members who would grab and shake her tea pot 4 times after she emptied it, hoping there was just a little more. I told her, no matter how hard she shakes, the only way her teapot was getting more tea was if she got up and made it. It was so great to see my team laugh together over that and more. Actually, it wasn't just great—it was awesome!!

The rest of the day with my team went great. There was lightness around us, something that hasn't been felt for a while. Everyone worked great together, we got a lot done and we were all in a good mood. I don't think I should be surprised by the atmosphere that tea creates and after the craziness it was wonderful to see that tea still works!

Tonight, I joined part of our wine group for an online meet up. I had some delicious sangria from Carrabba's Italian Grill thanks to my friend Boris. My dinner was awesome too! Our group usually meets up at Carrabba's for their monthly wine night, so we had to keep things normal. OMG, we laughed and laughed, caught up on what each other were doing. Before we knew it, we had been online for over an hour and a half. While it was a nice night, I am really looking forward to having wine night in person as soon as restaurants reopen their dining rooms.

Overall, it was a pretty fabulous day! Yea, there were bumps along the way, but what day doesn't have that?! None. It's how we deal with it, how we hold our head up and do the right thing that ultimately determines how our day, week, month, year and life go. I am very happy where mine is and where it's going! Can you say the same?

April 12, 2020

The day started like any other Saturday, for the past few weeks anyway. I still can't get used to not going to my shop and getting ready for our busy Saturdays. It still almost feels surreal to me that on Saturdays my shop is closed.

I spent the day at the brewery. It was somewhat busy, but I didn't feel like I got anything done. I always try to use my time wisely there, working on my laptop and such. However, yesterday it just felt like even though I was working, I wasn't getting ahead at all. I know we all have those days but even with the slowdown and "Safer at Home" order, I still like to feel as though I am getting something done.

Yesterday we went through inventory at the brewery. Holy cow do people like our beer! It's time to get brewing again, starting next Saturday! Don't get me wrong, it is an awesome thing! I am glad the beer is going and that we can make more. To me it shows that Bryan and my intuition were right about opening a brewery, and for that I am so thankful!

Tonight, we had a quite night at home, just the two of us. We had leftovers and just vegged out. Believe it or not, I didn't even have a book or my laptop with me. You know, I bet if they had been diagnosing ADD back in the 80's, they would have found that I have it. I am not one who can just do one thing at a time. I need to constantly be moving and doing, going from one thing to another. Even if it's slow, my brain is always on to the next thing. So, for me to just "veg" is a relatively new and uncomfortable thing. I have to say it wasn't bad, but it did make me very tired, and had me going to bed early. That's not a bad thing either until you are wide awake at 5 a.m.

Well, here's to another day in the books. They all seem to be running together and that's ok. At least each one has its slight differences, so my stories don't get too boring.

April 13, 2020

I wasn't sure what to expect from Easter this year. With not being able to really go out, and I just knew it wasn't going to be like any other.

We started our morning off by taking my mom and my mother-in-law to the National Cemetery in Bushnell. There we visited different family members and put flowers at their graves. It was a nice feeling to be able to do that, and it was wonderful seeing so many other families there doing the same. It gave me a sense that even though we couldn't celebrate with them; they know they are still important in our lives.

We spent the afternoon at my mom's house. From wrangling a black snake on her front porch that was blocking the front door so Bryan and I couldn't get in (she absolutely hates snakes by the way), to enjoying watching Easter Parade with Judy Garland and Fred Astaire—it was a great afternoon.

To make things even easier, we decided to have our Easter meal catered. Thanks to Arlisa's Events for the amazing food. Maybe I could pay you to make me that amazing mac and cheese every week! It made for an enjoyable and stress-free afternoon.

In the evening, we hung out and watched movies. We also got to watch things on our phone. We found a video of a bird feeder that, when a squirrel jumps on it, it spins and spins, and the darn squirrel never lets go. It looks like an Olympic sport! OMG! We laughed so hard we were choking! Apparently, there are a ton of these videos out there! And now my husband wants one of these bird feeders so he can watch the squirrels try to get on it while he is sitting in his home office. I can see him getting so much work done while he waits for the squirrels. LOL.

I hope you had a wonderful Easter. I know it's probably not what you were expecting but hopefully it was still nice!

April 13, 2020

For those who know me well, know that I am huge fan of this man, Robert Iger. I have so much respect for him and how he runs business and makes decisions. Truly a class act and someone who can ensure Disney's success once the threat of this virus has passed. He will have to think of new and unique ways to keep Disney guests safe across the globe and come up with new ways to run their business. I can't think of anyone better to oversee this massive company.

April 14, 2020

A boring, then productive day...

I got up this morning without much of a plan for the day. I thought it would be nice to take the day off since the next few days will be spent at my tearoom. So, I went about my normal routine: got showered, put on make-up, got ready to go and sat down. Now what?

I went into our home office where Bryan was working and thought maybe that would give me some motivation to get things done. NOPE! After perusing social media for what seemed like forever, but was really only ten minutes, I realized I was completely bored with my day. If I didn't do something quick, I was going to close my eyes from boredom and sleep the day away. Now, anyone who knows me knows that's not remotely normal for me.

Then I remembered I had a beautiful office upstairs from my tearoom where I could work. So, I packed up my laptop and files and headed to my office to work. And work I did! I didn't feel too productive for the first thirty minutes (my office is new so I'm just getting used to it and learning where to put stuff). By the time Bryan came by around 3:15 pm, I was in the thick of it and didn't want to leave.

This afternoon we went over to see our friend Brad at Astro Cycle. Bryan has wanted a cruiser bike for a while. I think he was jealous of my awesome comfy ride. LOL! Brad built him the perfect bike. He even rode it home from the shop! I can see more bike rides around town in the future!

Tonight, we enjoyed dinner at my mother-in-law's house. I'm so glad that she lives close to us. We brought the food, and my mom and Wendy joined us. Now, before you get worked up that we have dinner together almost every night, don't forget that we are all together almost daily and we aren't around anyone else. They both help us with our businesses every day, and we are keeping them away from any public. They are the only people we are around these days and I'm kind of glad. Our lives got so busy that other than working with our moms, we never spent any time with them.

One thing this "Safer at Home" plan has done is give me more time at home and more quality time with the people I love. And now for the hard part…trying to maintain being together and running our businesses when things get back to normal. I know that this time has been hard for a lot of people, but for me it has been a blessing. And I truly am going to look for that balance when all of this is over.

April 15, 2020

It's times like this that you learn the truth about people's character. How they treat others and the decisions they make really tells you where their moral compass points and about their integrity or lack thereof. It's so sad that in a time when so many are struggling, people can't find it in themselves to be decent human beings to each other.

April 15, 2020

Yesterday we worked in the tearoom during the day. We are starting to get some things cleaned up so it's good. For a while, we were tearing things up and cleaning; now it's time to get things together so we are ready to open when we can. We also started our Scones and Afternoon Tea to go this week. Many people asked me why we didn't start doing take out right away. The honest reason is that I needed a break. I needed to take a step back, reassess, and figure out how my shop could be a bright light in what seemed like a dim world. I also had to do it for my own sanity.

When this whole thing started about a month ago, I went through a period of disbelief that this couldn't really be happening…then one of I can't believe it was happening.

Everything I knew, my way of life and my business were all stopping. In order to gain some control and not have a mental breakdown, I decided to take a step back. My team still worked and so did I, both in limited capacity. But to best be able to be there for my guests, I needed to take a break and figure out what was best for all of us.

Last week we started making 'scones to go'. During the two-day period we sold fourteen dozen scones! Today alone, we sold twelve dozen! We also started our 'Afternoon Tea to go', with fourteen orders. I am in awe of the love our guests have shown us. One guest was moved to tears, and so was I when she thanked us over and over and told us that us doing what we were doing was the best thing that had happened to her in two months. That means more to me than anyone will ever know. Truly, that is why I get up and work so hard every day. If I can provide a little joy and hope for one person, I will have fulfilled my goal.

For those of you who have asked, Bryan is doing well. My home office is serving him well working from home. I'm glad he's getting some use out of it, but it leaves me typing on a snack tray. I have to say that I am looking forward to finally getting my office upstairs from where my teashop is situated.

The brewery is doing well. We are beyond blessed to be able to continue to serve our guests and provide our beer to go. Truly, it's been a wonderful blessing and I thank God every day for the opportunity to do what we do. Bryan has even run out of one of his beers, so this weekend we start brewing again. That's a great sign. Oh, and I get to go on another adventure to St. Augustine to pick up more growlers. Who would have thought we would sell over 300 of them so far! Then, because we can only get 1/2 our growlers this weekend but we are completely out, I will have to go back in a week or two. What can I say, a girl's got to do what a girl's got to do!

Nothing else is new at this point in my life. My highlight is waiting for eighty tea books to arrive that I purchased from another tea professional. The three boxes were supposed to be delivered on Monday. When I checked on them, they were in the distribution in Memphis, TN. Yesterday they were in Jacksonville, and today they were back in Memphis! Good thing they aren't travel books, otherwise I might never get them. LOL!

Hoping everyone out there is doing well. I miss everyone and I can't wait to sit, have a drink and catch up (though I bet most of our stories are similar, home, cooking, etc.). Love you all!

April 17, 2020

Thursday went quick for me. My normal routine these days is to go into my shop and work on certain projects with my team or be open for orders to go. I seem to be getting quite a bit done overall, though some days it doesn't seem like it.

Thursday afternoon I hosted my first Facebook Live from the tearoom. I set everything up as if I was having a tea party and I talked out to Facebook land. It was kind of fun and I'm looking forward to doing it again in the coming weeks.

After we got done taping, Bryan and our friend Travis enjoyed the food from my tea tray. Apparently, I didn't realize how much my husband missed having our Devonshire cream. Once I gave him the go ahead, he proceeded to enjoy a tiny bite of scone with a boat load of cream. Tiny bites and more cream, over and over again. I actually caught a photo of it!

Today, we were so blessed to have so many take-out orders. Truly, our guests were so amazing, and I feel so blessed to have the opportunity to say hi to them and make sure they are doing well. It also feels good to provide a positive light for so many. I have been so blessed during all of this and I'm glad to help others!

This afternoon I took another trip to St Augustine. Yes, the brewery ran out of growlers, and I needed to get more. We have sold over three hundred actual growlers so far, and another more than three hundred and fifty fills, in addition to the initial purchase and fill. Kind of exciting, though it makes for a long day. And I have to tell you, I can't wait for the day when I can go over and spend a day or two sightseeing and enjoying our favorite restaurants. It's hard going over and coming right back when I want to just stay and hang out!

The trip over and back was uneventful for the most part. I mean, on the way back, heading the opposite direction, there was a semi-truck on fire. Well, it looked like the back wheel blew and caused it. The fire department was there, and they were putting it out. I looked at my mom and said, "Well, you won't see that on an airplane!" That has been a running joke for us any time we see something unique in our travels since we mostly travel by car (as I don't fly). It gives me a sense of the cool stuff I wouldn't see if I flew. LOL.

So, now I'm home and getting ready for bed. I'm helping at the bar tomorrow while Bryan brews. Yes, beer is starting to get low, so we want to keep ahead of things. It's a great thing to be able to keep going, and I'm looking forward to seeing everyone tomorrow.

I hope you are doing well. If any of my friends need anything, please let me know. I'm always here and we are in this together!

April 18, 2020

I'm not sure about you but the day started off a little rocky...they skies were rocking with some great thunder and lots of rain. I was sure that it would be one of those days that I would be unproductive. I would want to sit at home, cuddled up in a warm blanket, and enjoy some nice movies or read a good book. But nope, I got moving in the pouring rain (thanks to my mom for being my driver, so I didn't have to park and run in the rain). The brewery keeps running out of my famous red sangria, so I set out to get the ingredients. The first Publix didn't have what I needed, but the second one did!

By the time I got to the brewery to "work," they were set up and ready to start their day. And Bryan and our friend Bob were deep into the brewing process, making our famous Market Fresh Wheat. I'm not usually at the brewery on brew days so all I can say is the brewery smelled amazing, I just wish our wonderful guests could have been there today to enjoy it.

I helped at the brewery, though I don't know how helpful I was other than making more sangria. We ran out of both types, red and white, so I had to make them. Then we ran out of the red sangria again, so I have to make more tomorrow. I'm still completely amazed at the growler situation. I never imagined that I would have had to go to St. Augustine two times in a month to get more growlers. Oh, and I can't wait to share our awesome new shirts for the brewery next week! They are so cool!

Tonight, I came home and felt like doing a little something different rather than eating dinner on snack trays in the living room, like we do most evenings. We have one of those coffee tables where the top lifts up and comes toward you, so you can use it as a table. It's been cluttered for months, well, probably years, so I decided to clean it off so we could use it. The dust must have been an inch think, holy moly!

Then I thought I might as well keep going and turn my living room from the dust collection of an old, haunted house to one that is cleanly polished. I only dusted four pieces of furniture so let's not get carried away, but my furniture looks shiny and pretty. Maybe now my five-year-old niece won't make tiny dust balls with her hands when she comes over. LOL. Yes, I'm not ashamed to admit it, I don't ever take time for my house…it serves its purpose and

I love it, and that's all that matters. I will admit though, that I do love it more with bright furniture!

Tonight, for dinner, we ordered from Sip on Grand. Since I had a clean table to use, I decided to get "fancy" and set up the food on my beautiful tier trays to enjoy. It was so nice, and the food was amazing. We really enjoyed having a nice dinner, a great glass of wine and relaxing. I think Bryan enjoyed it too, having a little down time after a long brewing day.

Tomorrow is going to be a busy day at the brewery, I can feel it! We have our friend coming in to engrave growlers on site and one of our musicians doing a live stream of his music from our place. I'm glad we can all work together during this time and do some good things for some good people.

Oh, and I have a lot to catch up on for both businesses. Here's to a great Sunday Funday! I hope yours is fun too!

April 19, 2020

This morning, I woke up, realized it was Sunday, and instantly began to miss the fact that I wouldn't be going out to breakfast. Before the "Safer at Home" order, Bryan and I would go to breakfast on Sunday mornings. It would be one of two places in town, and it made us feel like Cheers because we knew everyone. The "good mornings" and light conversation were always a highlight of our day, and the longer I don't have it the more I miss it. So, this morning I decided to make breakfast at home for us. I made biscuits and gravy...one of my all-time favorites. It was a nice meal to enjoy since we couldn't go out.

On our way into the brewery, we stopped at Winn Dixie to get some ginger ale to make another batch of our new red sangria.

When we got to the store there was a gentleman dressed as Batman, asking people if they needed toilet paper. If they said yes, he graciously gave them 2 rolls. It was so sweet the way he talked to people and the way people were so friendly to him. It made me feel like there truly are people out there who want to help those in need.

By nature, I have learned that most people are good. They truly have good hearts and would never wish anything bad on their fellow man. What's most heart-warming is when we see it first-hand. Such a small gesture can really help someone, like today. Some people took toilet paper while others said they were ok and to give it to someone who needs it more. See, humanity can be good!

Tonight, after a few short hours at the brewery, we went to mom's house for dinner. She made a roast in the crock pot, mashed potatoes and gravy, and corn on the cob. It was great to sit around the dinner table, talk and enjoy each other's company. After dinner we watched a movie, and then we went home in the golf cart. The weather was perfect, and I remembered how much I loved night golf cart rides. I'm looking forward to more in the future.

Tomorrow starts a new week and I've got lots going on. There's never a dull moment when it comes to our businesses, and I guess that's why I haven't been too crazy about the "Safer at Home" order. I'm rarely home as I'm usually working to prime my businesses to be ready to reopen. Until then, we continue to plug along!

April 20, 2020

I was up bright and early this morning...well maybe not for everyone else, but for me. I had an appointment for my quarterly blood work at 9:30 a.m. I made myself a promise this year that I was going to follow through with my appointments. See, I am supposed to go have blood work every three months because I'm diabetic. I also have non-existent Vitamin D, so they have to check my levels to see if we can get them up. It's been three months since I was put on prescription Vitamin D, and we have to see where my numbers are now.

For about four months, I have been having severe exhaustion and couldn't figure out why. I could barely get out of bed. Once up and ready to go, I would have to take a nap, and this dance would continue all day until I came home and went to bed. When I finally made the commitment to get blood work, we found I was completely deficient in Vitamin D. Over the past three months, since being on medication, I have felt a little better. The best days for me are the second to third days after I take my meds. That's when it's in my system the best, then for a few days I'm tired again...

I'm just not sure that this was the best time to get blood work for my diabetes. With all the stress I have been under, I am sure it's affecting my health. But, this year, I am not going to be afraid of it. I'm going to own up and face it. I will know the results in a few days, and I am excited to meet with my doctor on Friday!

I am glad that I had an appointment for my lab work. My wait time was only twenty minutes. I went early, so I was home before that horrendous thunderstorm hit!

This afternoon I spent some time at the tea shop. I was working on a project to get some press that shows the unique things we can do with tea. I designed four new tea cocktails that have been sent in for consideration. Thanks to my amazing friends, Joe and Lou, over at Boulevard Beef & Ale for letting me play at their place today! It was fun experimenting and putting things together! The drinks came out surprisingly well. Personally, there are two that I just love! I can't wait to share them with all of you!

Tonight, we continued working on setting up my office. I got a new printer and Bryan got it all set up. I'm excited about that! This week I want to start getting more stuff set up in my office, if I can get the stuff up there. It's exhausting going up and down those stairs. I can only do it a few times before I have to quit for a while. If anyone ever wants to help, let me know! LOL.

Tomorrow is an organizing day for me. We are getting into a good routine, but I can't wait until they tell us we can reopen. I love seeing our guests when they come in for to go orders, but I can't wait for the day when I can visit with them more and hear how they have been doing.

I hope everyone has a great night, and I'll holler at you tomorrow with more adventures.

April 21, 2020

Has it really been twenty-nine days since I started writing?? I mean, I know it feels like forever, but then it doesn't. Time has flown by for me, but that is probably because I've tried to stay busy. All I can say at this time is my two businesses have saved my life. I just couldn't imagine not getting up every day and having a purpose for the future. I guess this time has taught me, instead of thinking of my shop as a chore sometimes (especially when it gets crazy busy), I need to see it for the blessing that it is, not just to my guests but to me too!

Today was a good day. I felt like I really never stopped running...

My day started with a trip to Largo to get supplies for to go orders. The restaurant supply wasn't too packed with people, and they seemed to have a good supply of what we needed. Except my employee who was with me had forgotten to put self-rising flour on her list, so we didn't get it. Talk about not being able to make scones! My mom ran to Publix where we got two of their 5-pound bags. Hopefully that will get us through this week...I mean, people have to have their scones!!

This afternoon consisted of a really nice phone call with a family friend (you know who you are!), shipping out more tea at the post office, going by the brewery, and getting some fun paperwork done, LOL.

Tonight was my weekly Tea Mastermind meeting. I've really come to love this group because they are very smart businesswomen in the tea industry, and we all are so supportive of each other. It's because of their support that I feel like I am thriving as best anyone could during this crazy time. And I've got some great ideas for the future thanks to them too!

I know my day wasn't much to speak of, but man did it keep me running, or at least moving, which after my blood work results is something I need to do a lot more of…more on that later!

Now it's bedtime and for some reason I am extremely tired. I'm hoping I can turn the brain off for a little bit and actually get some rest. Sweet dreams!

April 22, 2020

Holy cow, I can't believe I have been at this for thirty days. I'm not talking about the "Safer at Home" order; I'm talking about writing these daily updates. Granted, I had to combine a few days, but I'm still impressed I've lasted this long.

Writing my update is usually the last thing I do before I go to bed, kind of like how people say prayers. Of course, I say prayers too, so my nightly ritual to get to bed has gotten just a few minutes longer.

Speaking of bed and sleeping, I'm not sure about anyone else, but the rest I get at night depends on a lot of things. Lately, I haven't been able to turn my brain off and I end up having the craziest dreams. It feels like they last all night, but I know they don't, and then I wake up feeling like I haven't slept. Other nights I wake up and just can't go back to sleep. I tried CBD, and holy cow did my dreams get crazy. Yea, no more of that stuff for me.

Today was a good day overall. We prepared twenty tea parties to go, and I think we sold 6 dozen scones. It's so nice to see so many of our amazing guests! And I love that they love their tea parties. It feels good to have my team working hard and bringing in some revenue. This whole challenge of running a business during this time has made me really reevaluate how I do business, how I promote, and really look at what people want. It's kind of fun for me!

This afternoon I spent some time at the brewery. We went through our grain and worked on preparing a big grain order to cover our next five brews. Yes, five brews! It's time to get making beer again because we are going through it! All good things!

Tonight, we enjoyed takeout dinner and watched a movie at my mother-in-law's house! I love that our moms live so close, and we can still spend time with each other. We are so blessed.

Normally, during times like these I would make them stay home. Since they are with us all the time, I see no reason why we can't hang out with them and have dinner or watch movies. The four of us have been exposed to each other since day one of the pandemic. Heck, my mom even drank my soda two different days a few weeks ago. If that's not sharing germs, I don't know what is!!

I know some of my friends up north are stuck in their homes and I'm so sorry. It's not that we aren't, but with our businesses, we do go out, though much more limited. I can't imagine being inside all the time. I need my fresh air and some sunlight, though not too much because my meds don't like me to be out in it. My mom raised me to use the fresh air and sun to keep me healthy. Now, that doesn't mean laying in the sun to tan, but rather using nature for healing. I think that maybe that's why I love tea so much...the nature of it is amazing. I could talk about that for hours so that's another day...

Congratulations to all of us for making it through these past thirty-plus days. I know we still have a long way to go, but together we will make it through, and in the end the struggle will have been worth it. Love you all, good night!

April 23, 2020

Another day in the books...and this one was like no other.

Do you ever wake up, start your day and just feel like it's going to be off? That is how I felt when I got out of bed this morning, and boy was my instinct right...

Before I left for work, I made this awesome ham and mayo sandwich. I was so looking forward to enjoying it. You know what I mean? When you just have a craving, and it looks so good, and you can't wait to eat it! Yea, so, I left for work and got to my shop and when I got out of the car, my sandwich fell out of my hands and on to all the dirt in the parking lot. Man was I so bummed! I had just wanted to enjoy that so much and in a quick slip it was gone.

I should have known from that point that the day just wasn't going to go easy...

This afternoon I got some sad news about a friend. While I know life has a way of working out and that God always has a plan, sometimes getting not so good news and knowing your friend is in pain does not make it easy. I've always really cared about my friends and feel bad when one is sad or in pain. She knows who she is, and all I can do is make sure that she knows that I am there for her. I always will be, and I love her. I'm sorry I can't say more, but I always respect people's privacy.

Tonight, I left my shop around 5 p.m. to go home and rest for a few minutes before Bryan and I went to the brewery to do his Virtual Happy Hour online. Well, we got in the car around 6 p.m. to head back and two of my downtown business owner friends started frantically calling me. It turns out that one of my front windows at the tearoom shattered. Now, before you worry too much, it wasn't done on purpose, and nothing was taken. In fact, this is the second time the window has shattered in the last three years. I'm not sure why, but we talked with our landlord about a possible fix. I'm confident that we can get repaired, so this won't happen again.

You would think with my day, and especially with my window breaking, that I would be upset.

But in reality, I'm not mad mainly because there is nothing I can do about any of it...other than not drop my sandwich. I know many of my downtown business owner friends came and offered to help and told me they were sorry I was dealing with my window...I appreciate every one of them so much!

For me, there is no reason to be upset or throw a fit. I can't change what happened. The only thing I have control over when things like this happen is how I respond to them. Being upset only causes more problems. Yes, I'm sad that it happened, but I'm going to have a positive attitude that I'm still more fortunate than most and that in the grand scheme of things this is just a minor setback. I am a good person and today was just a minor pothole in the grand road of life.

Now, I have to admit that each day, as I go through my day, I always wonder what I'm going to write about at night and most days I'm given so much stuff that it's hard to choose. Today was just an exceptional day of happenings! How lucky for me!

I hope day thirty-two is a little smoother than day thirty-one, but any day we all wake up is a great day!

April 24, 2020

Unlike most of my friends, I was not woken up by the emergency alert on my phone or the emergency phone call from the county telling us of a tornado warning for our area. Sad to say, but we had some crazy lightning and instant thunder around 5:30 a.m. and Bryan and I both woke up, agreed that it was close, and immediately fell back to sleep to the enjoyable sounds of the rain outside. It's very strange that I missed the event as I am a very light sleeper. I guess it goes to show that I must have been really tired!

Later this morning I had a doctor's appointment. This one was my quarterly meeting to go over my blood work for my diabetes and to see if my critically low vitamin D levels happen to come up at all. Of course, I knew exactly what to expect, I had received the test results from the lab a few days ago. Despite rising numbers, some bad and some good, my doctor was courteous as ever as we discussed a plan on how to reverse the bad numbers, even during this crazy time.

I also told her I have been having anxiety and stress to the point that I feel like my heart is fluttering or that my muscles get really tight. Wow, that bought me a trip to a cardiologist, but I'm glad because heart issues run in my family. I do not want to suffer some of their fate at a young age. After a lot of discussion, we determined that it's most likely stress and anxiety compounded by my already crazy nerves and muscles, but better safe than sorry…so Monday I call a new specialist.

This afternoon the tearoom was open for takeout orders. Everyone seemed genuinely excited when they came in, and from their photos and shares on Facebook they all seemed happy. That makes me smile. However, I would be remised if I didn't acknowledge that going to the tearoom is hard because it still lacks the vibrancy or having our guests coming in. That part, and the drive to keep going, is starting to take its toll on our team and I can see it. As a business owner you always try to do the right thing for your team. When this started, I promised them I would do whatever I could to keep them working and keep paying them. Now I feel it may have been better to not do that and let them collect unemployment for a lot more money. I wonder if they are feeling the same thing too.

The brewery is continuing its march forward! Bryan got his system ready to brew the Irish Red tomorrow and guests are still coming in for refills. His new shirt was a hit and is selling like hot cakes (yum, those sound good for breakfast). I'm so proud of him for taking risks and continuing to press on. You find out what you are really made of in times like these.

So tomorrow will be a fun day at the brewery. I am hoping to get up early, head into the tearoom to play a little in my kitchen, and finish cleaning up the mess made from my broken window. Then I'll head to the brewery to help there while Bryan brews. It's a good thing he and I make such a great team. LOL.

I know being home all the time together can bring out the worst in a couple, and boy, am I glad that's not the case in our home. He puts up with my still crazy schedule, my crazy idiosyncrasies, and still does most of the housework. When we are actually at home, I'm lucky to be home with my best friend because I really don't think anyone else can handle all this.

Here's wishing you a good night's sleep, and that all of you don't get woken up by a crazy tornado warning again while I sleep peacefully.

April 25, 2020

This morning started out with a trip to my tearoom to get some online orders ready. We've been doing decent holding our own with the online orders. I like to get them out right away, so people don't have to wait.

After getting all of my packaging done, I went to the post office. Today it wasn't too crowded, and I only had to wait in the first lobby for about five minutes. Man, I'll tell you, as someone who runs to the post office up to three times a week, I'm always amazed at how quick they move that line. And they are all still working! Apparently, I am not the only one who appreciates them…as I came out from shipping my packages someone wrote a thank you message with chalk on the sidewalk just outside—thanking the postal workers and recognizing them as essential. They so are essential, and I am thankful for all they do for me!

Next was a trip to Publix to pick up stuff for the house and restock items to make the red sangria at the brewery. Thank goodness I did because we blew the keg within the first 20 minutes of being open today. I know we are all craving human connection now so if you want some, all I can suggest is a trip to Publix. The staff is so friendly, they all say 'hello' through their masks, and just the look in their eyes tells you they are smiling. I just love that they are so friendly, even during times of stress. I made sure to smile and say 'hello' to them as well, to give them a sense that I'm proud of them and thankful for all they do.

That got me thinking, how many people perform the little daily tasks we take for granted?

I'm sure there are too many to count. The important thing is that we know, and they know they are important. Like farmers, grocery clerks, health care workers, post office workers and first responders. Have you ever taken a minute to think about how different our world would be if these people didn't do those jobs? Now go a step beyond that and think about everything we do in a day. Well maybe not today, but in past normal days—riding in a car (i.e. gas station attendants because we all don't have electric yet, mechanics who keep us moving, and car manufactures, truck drivers and train conductors that get our vehicles to us), using a cell phone (i.e. computer programmers, people who build cell phone towers, cell company employees), eating a meal (i.e. farmers, factory workers, truck drivers and grocery employees), and the list goes on and on.

Think about everything you touch, you have, or you do. Someone else, a stranger, helped make that possible. So why, knowing all of this, can't we all smile at each other and say 'hello.' and treat each other with compassion. I'm not saying become their best friend (but you might want to be), but recognize that everyone has a worth, a purpose and a value.

This afternoon I spent time at the brewery. Bryan was brewing with our founder, Marty, so I was on duty to help Tara out front. I don't know how helpful I was—I tend to socialize more than anything. But hey, it's something I enjoy, so I consider it a win for the day!

Tonight was a quiet evening at home. I watched a movie, and we ate leftovers. One thing we are not lacking in our house is food! We tend to order out a lot, but we never eat it all, so this weekend is consisting of a lot of leftovers. I don't mind at all. It should give me a cleaned-out fridge to order more this week. LOL.

Well, tonight is going to be an early night for me. Tomorrow morning my goal is to get up, make breakfast, go to Office Depot and Home Depot, and then to my shop where I am going to spend some quality time in my kitchen working on some new recipes. I'm looking forward to that, and then finishing cleaning up the mess from my broken window and giving the middle room a good vacuum. I really don't mind any of the work, especially the part where I get to create things!

So long for now, until tomorrow!

April 26, 2020

My day started out at home, with Bryan making us sausage, egg, and cheese bagels. It was delicious and I love that we are making breakfast at home, though I will say I will be much happier when we can go out on Sunday morning for breakfast. Before all the shutdowns, we had made going out to breakfast on Sunday morning a weekly ritual.

After breakfast, Bryan went down to the brewery, and I went to vacuum my tearoom. We have been using our middle room as an office and work room and in an effort to keep it clean, it was time for it to be swept and straightened. I also worked a little on getting the rest of my broken window cleaned up.

About midway through cleaning my mom called, and I went to Office Depot to help her pick out a new printer. Oh boy, were they picked over for printers. After looking for a few minutes, she decided what she wanted, and we resolved to order it online. As we walked down the aisle to get some other supplies, we noticed the printer she wanted, sitting on the ground next to a shelf. How lucky! So, we put it in the cart and finished shopping. I mean, seriously, how lucky!

After shopping, I returned to my tearoom to work on a new scone recipe so I can put it out on social media for our guests. It felt so good to be in my kitchen playing around and trying some new things. I saw a recipe for a blackberry scone that uses Earl Grey tea, with a lemon vanilla drizzle. I always change recipes and make them my own, so I decided to do just that with this recipe. In my tearoom kitchen I usually have all my equipment at my disposal. In an effort to keep dishes to a minimum today, I decided to mix by hand, so I didn't have to clean the mixer. Man was that a challenge, but worth it not to have to clean that machine.

All I can say is—oh my gosh!! The scones came out so good! The only thing I don't like about blackberries is the little seeds, but honestly it wasn't enough to deter me from eating them.

I spent the later part of the afternoon at the brewery. I didn't do much except work on my computer. I am working on this week's social media for my shop, so it was good to have some time to do that and get caught up on emails.

Tonight was a low-key night at home. As much as I want to constantly run, I admit that sometimes it feels good to not do anything. So, that's exactly what I did. We ate leftovers and vegged on the couch. At about 9:30 p.m., I was ready to fall asleep. Unfortunately, that's what happens when I stop, and then I don't sleep well in bed. So, I'm up now, just waiting for bedtime.

I'm sure I'm exhausted because my brain goes nonstop. I'm constantly worrying about our businesses, finances, my employees, how long this is going to last, and so much more. I just wish I could have 2 to 3 days of not dealing with anything—to truly get a break. You know, run away, stay in a hotel, rest and hang out, and not worry about all the things that have been on my mind since this craziness started. I know, wishful thinking, but you can bet when I finally can take that break, I'm going to take it.

April 28, 2020

The days seem to be running just about the same, not a lot of changes from day to day anymore...

This morning, I got up and got around like I do every morning. Then I headed into my office.

Today was a numbers game. I hadn't reconciled the books for either business since January, so I decided to spend my day getting that caught up. I didn't take long, but I've never had more than one to do. I have been so good about doing it monthly. Still, there were no major surprises with it, other than the lack of transactions happening this month compared to others. Despite doing all I can, we are still down 80% over this time last year. That hurts.

I've never been a doom-and-gloom person, but the reality of what is currently happening can be seen that way for most businesses. The reality is most businesses operate on such a small margin that they can't sustain for long without a steady and consistent stream of revenue. We have done it for five weeks. Well really six to seven because our reservations started falling off sooner than we were closed because people were scared. I don't know who could keep afloat with bills and keep employees on regular schedules longer than four to six weeks, even with financial help. Even though we have been blessed to have help, it's supposed to help multiple facets of the business. That's great that staff are kept on, but with little revenue coming in, you struggle to pay the operating expenses. Now, for the first time in my business career this is where I find myself torn. I am torn between keeping things afloat for the next two to three weeks as they have been all along and praying within that time frame things will reopen a little to provide a steadier revenue stream. Or do I wind down the business and employees and conserve funds so that we have the money to reopen strongly when we are given the go ahead? It's a tough decision, and one that impacts more than just me.

The other scary part of this is the mental game it's playing. I'm not talking about depression or anything like that. For me, it's making me question if I want to go back to it all. I've enjoyed working less hours, feeling a lot more relaxed, and being less exhausted than when I juggled two businesses and a home life (a very little one at that). The sense of urgency isn't there like it was…and while there is still pressure (just a different kind); the pressure now is on decisions and daily operation. I wish there was a happy medium—a place in the middle where I could enjoy my businesses but have more time for myself. A place where Bryan and I could spend a few days away like we used to; where we can eat dinner together more than one night a week, and not always be at our businesses.

Gosh, if someone would have told me when the year started this is where we would be, I would have never guessed. Now many people, including me, are left to make some major decision about our and others' livelihoods, and no matter which one we make, it is bound to be wrong for someone. I'm sure I'll get it wrong, but it's my decision to make and I hate it. I mean, I love it because I am in a position to make these decisions, but I hate it because both options are wrong.

That's what I contemplated today...while working in my office, while enjoying an awesome lunch from Boulevard Beef & Ale, while reconciling my books, and while writing out 'thank you' notes to our guests who have purchased tea online for shipping. All day, for the past several days or longer, this is pretty much all I have thought about.

I worked in my office until 6 p.m., then went home, had dinner and watched a movie with Bryan, my mom and mother-in-law. They are the one thing that has stayed consistent during this difficult time, and despite the hard road ahead, I am so thankful for them.

April 28, 2020

So, I didn't sleep well last night. It's like every time I was almost asleep, I woke up. This continued all night long. I'm not sure why. I know I'm stressed, but usually I am still able to grab a few hours of sleep. I don't know if I am staying up too late or being on my phone or computer too late. All I know is this whole crazy situation has my internal clock all screwed up! Maybe going to bed earlier and getting off the electronics will help.

This morning, I thought it would be nice to surprise my staff by fixing them some tea when they arrived at the tearoom. We sat around together, visiting for about an hour, laughing and sharing. We talked about the pressure this pandemic has caused, and about depression and anxiety. It was important for me, as their leader, to talk to them, acknowledge that I know they are going through hard times, and to let them know they are not alone. I also shared with them where our company stood and what I'm doing. I felt they needed to know the reality of the situation and how I'm trying to conserve, so we can open well when we have the option. I also think it's important that they aren't disillusioned about our struggle. I realized that we all hadn't talked, and I hadn't let them know that I understood their fear and frustration.

I also decided that every week we are going to play a game or do something unique to bring a little fun to our place. We have so much fun every day with our guests and that has been lacking between the team, so it's time to bring it back. I hope they enjoy what I have in store for them. A little game with prizes!

This afternoon I made a new scone recipe. I'm working on a little project with it, so I have been trying out new recipes. Today's scone was savory with ricotta cheese, scallions, parsley, thyme and rosemary. OMG, it was amazing!! I made sixteen of them, and yes, I have only eaten one. Tomorrow I am going to get some soup and take a photo with them. I'm so excited that my project is moving along and that my recipes are working out well!

Tonight, I had my weekly tea gathering online. I just love that group! It allows me to converse with people in the tea industry; we share ideas and encourage each other. It has truly been a light in my week during this time.

Well, it's 9:30 p.m. and I'm starting to cook dinner. Tonight, it's going to be grilled cheese since it's late. We have tried to eat out and support our friends who own restaurants, but tonight I'm looking for something simple. I hope it's yummy!

I hope you all are having a good week so far! For those who aren't keeping track, tomorrow is Wednesday. It's the middle of the week and we are getting closer to the weekend, not that it matters because we can't do anything. LOL.

April 29, 2020

This morning started like just about every other. Though, I think it actually started out a little smoother. I didn't drop anything or knock anything off the counter, and I felt like I was on my game when I left the house.

Now, I bet by that start you are thinking that the ball finally dropped and ruined my pretty good day, and today you would be wrong. Usually when my day starts out smoothly something always happens to throw the day off, but not today.

The tearoom was busy with to go orders, which I love. It's always so nice to see everyone, all of the smiling faces. It really does give us a chance to remember why we do what we do.

Before we closed for the day, I decided to try my hand at a new scone recipe. It was a strawberry lemon scone with a vanilla lemon glaze. I used our Lady Londonderry black tea in it as well as fresh strawberries and lemon zest. Let me tell you, oh my gosh, it was pretty amazing! I let some of my downtown neighbors try them and they were totally amazed. I love it! Another recipe is good to go.

After all the orders were picked up, I went up to my office and attended a zoom meeting with the city and their marketing planners. I felt like it was a really good meeting. I was on there with other business owners and I'm so proud at the way we see our town and what we want it to become. The potential is tremendous, now and after the pandemic calms. That makes me so happy!

After that meeting, I went downstairs to Rose's Bistro and got a bowl of soup that I could use to take a photo with my savory scone from yesterday. They are just amazing people—always so supportive of my crazy ideas. Actually, both of my building neighbors are awesome! Last week Boulevard Beef & Ale let me work on some tea cocktails, this week Rose let me use some soup and take some photos in their place. If that's not teamwork, I don't know what is.

The best part of my day was watching the Governor's talk tonight and seeing that restaurants can open their dining rooms to 25% capacity. For my capacity, that only equates to eight and a half seats inside. When we are used to eighteen to twenty-five guests per seating, it's hard to imagine doing business at 25%. However, if I can add that to what we are currently doing, that's helpful. I'm also looking to see what we can do about outside seating now that all outdoor seating can open, with CDC (Center for Disease Control) guidelines being followed. Tomorrow, I will meet with our contractor to discuss ideas, followed by the process of filing with the state and local authorities. We will see if there is anything we can do, fingers crossed. Now is the time for invention and unique ideas and I've got my thinking cap on.

After my day, I came home and relaxed. We had dinner and now I'm ready to turn into bed. I've got to let my brain rest before my "crazy idea" day tomorrow. Wish me luck!!

I hope you and your families are well, and I can't wait to see and hug all of you soon (I hope)!

April 30, 2020

Well, all my good vibes today from yesterday disappeared. I should have known first thing this morning when I was getting ready. I always do my deodorant first and then lotion on my face, and today I grabbed the lotion first. I grabbed it, looked at it, put it down and thought, "No,

I can't do this today." That was the start of the day being off.

Now, I know this craziness didn't happen because I was tired. No, no, I actually slept great! That storm everyone heard late last night, yeah, I slept right through it.

I got to my store a little late today because I was in the middle of getting ready for work and my husband informed me that he had to use the bathroom now. So, I sat on the couch waiting, and waiting...I really need that master suite built with a second bathroom.

Once settled in my store, I was going to sit down with my team to discuss our plans for reopening. However, our phone had other ideas. By 10:30 a.m. we were already up to thirty carry out afternoon teas and we realized that I would have to take a trip to Largo for supplies.

Before leaving, I met with my contractor to talk about ideas for some outside seating. We can only open to 25% capacity inside, but we can also utilize outside seating. We need to see how we can accommodate our guests and keep our quaint and beautiful atmosphere. It's going to be a balancing act and I know we can hit it out of the park, but it is going to require a little planning. I hope we can get it moving quickly, I'm so excited!

Around 11:30 a.m., off I went in my trusty gold steed (my truck) to get us restocked. The restaurant supply store was crazy, to say the least. While trying to run around, I kept seeing lots of couples walking around. Yea, they opened up our restaurant supply for the public. While this doesn't tend to bother me, I was on a mission and needed to get going and they were just wandering in my way. The highlight of my trip was running into Sean from Sip in the refrigeration section. It was so good to see him, and I am so glad he is doing well across the street!

Running back to my shop, I had return before 3 p.m. so that I could do my online virtual tea party... but first, I had to talk to my team. I wanted a meeting where we could talk and discuss several things, but it became a rushed conversation. We got done what we needed quickly, and I got online with my virtual tea party. Or at least I planned to.

These days, nothing goes as planned. I went to get online using my phone and I had no sound. I tried again, no sound. Tried on my laptop and I couldn't figure it out. I tried again, nothing. Then, right about 4 p.m. I got it figured out and I went live, finally, only an hour after I had originally planned! I had a great time chatting and sharing with my guests. Now I know how to get my live programs going, so I won't have issues again.

This afternoon I had a great conversation with my dear friend Julie. I love her so much; she is one of the strongest people I have ever met. She is facing a challenging time ahead and I will be with her every step of the way. My faith is strong, and I know she will be okay. In my heart I feel it.

After my wonderful conversation, it was time to start helping get the teas together for tomorrow. My friend Travis came over to help get our new chandeliers ready to be put up in the tearoom. I can't wait for our guests to see the new lighting; it is so beautiful! I also helped my mom, who has been the biggest trooper in all this, with her work on getting teas ready. The orders are all good to go for the morning, and I have my amazing friend, Samantha, along with my first-class team ready for "battle" tomorrow.

Bryan did a virtual happy hour at the brewery tonight. He did really well, and I felt bad that I couldn't be there. I was tied up with tea. He has gotten much more comfortable with making online videos. I am proud of him for embracing his business and doing some new things to keep it thriving.

Tonight, after my crazy running around day, we decided to get takeout. We enjoyed a family dinner at my mom's with my mother-in-law too. I am so blessed that my mom and mother-in-law get along and like spending time together with us. I know it sucks for both of them being widowed, but for selfish reasons I'm happy I get to spend so much time with them. Time goes too fast and it's so important to spend it together now.

Well, time to go to bed. I have to get ready for a crazy busy day tomorrow. I'm so excited!!

May 2020

May 2, 2020

It's May Day and at first when I heard that, I thought, why would there be a day for a distress call. I mean, when the ship is going down, don't they call "Mayday, mayday!"

Actually, it was funny because my day was going to be crazy, so all I could think was if I had to make a distress call, today would be the day. How perfect!

I arrived at my shop early (for me) and found my team hard at work. We had fifty-six Afternoon Teas To Go, twelve dozen scones, and some catering platters to be ready by 11 a.m. It was a race to the finish line, but we did it! Thanks to my awesome team, Dawne, and Lily, for keeping it alive in the kitchen and putting up with my craziness trying to help. I'm sure it's not easy when your leader comes in and tells you about the order count for the day, but they make it happen thanks to Dawne's leadership and always being as prepared as anyone could be on the kitchen side.

I thought we made a pretty good team as things moved from one task to another. How awesome it was when we all came together! And, I must admit, I enjoyed having the opportunity to get into the kitchen for a little bit!

Up front my mom was amazing. I'm so proud of all the things that she has learned. I'm sure when she decided to come to work for me part time, she never imagined learning or doing so much with tea. And then there's my amazing friend, Samantha. Talk about someone who is beautiful both inside and out, and probably the most selfless person I have ever met. Not only has she been helping me out at the brewery, but also when I asked her to come hang out and help me as a friend at the tearoom, she didn't hesitate. She embraced the whole experience and was truly a blessing today, as she is every day.

I guess the moral of today's story is that "no man is an island." It has been great that we have been able to grow both of our businesses and keep them busy even during this time, but a person cannot deliver success alone. Yes, I may be the leader, but my team together with my leadership makes all of us a collective success.

In fact, in every facet of life we play different roles, but with equal importance. We all coexist, survive and succeed together. Yes, sometimes we fail together too. The important part is to realize we are together, a team, and to appreciate and preserve the team.

I'm so proud, with our busiest day since the "stay at home" order was put into place that we didn't have to sound the "mayday" call because as a team we succeeded!

I just hope that when this is all over and we start moving toward wherever the new normal is headed, that we all remember we are a part of a team and continue to love and respect one another for who we are and for the part we play.

XOXO

May 2, 2020

Day forty wasn't bad at all. For the past two nights I actually slept pretty well, so that makes for better days all the way around. In addition, yesterday was my day to take vitamin D, so for the next few days I will be a little more energetic and able to accomplish more than I do on my down days.

This morning called for a quick trip to Publix before heading into the brewery. It was nice being out and the place wasn't too packed. I had to go for two main reasons: 1. Poor Sam was out of cat food, so to get her by this morning she got a handful of treats, and 2. I had to get more items to make another batch of red sangria.

I spent half the day at the brewery—really just making sure everything was good while Bryan brewed. He has had to start brewing again because we were getting low on beer. Honestly, it's quite a spot to be in, to be making beer, when so many others are dumping beer for sitting too long.

Later in the afternoon I spent some time in my kitchen at my shop, working on another savory scone recipe. It was prosciutto and gruyere cheese with parmesan, green onion and parsley. I got the prosciutto and gruyere from my friends at Heros Downtown Subs and Salads, and it was perfect. The scones came out amazing! In fact, it was hard to eat just one...I wanted to keep eating them, but goodness knows I don't need them!

Apparently, they were a hit because everyone who tried them said they were very flavorful and really good. Yes, another recipe for my project!

Tonight, while enjoying leftovers for dinner, I watched the movie "The Art of Racing in the Rain." It was a great movie. A little soft...I don't really cry, but I could feel the emotion building. Let's be realistic though, anyone else would cry, including my husband who had to keep getting up to leave the room because he hates movies that make him cry. LOL. Still, it was a great movie, and it featured a golden retriever that I want so badly! Unfortunately, our lifestyle doesn't allow for a dog, but I look forward to the day when it does.

Well, I'm heading off to bed. I have a lot going on tomorrow as I work to get prepared for our minor reopening later next week. It's exciting and stressful all at the same time! Wish me luck!

May 3, 2020

Did you ever have one of those days where you wake up on the wrong side of the bed and everything bothers you more than it should?

Today was that day for me!

It started when Bryan didn't ask me about something before he did it. To be clear, he does stuff all the time without telling me and it doesn't bother me, but this had to do with the scones I made. Normally, it wouldn't have bothered me, but today I flew off the handle. In fact, I was so upset that I sent him to the brewery alone and I stayed home for thirty minutes to sit on the couch to try to calm down.

I'm not sure if my tolerance level is lower these days because of all we are going through but man, I could have ripped someone's head off. I have remained pretty calm during this whole thing. When I feel like this, I know I need to just take a break from everything. Otherwise, I will say or do something I regret, and really with no justification. That's not what I want at all. I tend to just remove myself, so I don't do something bad.

I finally calmed down and eventually made it into my shop to make another scone recipe.

Today was a triple chocolate scone with vanilla glaze. I used white, milk, and dark chocolate chips. I think it came out really good and it's a nice thing to enjoy instead of the usual chocolate chip cookies. I haven't taken any photos yet, but plan to tomorrow.

I ran to Lowe's this afternoon. I usually prefer Home Depot, but I wasn't willing to stand in line when all I needed were some light bulbs. I also looked at some smaller bistro sets to possibly use for outside dining in the alley way of my building. I found a set I like but, I'm not willing to get it until I get the okay that I can put the fence up and block off the area for private dining.

Afterwards, I went back to the brewery, stayed a little while, and enjoyed some pizza. Then I decided the best option for me was to go home and watch a movie, maybe take a short nap, and just keep to myself. I could feel myself getting worked up a little for no reason, so it was truly necessary.

My night was low key. Bryan and I took a nice golf cart ride. It was nice to get some fresh air. We toured some different parts of the city that we don't often see so it made it fun to look at the houses and get ideas of what I want to do with ours.

Here's to a good night's sleep and the hopes that tomorrow I get up on the right side of the bed.

May 4, 2020

Today was a decent day...I slept in a little and had a hard time getting moving. I have been trying to figure out why it is so hard for me to get up in the morning. I lie in bed and feel great, but then trying to get moving is a rough go. Today, I decided to check my blood sugar, and yep, that would be why. It was high, not go to the hospital high, but high enough that the day warranted being a little careful on what I consumed.

I got to my shop a little later than anticipated today but got right to work. We are getting ready to open with very limited seating, so I have lot of things to do before we welcome our guests back. Last week we added new chandeliers to the tearoom, so today we got the lightbulbs in, got the tables cleared off and moved back into place, hung some of the curtains we had taken down for dry cleaning, and dusted all the fans, and lights! Tomorrow, I have a list for my team to continue getting ready. It's awesome that we are in this position to be able to get ready to serve guests again! Though I am not sure everyone will like cleaning, it's a necessary evil if we want to be ready and be on the top of our game. My mom was a trouper today, working with me, side by side, doing some of the grunt work. LOL.

Today for lunch, we did the unthinkable that was finally allowed—we went out to lunch. We walked over and sat at our downtown neighbor, Rose's Bistro. We sat outside under their patio and enjoyed eating in the fresh air. It was wonderful and I love outside patio dining!

Tonight, I treated my mom to a drink and some appetizers at our other downtown neighbor Boulevard Beef & Ale. Again, we sat out on their patio, just enjoying the night. I really liked seeing other friends doing the same. Everyone was keeping a safe distance, but just hearing other conversations and laughing was enough to warm my heart and remind me why socializing is so important to us, as human beings. Truly, it was much needed after the past 6 weeks.

To my friend, Melissa, I don't think I have laughed so hard in a long time. I finally realized that I'm not the only French Onion soup eating weirdo! I mean, truly, who else eats the whole soup, allowing the cheese to soak in the broth, and then eats the cheese at the end! OMG, my soul mate!! P.S. This week I am going to wear my Carol dress!! And Jean, I feel a sunset coming soon!!

After so much seclusion during the past six weeks, it is easy to see why people have suffered from depression and aggression. I have been fortunate to at least escape to my shop a few days a week, and to the brewery as well. I feel for the people who can't or don't go out. The seclusion must be enough to make one go nearly crazy. I pray for the people up north, as we know nothing of what they are going through. We are so blessed to live where we live, have this beautiful weather we have, and be allowed to begin living our lives on a small level right now.

I hope you continue to stay healthy, and if you go out, remain diligent and be careful. We don't want to go backwards during this time!

May 5, 2020

I'm writing early tonight in the hopes that the rest of my evening will be uneventful, and I will be able to sit back and relax a little.

Today wasn't a bad day; I just had a lot going on. Still, despite it all, it ran smoothly. I was at my shop by 9:30 a.m. this morning, and my awesome manager, Dawne was already working. She was doing a good cleaning of the kitchen, so we are ready for our minor opening this week. She cleans the kitchen all the time, but we removed everything out of it this week to have some tile replaced. It was a good time to clean behind things and really make sure we are good to go.

Mom worked on answering the phone, which barely seemed to take a break today until later in the afternoon, and she got our teas ready for pick up tomorrow. I am so glad so many people are excited about the Afternoon Tea to go. I just love that people are taking the time to enjoy tea and relax a little among the stress that is "Rona."

I worked on getting our five hundred tea bags out to Sips By. This has and continues to be a huge chore for us, but it has brought recognition to our brand along with the opportunity to ship our teas all over the country. I mean, we must be getting known when the young man at the UPS store asks my phone number and pulls up my tea company and says, "Oh you're the tea company with the shop downtown!" Score one for branding, marketing and repetition! Needless to say, I gladly sent those teas out with a big smile on my face. No, I didn't wear a mask, so everyone could see how excited I was in the shipping store.

This afternoon was probably the most 'exciting' part of my day. My husband walks into the tearoom and tells me that our fridge at home is broken and things are thawing in the freezer, as the Paula Abdul song played in my head: 'one step forward, two steps back.' Yea, you know the one!

I headed home to remove everything from the house fridge and take it to the fridge in the shed. Then it was a dreaded trip to Home Depot to look for a new fridge. Look, I like the store normally, but these days people are crazy! I mean, really... Do we need a new fridge right away because we always eat at home and have it stocked? Well, not really, our fridge is more of a holding place where leftovers go to die a long and slow death. Low and behold, we got the freezer emptied and one big garbage bag of food to throw away. The oldest thing I found in there was from 2018, not too bad for me! But then the darn fridge started working. Now it's blowing cold air, running normal, and freezing my awesome ice packs I use for my neck spasms, score! After that, we decided not to remove items from the fridge and to see what happens. Here's hoping I don't come home tomorrow to the fridge being warm and that I can hold on to my stimulus money a little longer!

Tonight, I came home to get on my Tea Mastermind weekly meeting. I just love them all so much. I mean, let's be realistic, being in business is hard. You have ideas, goals and things you want to accomplish. Sometimes there just aren't a lot of people to bounce ideas off of, so that's where this amazing group of tea professionals comes in. Granted we talk about tea, but sharing ideas about expanding businesses, how we operate those businesses, and what we could do differently or better is a great resource and outlet for me. When I have those days where I wonder what all of this is for, they lift me up. We talk about tea and our businesses, offer suggestions when needed, and cheer for each other's successes. Truly, I need a group like that because sometimes sitting out on the business owner limb can be pretty lonely.

Now, it's time for dinner. Cinco de Mayo! I think this is the first year I am not going out to dinner at a Mexican restaurant, how strange! But strange times call for weird measures or something like that.

So, I'll leave you with this, a toast: Cheers to the beers that we drink, cheers to the tacos we eat, and cheers that next year this holiday won't be interrupted by a virus that keeps us apart!

Cheers!

May 6, 2020

We are making the hill to fifty days of me sharing my writing! Before we know it, it will be all downhill.

You know, as I think about the comment 'over the hill', I don't really think it pertains to the fact that things go downhill or get bad, as much as it takes longer to go up hill than it does down. Think of it this way, I love to hike in the mountains and the last time I hiked Mount LeConte it took me seven hours to get to the summit. On the way down, it only took five hours. The same amount of distance takes less time going down. So, when I started thinking about 'it's all downhill, I think it relates to our perception of time. When you're young, you look at forty and think it's so far away, then you reach forty and all the sudden you blink and it's fifty. Same decade of time, but it seems to go by faster.

Don't ask me why I went off on that tangent. I was looking at how many days I have been writing this daily update and all of the sudden it got me thinking. Gosh, I hope that when I hit fifty days, a magic button will be hit, and the days will go fast. Before we know it, things will be closer to normal, but it won't feel like so many days.

Oh boy, I think I'm delusional tonight.

Today was a good day. It started with a big smile when I arrived at my shop and noticed a white envelope at my front door. The absolutely amazing J. David eft me some beautiful photos of me with my husband and niece that he took at the Chasco King and Queen gathering we hosted at the brewery in March. I just love them, and they gave me the biggest smile! I can't wait to put them in my office! Thank you so much J. David! You are a true gem and an amazing person, and I'm so blessed to know you!

The rest of my day was filled with getting orders shipped out, working on cleaning some things up at the shop, and putting some finishing touches on the tearoom for the reopening tomorrow. We only have two tables for reservation, and I am so happy for that! It's truly an honor to be able to welcome guests back. When we make our official announcement tomorrow about being able to take reservations, I know it's going to get quite full—well, as full as we can be with nine people.

Tonight, we went to look at refrigerators. Since yesterday, ours at home has stayed cold for the most part, but it's showing signs of wanting to act up. I just don't want to take the chance and have it break when we aren't around. What a mess trying to find one that fits our space. Who knew that in ten years these things would get so big? I mean, honestly, we barely even use this thing and now trying to find one to for the space is hard. We currently have a side by side and it's been good. But the side-by-side ones are at least two to three inches bigger than what we have now. In this situation, inches really do matter…Bryan is looking at a freezer on top and fridge on the bottom. You know, the only way they came in the 80's. Think about your first apartment. I really could care less, but I want it to look nice. We will see what the next few days hold as we continue looking.

Tomorrow night is the return of our girl's night. We aren't able to go to Carrabba's, so it's going to be a makeshift wine night at Boulevard Beef & Ale, yea liquor!! Just kidding, I don't really drink but I'm looking forward to seeing my girls!

So, time to turn in. I've got an exciting day ahead, and I can't wait to tell you how it goes!

Nighty night!

May 8, 2020

Yesterday when I got home, I was so exhausted that I actually fell asleep on the couch and didn't move until 1 a.m.!

Yesterday was our first day back open to the public. We have done a very soft opening, as we do not want to overload ourselves and also want to make sure we are prepared for our guests. It's actually a little strange being back open. It's almost like we are starting all over.

Last night we got the gals together for dinner. We didn't go to Carrabba's because we were looking to sit outdoors, so we went to Boulevard Beef & Ale. We sat on their back patio and man did we have fun. It's so true that it's all about the company you keep, and I am so blessed for these ladies in my life. They have been through some major stuff this year and still we manage to get together and laugh. It was so needed for all of us! Personally, I don't think I have laughed or smiled that much in several months.

Today was a busy day at the tearoom. We had twenty-nine Afternoon Teas to go, and some scones being picked up. We also had a few tables in for tea, so that was nice. You know, I don't mind doing the 'to go' packages, but it does make it a little more difficult when we are open and having guests in too. For our tiny kitchen it sure is pressing our limit. Still, I am trying to make up for six weeks of no revenue. While it may look like we are making lots of money, we are down for the year and behind on our budget that I doubt we will ever catch up, at least not this year. I really just want to get to the point where the bills are all good and we can actually pay them all. Don't get me wrong, we were doing great before all of this happened. Now we are trying to catch up and it would be nice to get back to where we were. The problem is we are going to have to kill ourselves to get there.

Tonight was a nice low-key night at home. I made dinner and the moms joined us. We watched a Tom Hanks movie from 1996 called "That Thing You Do." I haven't seen it in years and it's just one of those cute, feel-good movies. It was a good way to end the day.

Tomorrow is going to be crazy! We have sixty Afternoon Teas to go and seventeen people in the tearoom between two different seatings. I will be happy when everything runs smoothly, and I can take a much-needed break at 4 p.m.

I hope you all have a nice Saturday! Stay tuned to see how we do with our largest takeout day yet!

May 10, 2020

Today started off really good. I was a little worried because it was going to be such a busy day, but things went smoothly.

I arrived at my shop at 9 a.m., which, for those of you who know me know that's early. I have never been a morning person. In fact, I will often decline to be on boards in the community if they meet before 9 a.m. At 9 a.m. I will still be five minutes late!

First thing I did was started helping to get sandwiches together in the kitchen. Because I have a great team in there, I usually end up putting the spreads on the sandwiches while they do the rest. Today was just that kind of day. I spread, they made. Then they put together the 'to go' trays. There was a lot today and we had to be done with the tearoom food and set up before our first seating, so it was a race against the clock, and we beat it. Way to go Team!

The shop was quite busy today. We saw guests for tea in the tearoom, guests for 'to go' tea service, and guests shopping for gifts. Overall, I think people were just happy to be out and about and having conversations with others. It was cute, some of our guests said it was the first time they put on makeup or did their hair in six or seven weeks because they never see anyone. I love that! It made them feel good too!!

I did spend a little time at the brewery this afternoon. Hey, someone has to make the red sangria! I didn't stay long because after our day, I was exhausted. Just the mental preparedness that goes along with busy days is enough to make you crash. So, that's what I did afterwards.

Tonight, I came home, and I honestly did nothing. I watched a movie, read a little in my book, and had some downtime. Now I keep thinking about all the time I wasted...oh well, I'm going to start calling it "me time," so I won't feel so guilty.

My biggest dilemma tonight is deciding if I should go down to St. Pete Beach and stay at the Don Cesar for the next two nights. We haven't been anywhere in so long. During this whole 'stay at home' thing we continued to work, despite the businesses being closed. So, I looked at the rooms and they are a pretty good price. It's just a matter of whether I want to spend it. See, I keep thinking about all the other things I could do with that money—like put it toward getting the house painted.

Decisions, decisions!

May 11, 2020

First, I want to wish a Happy Mother's Day to all the moms out there. Actually, to all the ladies out there! You may not have given birth, but you have probably acted as a mom in some way, shape, or form at one point in your life, and for that you deserve a huge thank you!

My Sunday was like almost every other before the virus happened. I had breakfast with Bryan and my mom.

Then, right after breakfast my mom and I headed down to Restaurant Depot to get supplies for the tearoom. It's our normal every other Sunday trip—we ride down, get our supplies and come back. I always enjoy those rides because we talk about all kinds of things, from work to family stuff. Sometimes the conversations get interesting, and I love it. Today was just the usual stuff. The shop is ok, but not great...what other things can I do to help it along? Maybe some restructuring, or different things like that. These are things I really need to take some quiet time alone and ponder.

The supply store was a mess! When all this craziness started happening, they started allowing individuals without business licenses in. While I get it, now that the restaurants are starting to reopen, there are hardly any supplies for them. It almost makes me want to write to the corporate office about it. I still may.

After shopping and unloading everything, I felt the need to play in my kitchen. While most of my experiments lately have been pretty good, today did not turn out the same. I thought it would be fun to experiment with making some petit fours with some sponge cakes that we had cut and frozen. In the past we have used them just as little cakes, so they were already cut to a certain size. Today I took them, added some preserves, put another cake on top, covered them with chocolate, and did a really cool drizzle design. While it definitely made the cakes taste so much better, they looked hideous. One looked like the leaning tower! LOL. So, back to the drawing board I go, and I will try again next weekend.

Tonight was a quiet evening at home. We made steaks on the grill for the moms for Mother's Day and watched a Disney sing along. Both moms had their "ears" on. Then we watched Forrest Gump. What a great movie! I've seen it hundreds of times but still enjoy watching it. I love the music. Not just the rock-n-roll, but the score as well. It's so beautiful.

Well, it's time for bed. I have a few things planned for early in the day, so hopefully I will be able to spend the afternoon relaxing...fingers crossed.

May 11, 2020

Today was a good day! I ran through my normal routine and got to my shop to prepare some outgoing orders. After getting those ready and packaged, I made my every-other-day trip to the post office. Can I just tell you; I love our post office team? They are awesome! They are always so nice and helpful.

After that, we picked up the moms and spent the day at the beach. We ended up at St. Pete Beach at the Don Cesar.

Can I tell you, the perfect way to be forced into relaxation is to be on the beach watching the waves? We actually sat at a table on the deck at the beach, but not on the sand. Because of my medications I don't do well in the sun. A lot of times I end up with hives or not feeling well, so I sat in the shade and just stared at the water. Of course, it's a great way to unwind, but it also is a great time to let your mind wander. Interestingly, I did have a few ideas that came to me. I can't wait to explore them a little more.

It's funny, I am used to being down here when the pool and beach are filled to capacity, and everything is open. Today, you could have your pick of places on the beach, and we didn't run into too many people. Those we did seemed mildly concerned at most, of any virus or pandemic. They all practiced staying away from each other and there were lots of comments about things not being open, even partially. I get it, but when you have a resort hotel, you have to accommodate your guests.

After a day of relaxing, I'm ready to get back to work tomorrow. In order to continue to take care of myself and my team, I decided to only open my shop Wednesday through Saturday, from 11 a.m. to 4 p.m., with seating times at 12 p.m. and 2 p.m. That gives us some time for reservations, but also the ability to continue to take care of ourselves. During this time, I have realized how important self-care is. Until we get to a fuller capacity, that is the way I am going to keep it. I mean, as much as I love working and what I do, I need to take some time for me to stay healthy and now that I've started, I need to keep it part of my routine.

Have you picked up any good habits during this crazy time?

May 13, 2020

My day started out on the beautiful St. Pete Beach. There's nothing like waking up at a beautiful hotel and opening the curtains to see the absolutely perfect beach and Gulf of Mexico in front of you. Eating breakfast at our usual table overlooking the beach and breathing in the fresh air was something I needed. I hated to leave, but it's time to get back to life.

Overall, the day was relatively relaxing. I did stop in my shop, and everything was under control, so I didn't stay long. In fact, I was so tired that I came home and took a short nap. I have found that when I spend time at home, I don't get much work done, but I do get some much-needed rest.

Tonight was my weekly tea group. I had a nice time with them tonight. I always get so many ideas and it's a good thing that I write them down because I will never remember all of them. Now I just need more time for all the things I want to do. More to come for sure!

Tomorrow our shop is open and I'm excited to be back on a more normal schedule. I've got lots to do, so I am anxious to get it started. Not only that, but I'm going to work hard, so I can get another beach break soon!

May 13, 2020

Onward and upward to day one hundred of this writing project. Let's keep going!

Today the shop did well, and we had a few reservations at our 12 p.m. seating time. They went well, and of course I just love seeing everyone! I feel so blessed that despite everything, we are still getting our guests to slowly come out and visit with us.

Today I got some exciting news about our teas. We currently place our teas with Sips By, a subscription-based tea service. We have been working with them on our summer teas and they asked us to make a tea that we did with them in the winter. When I asked why they wanted to do it again, they said it was because that tea is currently ranked #6 all-time highest white teas they have ever offered.

I was so excited to hear that. That means all of the white teas they have ever brought in and sent out through their service; this is the #6 favorite. They feel if they can do a full run of this tea again that it may just move a lot higher. Take that big tea companies. My little tea company is making great blends! Oh, the tea, you ask? Why it's my very own blend—Strawberry Dream! Yea, happy dance!

This afternoon I met with extraordinary artist, Jenny Pearl. We talked about the potential of a small mural on the side of our tearoom building, in the alley where we hope to have some bistro seating. We have a few ideas, but first I have to see what grants are out there to make something really cool. It's going to go along with what we are doing in the alley. It's so exciting working on a new project and I can't wait to see where this one goes. Oh, and we also talked about our main window. Jenny paints it up for us each season, and I can't wait to unveil our new window in a few weeks!!

Tonight, Bryan and I had a really nice dinner at Thai Bistro in downtown. It's funny, I go there quite frequently but it's always when Bryan is at the brewery. I usually bring him takeout, but tonight it was nice to actually go there and sit down with him. The joy that came from all that has gone on is that we have gotten to eat together and spend more time together. I know things will start to move back to the way they were before. I'd be remiss if I didn't say I kind of wish they wouldn't, just for the selfish reason of feeling like we have a normal life and a normal family.

Well, it's time to start getting ready for bed. This whole day mix-up has caused my sleeping pattern to be messed up badly. Last night I went to bed at 1:30 a.m.! I know I'm a late-night owl, but not usually past midnight. No wonder I'm having issues getting up in the morning!

Night all! Ready for another day of adventures tomorrow!

May 14, 2020

Do you ever have those days that are good and bad at the same time? If ever there was one of those days, today was it!

My day started off good. We received word that our growlers were ready, so Bryan and I decided to take a trip together to St. Augustine and make a night away of it. Why not? Did you know that during this time you can get some amazing deals on great hotel rooms? You know the kind you wish you could stay at, but never do because one night there is as much as your entire car payment. Turns out right now, if you can stomach traveling, those places are now available in abundance.

So, since we have to travel, we might as well stay in a great hotel right in the heart of the historic district. So, we are!

The ride over was pretty standard. I've made the trip so frequently that I know where all the turns are now. As we traveled, that's when the day turned.

First, we are ok, no issues for us. We received some very devastating news. One of my beautiful cousins passed away unexpectedly this afternoon. She was 2 years younger than me and had such a beautiful soul. And her kids are amazing! I am her daughter's godmother, and I haven't been there like I should. We used to talk all the time when she lived closer and today, I regret letting time and distance get between us. I still love her though, and her daughter and I'm hoping that I can step up and be a positive person in her life. She is an absolutely extraordinary little girl, and she loved her momma so much. I hope l can show her love and be the godmother she needs now and in the future.

I also find that when someone I know who passes away so young, I question my own mortality. I think that's only natural, but this one got me thinking about my health, my actions, and what would happen if I wasn't here tomorrow. Now more than ever, it's time for me to put things in order. The last thing I want is to have something happen to me and the people around me to not have my wishes for myself and my businesses laid out. I guess it's time to sit down and get serious about a lot of things in my life.

Tonight, Bryan and I are in St. Augustine and I'm glad we took the evening to come over here. Life is too short, and we need to take the time to be together. Even though we own businesses that are important to a lot of people, they are nothing if we don't take care of ourselves mentally and physically. Before all this, we would sleep in the same bed but hardly talk and we would have dinner together maybe one night a week if we were lucky. That time together, that break, I see that as a priority now and know changes are coming to our businesses, so we can make sure we stay together and spend that quality and much needed time together.

So, my advice to you as we start to move back to some sort of normalcy: take time to relax; take time for you; and find what is important to you and do it. Finding balance is the trick and without it your time will be short.

May 16, 2020

Today, if I had to compare it to any of the past few, was one of those days that I would call uneventful.

This morning, we woke up in beautiful St Augustine. Just being away for the night brought my heart rate and blood pressure down. It's good to get away and really relax, even if it's just for the night.

We left our hotel around 10 a.m. and stopped at The Blue Hen just south of downtown, in the neighborhood of Lincolnville. We enjoyed breakfast there when we stayed in the area a few years back. Today they were serving to-go meals with tables to sit at outside. Bryan got the tomato and scallion omelet with bacon and gruyere. I got the same without tomatoes. It was awesome! And the freshly baked from scratch biscuit was so good. You know, you can definitely tell when something is made from scratch verses something done by food service. Anyway, it was an awesome way to start the day.

Afterwards, we met up with Chris from Skinny Lizard and picked up our brewery's growlers. He is so nice, and I am so glad that we have been able to give him business during this time to help his small business and his staff out too. That's why small business is so vital. We all work together and support each other. We buy a lot from small businesses and that helps them out. It's so important!

We got back to the area around mid-afternoon and my team at the tearoom didn't need me, so I stopped by the brewery quickly, and then went home. Instead of sitting down though, I started working on the house. I folded laundry, emptied the dishwasher, and cleaned up some other little messes around the house. I hate doing those things normally, but today I set a time limit and tried to see how much I could get done. I find that's one way for me to get moving without feeling so overwhelmed. I got some stuff done and spent the rest of my time reading a book on the health benefits of tea. I know, I know! I already know so much about tea, but the reality is you can never know it all and the more I read, the more I keep up on it.

Now it's time for bed. Tomorrow is a slow day in the tearoom so I'm hoping to spend a little time in my upstairs office and getting that better organized. Wish me luck! If anyone ever wants to help, I have a ton of files and books and other stuff to carry upstairs...I hate going up and down the stairs! LOL!!

Here's to another day in the books!

May 18, 2020

I skipped the past few days because, let's be honest, life just isn't too interesting these days. While I always have something going on, sometimes it's not worth talking about because it truly is nothing.

This weekend the tearoom was open on Saturday. I think we had ten to twelve people total. Unfortunately, looking at the numbers, the tearoom will not be able to continue to survive in the long term if it can't generate more revenue. The only good thing is that I am looking at additional revenue streams for the business. Trying to think outside the box was a little easier for me about three weeks ago. I'm not sure what has changed, why I just can't seem to focus or come up with anything these days. I really shouldn't be tired, I mean, seriously! I've had more down time in the past eight weeks than I have in the past twenty-five years! You would think that I would be full of ideas and motivation. Yet, here I am, facing the very thing that kills half the successful authors after their big novel success...writer's block. Maybe not so much writer's block as it is a creative block. That's right, instead of working on my newsletter, generating additional ideas for added revenue, reviewing my five-year business plan, etc., I am here on Facebook writing this! Oh, and eating a chocolate lollipop!

I'm not a big believer in tarot cards or things of that nature, but I do believe in fate and signs. So, this morning while I was sitting in my office trying to concentrate, I decided to pull a deck of wisdom cards from my drawer to see what the "cards" were telling me. After thinking long and hard about a question I had or something I needed, like guidance to know that I am where I am supposed to be and doing what I am supposed to be doing, I closed my eyes and drew a card out of the pile. LOVE! LOL, I know that I have great love in my life; I am so blessed by it. But, as I read the meaning, it didn't just mean people, it means what I do. Do I love what I do, what I represent? Yes, deeply yes. What it means is that love is present in all areas of my life, not just in people. It also says that love has come to guide me into an important experience and that I need to trust love.

So, here I am, trusting that my love of what I do is going to continue to lead me in the right direction. It's going to guide my decisions and help me forge ahead. So, if you see me acting all "lovey" you know why, LOL!

Now I'm going back to my brainstorming, as no one else is going to do it for me. No one is going to make sure my businesses succeed. No one is going to save me, it's up to me. These days I am just wondering if I am up to the task. I hope so.

I hope you all have a great day filled with love too!

May 19, 2020

Well, I must be getting really lazy as I have really enjoyed lying in bed until around 9 a.m. each morning. It's not that I don't want to start my day, but to be honest, my neck has been really bothering me lately. I noticed the spasms have gotten worse and more frequent. It makes it hard to get out of bed because when I am lying down, I tend to have more control. Just the thought of having to get up, shower and deal with my hair is enough for me to want to stay in bed. I swear I can't get a ponytail to be in the center of my head no matter how hard I try...darn dystonia! Tomorrow, I go for a massage and I'm hoping that it feels better or at least maybe I will have some temporary relief.

Today was a good day overall. We received clarification from the Florida Brewer's Guild that breweries are able to open as long as they follow the guidelines set out for restaurants. Boy, I was not expecting that today. I am very happy about that because I know that it will be busy, as busy as safely possible. There are quite a few things that we need to get ready for outside seating and such. I'm glad we kept things running pretty well on a limited basis, so getting back into it won't be hard. I'm sure our team will be happy to serve our guests again too.

I was able to get quite a bit of work done this morning before my afternoon running began. I had to go to Dunedin to get some things for the brewery, and then stop at Tarpon Home and Garden, which always tends to be fun because I find lots of cool things. Then it was lunch at Rose's Bistro, a meeting with John from Hero's, getting an application notarized by my awesome friend Helen, and meeting with Jeff at Wrights, and Margo at Juan-a-Taco. One of the caveats of us being able to open is that guests must buy food with their drink purchases, so we can either have a food truck or work with our local businesses. Of course, our first choice is to work with our local businesses, so we worked this afternoon to get that ready. Everyone is on board for when we open on Thursday.

Now the hunt begins to find tables and chairs that we can put outside for guests. It is not an easy task, and I don't want to spend a lot of money as the outside seating is only temporary until the restaurants get up to higher capacity inside. I have a feeling the two tables from my tearoom may end up over at the brewery simply because they don't get used much outside and Bryan would get much more use out of them.

As things start to come back together, slowly, I find I am getting some more stuff done. That is a really good thing because for a while I was feeling a little useless. This week I finished our shop newsletter, started a class from the US Tea Experience, registered for a class with the World Tea Academy, and finally got caught up on both companies' bookkeeping. Also, I'm really excited about Thursday—it's International Tea Day. I am going to drink and enjoy tea all day and watch an all-day conference with some of the world's leading tea experts. Yea!

Well, here's to another day in the record books. It feels good to be useful and feel like I am working toward something. Even though I feel like I never quite get ahead, I am so happy I am starting to be busy, and useful! I can't wait until things start to fill up more!

May 20, 2020

Boy, you would think by now that I would be running out of things to talk about or that my days would slow down but that's just simply not the case. LOL.

This morning, I got to work at my shop and got some orders shipped out. I'm so glad we are still getting orders! Before I knew it, it was noon, and I went running upstairs to join a virtual meeting for Main Street. I am so honored that Liz asked me to sit in and be a part of the meeting. We discussed ideas for some upcoming small events that can help generate revenue for them and create foot traffic and increased exposure for the businesses. It's a hard balancing act because you want to have things, but not with too many people, so we keep everyone safe. I can see good things coming as we all work together.

This afternoon I had to take a drive to State Road 54 to find a piece of my mom's car that came off yesterday. I know, you're probably thinking, "what the heck?" So, she was at Bealls and when she backed up, she hit the curb. Apparently, it knocked the covering by the wheel off, but it wasn't all the way off, so she drove away with it. She got going down SR54 and the tire caught it and ripped it off. Instead of stopping to get it or calling me to come get it and put it in my truck bed, she kept going. So, as she's telling me this story today, I thought it would be good to go get it. There I was, in my dress, pulled over in a turn lane, loading this large wheel well thing...in the blazing sun! You know, normally she would call or get it, but I blame this craziness and her lack of thought on this pandemic. I have noticed not just her, but others doing crazy things and I just shake my head. Truly, are we all losing our minds?!?

Since I was out in the sun doing my good deed, I thought I deserved a treat. Of course, I stopped at my friend's cupcake shop, Mmmm Delicious Cupcakes. I always love picking out cupcakes. I felt I needed something to take to our awesome mechanic and his team at Master Mechanics, especially because he is going to have to fix my mom's car now. Any time I can do something to bring a smile, I like to do it. Oh, and if you ever get their cupcakes, get truffles too! They are to die for! I'm actually thinking about adding them for sale in my shop, they are that awesome!

Later this afternoon I ran to Old a Time Pottery to get some new bistro tables and chairs to use outside of the brewery. Oh yes, the brewery is opening tomorrow. We got permission from the state! The only caveat is when you order a beer you must order some food. So, we worked with some of the local downtown restaurants and will have some food on-sight. Guests can also order from any of our neighboring restaurants. We have asked to extend our outside area and that application went to the city today. I hope it doesn't take too long to get approved—like when we no longer need it, LOL!

After a massage that I so sorely needed, I spent the rest of my night at the brewery. Yes, I finally went to get a massage. My neck has been pulling so badly and the nerve is pinched so hard that sometimes it's hard to move. The massage helped a little and I'm hoping the heat and ice rotation will too. I mean, it's never going to get better, but I just need it to be tolerable. I have another massage scheduled for next week and I'm going to start seeing my amazing acupuncturist again in the next few weeks! Yea! Finally, it seems like life may be getting a little closer to what I used to know...maybe just a little.

Tonight, we built six bistro tables and got things cleaned up at the brewery. Now, we are ready to welcome guests tomorrow. Of course, we had help, which was awesome. Still, it felt like before we opened the brewery, when we would be there until late at night and grab fast food. And so, it starts...is it bad that I want the brewery to only be open Thursday to Sunday, so Bryan and I can still have some nice early nights with dinner together? I really think I may petition management for that!

Ok, time to turn in. Tomorrow is International Tea Day, and I am going to be watching the Sofa Summit with tea industry leaders all day. I am so excited!

Hope your hump day was good...now on to opening day!

May 21, 2020

Wow, what a day! Do you ever have those days when you wake up and think: something just isn't right? Yep, today was it, and to be honest, I probably should have stayed in bed. But I couldn't and I wouldn't, because today is International Tea Day. No matter what happens, I have tea!

My day started out at the tea shop where we worked to get out some online orders we still receive and got ready for our tea parties. Today we had two amazing sets of ladies who have become like family to us, though almost all of our guests are like family these days. They wanted to continue supporting us because they know it is going to take a little while to build back up to where we were. I appreciate that more than anyone could ever know. That part of my day was great.

Then there's the brewery, which is great too. But, today felt like our original opening day. We had some things to get done so it put pressure on me. It's not that I'm not used to it but let's be realistic, the brewery hasn't had any sit-down guests for over 60 days. Getting things ready with new guidelines is a lot like gearing up to welcome guests for the first time. Being pulled in different directions is all well and good, but for the past 2 months I have enjoyed the leisure life of it just doing my own thing.

All of this leads me to the utterly uncalled for and crazy part of my day. In an effort to not scold or make a poor showing on people in our town, I am not going to discuss what actually happened...only to say a few very direct things.

First, before you get mad at me for something I didn't do, remember all I did was ask a question. I have the messages to you from yesterday where I wrote, "And I'm not mad, I just wanted to know how you did it so I could get them too." I'm sorry, not sorry, that you felt the need to create this whole issue because you didn't go through the proper channels. As you may or may not know (ahem, I believe it was this person that even told me that everyone knows that I always play by the rules), and if that causes you grief, that's on you, not me. The other thing I am not is a "tattle tale." I could care less what anyone does, but when I am told 'no' and you are told 'yes,' I want to know why.

However, I didn't even have a chance to ask because I was too busy today worrying about my own businesses.

Second, to the third person who interjected and didn't know the whole story: before you accuse me of something you should first be professional enough to ask about a situation.

Third, if you are upset with someone and they come to talk to you about it, you should act professionally and not start yelling at them. You should also treat everyone with respect, not just my husband when he chimes in. I don't care that you are a man and I'm a woman, I deserve the same respect as any person, and I will not be talked down to or yelled at only for you to treat my husband better. My husband should not have had to interject at all, but yet you wouldn't even let me speak. Is it because I am a woman, and you are threatened or that you feel women aren't your equal?

Fourth, when someone comes at me and accuses me of something and said you told them, and I ask you to straighten it out with them, don't tell me it's my problem and to deal with it. You act like a decent human being; admit you were wrong and fix it; after all you created the issue.

Finally, I have never worked so hard in my entire life to help secure our downtown area. I have never tried to support so many businesses, including yours. For you to accuse me of not being a team player and wanting "everyone to get along," maybe you should find out all the facts first.

I know that times are hard, and everyone is concerned about their businesses and finances, but that does not give anyone an excuse to disrespect others. I don't care who you are. So, to the person who caused the issue today, we are done until you can apologize for how you treated me.

The End!

May 22, 2020

Nearly two months have passed since I started my daily posts. I have enjoyed them tremendously. More so, I think, because it forces me to sit down and write something, anything. Even on slow days I made the commitment to write something, so it keeps my mind fresh and my creativity flowing.

Today was a great day! It was one of those days where you wake up and realize the day is going to go your way. I used to have those almost daily, but with all the craziness that is COVID, it hasn't happened as often. Still, today is one of those days.

I actually got a lot done, now that I think back. Before heading into my shop, I returned and purchased some items at Old Time Pottery for the brewery, took a package of four hundred and fifty teas to UPS to be mailed, and then went on to the tea shop.

When I arrived, my assistant Dawne had a pot of tea waiting for me. It's funny but a few different times while we were closed but staff was coming in, I would go in and fix tea for the team. This way we could sit down and visit before we got to work. It's true that great conversation and relaxation happen over tea, and we found that to be true during this time. So, imagine my absolutely pleasant surprise when she did that for me! She felt that after all I was dealing with, I needed to have some tea and relax. I appreciated and enjoyed it more than she will ever know.

By mid-day I was off and running again. An adventure to the Post Office to ship five packages of tea, Walgreens to get some things for the house, and Home Depot to get plastic chain for a barrier for in front of the brewery. I also picked up lunch for my staff, and then headed back to the tearoom. Of course, they had everything handled perfectly so I kept moving on.

The brewery officially had the new front street-side seating area tonight. We got it all set up and it looked beautiful. It was very classy, everything matched with the theme of our brewery design, and the barrier came out great. It was made by our friend Travis, and I love that as we downsize the area, we can still use what we built! The perfect little plan! And might I add, it looks like a natural part of downtown. Making this evening even more perfect, my dear friend John and his team at Heros made some amazing sandwiches for enjoyment onsite and great charcuterie boards to go. Now our guests have an even greater selection of offerings.

After working in the hot sun, which my medication says I should stay out of, I had to go home and clean up. It actually felt like I had a shower before I did. I was glad to finally cool down. The rest of my night was spent working.

I hope everyone had a nice Friday. I know many of my friends were looking forward to a nice long weekend. I'm looking forward to using the time to get ahead. With so much going on, with our tea becoming a recognizable brand throughout the United States, it leaves little time to get caught up. Shipping and promotions have kept me busy, but my goal is to bring that brand into the national spotlight. I am going to use my "spare time" to work towards that goal. I'm also working on some videos about tea and trying to write about tea a little more. These are just more things to bring our brands into alignment and make them even more successful. Honestly, for me it's fun!

Here's to a great long weekend and to the continued success of everything we put our minds too!

May 25, 2020

Saturday was a nice day. The tearoom was slower, but with a holiday weekend it was expected. Still, our guests that came in were super excited to be there. I'm so happy we are able to provide such a nice environment for them. Now, Tuesday, we have postcards mailing out to our guests, so they all officially know we are open on a limited basis. That's very exciting!

The brewery stayed very steady on Saturday. I am so excited to say that our extended outside area was well received and utilized. Yea! We had over 5,000 views and 300 likes on one post where we shared the photos of the new area. I can tell our guests will enjoy it, especially as the sun starts to go down.

Saturday night I got home at a decent time, so I made some stroganoff. It's something I have been craving but am usually too tired to make when I get home. Now I have leftovers, yea! It's good, but in reality, I probably won't eat it all. I don't know why, I'm just not a leftover type of person. I know that's probably weird, huh?

Today was a lazy day for me. Thank goodness my mom told me she was going out to Pier 1 to check out sales; otherwise, I probably would have stayed in bed sleeping all day. It's not that I had nothing to do, because we all know that's not the case. Actually, for the first time in a long time, I felt like being lazy. Now I'm regretting that tonight because I wasted a perfectly good day, but it felt good while I was doing it. Tomorrow is a different story. I truly have so much to catch up on that I think I am just dreading doing it.

Since tomorrow is a holiday, but I spent today being lazy, I think I am going to try to get some work done. Maybe I'll have ambition to go work on my upstairs office...and maybe Tuesday I will blend some teas. I'll keep you posted!

I hope everyone enjoys the Memorial Day holiday tomorrow. Remember to take a moment and remember those who have died while protecting freedom. They are our real heroes and deserve every ounce of our gratitude.

May 25, 2020

Memorial Day

I usually have off every Monday, so it wasn't weird to have today off at all. What was strange is that it was a whole day I got to spend with my husband.

It was a nice day. We went to breakfast together, watched a movie, took a nap, and had hotdogs on the grill for dinner. It wasn't a glamorous day by any means, but it was nice that we weren't rushing off to do things.

In the process of our day, we realized a few significant things this weekend stood for. First, ten years ago this weekend we moved into our house. Despite its small nature, we still love it. We both agreed we need to clean things up and get rid of stuff to make it more comfortable. Honestly, this little 635 square foot house is ideal for us and our busy lifestyle, and we would never want to be anywhere else.

Nine years ago, today we lost one of the greatest men I have ever known. His influence on my life led me on an incredible journey doing things I never would have thought possible. I miss Don every day and make sure to remember him in everything I do.

It's funny how time goes by so quickly. I know that today seemed to pass rather slowly, but the busier we are the quicker the days go. They also stack up into years a lot faster than I could have ever imagined. I mean, if you would have told me that in the blink of an eye, Bryan and I would celebrate our ten-year anniversary this year, I would never have believed it would come so quickly.

Still, I look back on the past ten years and realize I have done so many things. Truly, they have been filled with adventure after adventure. I am so grateful I have taken the time to have fun, and no, I'm not always about work.

Time goes by so quickly that we must take a break every once in a while. Although it is hard for most of us to do, a little downtime makes the adventures that much more rewarding.

Wishing all of you a great week ahead!

May 27, 2020

Today was a good day overall. Being that it was another day off, I have learned to take time and not spend my entire day working.

Don't get me wrong, I did spend a few hours in my office working and getting my books done. It took a little while since I haven't kept up with them over the past few weeks. I am glad to say that both companies are hanging on. That's a good thing for these days and all we have been through.

Tonight Bryan and I went to Back Draughts Pizza in Tarpon Springs. It's one of our favorite places to visit and we find that we go there a few times a month.

When we arrived at the restaurant, I have to admit that I was a little disappointed that we couldn't sit inside. However, my disappointment quickly turned to joy. As we rounded the corner of their building to pick a table outside, and I was amazed at what I saw!

Their outside seating area was moved from against their building to the middle of the street. Yes, their side street was closed and the restaurant and the eatery behind them were sharing the road with tables, plants in beautiful planters, and outdoor A/C units.

So, let me share this: their city sent out $1,000 checks to 150 businesses to help them when their businesses shut down. Now the city blocked off this side street for them to serve customers, and they don't have to put everything in every night...and it's decorated so beautifully by the businesses utilizing it.

As I sat there, enjoying a beautiful early evening and watching each table around us fill up with guests; I got the overwhelming feeling that I was sitting some place other than Florida, like some place in Europe. What an unexpected and wonderful feeling.

It turns out that this evening the Suncoast News posted a story about what Tarpon Springs is doing to help their businesses. What's better, they profiled Back Draughts in the article. They also spoke to the economic development director for the city, and they talked about their desire to create these unique spaces, how it was part of their future vision and continued goal to move the area forward. It is the hope that the trial of using this space now may become permanent. All I can say is that I hope so!

I'm not saying our city hasn't tried to help but if you look at Tarpon, you'll see their desire to create something beautiful and unique even during crazy times. I'm not trying to knock Railroad Square, but it has nothing on Hibiscus Street.

I can't wait to visit again next week and enjoy some delicious food in a unique and inviting environment. I love the bistro lights that were hung from building to building with the city's encouragement. I wonder how it would look to do that across Grand Blvd. from our building across to Sip? I wonder if we would even be permitted to do such a thing!?! Lol!

BTW, their staff is wonderful, and their food is amazing! If you have a chance to check this place out, we highly encourage it!

May 27, 2020

Today was a good day overall, but nothing much differentiates it from any other day. The shop was open, my team is awesome, and we are living to fight another day!

Oh, and Bonnie delivered my awesome newsletters. Now I can get those out to all of our awesome guests, so they know we're open again. She and her team at Minuteman were lifesavers!! Tricia, you are awesome too.

Now it's time to start thinking more outside the box. Yesterday's post proved that our town wants great things, and we all know we need to work together to get there. 'How' is always the big question, but I'm not going to be afraid to ask and share ideas. Despite the virus and the closures it caused, we need to push and move forward, and we can. By bringing ideas up and talking about ways to move our town forward, we can create the traffic and guest environments to become a first-choice destination. So, let's all start thinking outside the box. What have you seen in other areas that might work well here?

And in addition to our town, what about our own individual businesses? How can we think outside of the box to create more traffic individually? This is something I have been struggling with myself. Before the shutdown things were rocking, and now they are slow. It's to be expected, but I also can't sit by idle.

I've thought of some ideas, new things to keep in line with our shop and our goals, but new ways to achieve them. I'm looking at how to expand our tea-to-go, how to grow our tea brand nationally, and how to provide additional services to our guests, like marketing, events, and promotions. My task is to really figure out where to start with this endless list. Well, actually, maybe my first task is to write all the ideas down and work through a plan for each. Then maybe I'll have an idea on which, if any or all, to pursue.

I know these are trying times for everyone and it's unfortunate that Darwinian evolutionary theory of the survival of the fittest is probably going to play out here. Businesses are going to jockey for position just like the horses running the Kentucky Derby. We all must be ready to run when the gate opens, to give both our businesses and our town a fighting chance.

For me personally, all I know is I really need to get a plan together, so I'm not wandering aimlessly. Then maybe I'll feel better about all the cool things we can do to move not just our businesses, but also our town forward.

May 28, 2020

If you would have asked me three hours ago what I was going to write about today, I would have said that I didn't have anything out of the ordinary. Boy how things can change quickly.

My day started out great, the tearoom ran smoothly, and my team did awesome once again. Truly, I don't even think they need me anymore! It's a good feeling, but one I have to get used to. I need to start using that time wisely so I can get some other stuff done. I wish it would motivate me, but I haven't had any such luck with that yet.

If you weren't downtown this evening, you missed a really fun treat. Tonight at 7 p.m., the outgoing class of 2020 graduates from Gulf High decorated their cars and participated in a "parade" to celebrate their accomplishments. This year, they didn't have the pleasure of a prom or walking across the stage to graduate, so this was extra special. Tonight, to show our support, Bryan and I went down to the corner of Main Street and Grand Boulevard and clapped as each one rode by, excitedly cheering. Some grads were even wearing their caps and gowns. I have to admit, it made me so proud to see them smile, and it warmed my heart and brought a tear to my eye. Their joy and optimism were infectious and for me, someone who rarely gets emotional, it was emotional. I am so proud of them and every other student who has faced these past few months with eagerness and steadfastness despite the world's uncontrollable circumstances.

Afterwards, I went home to relax and enjoy some dinner. All was good until around 9 p.m. when my husband called and told me that during the storm we had earlier, the brewery building was hit by lightning. Oh great! Good thing it didn't do too much damage. We lost a cable box, our radio, and our camera system. That's what we know so far and hopefully that's it. The good news is the cooler is good and the fermentation room is good. Tomorrow, we test the brewing system and then we go from there. Hopefully our other business friends in our building faired ok. I mean, it really could have been so much worse.

In addition to all that, my dystonia has been so bad the past few days. My neck muscles have been spasming so bad and pinching my nerve to the point that sometimes I can't even move my neck. Normally I don't have any pain. With my stress lately, I think the muscles are just so tight that it's really creating some issues with balance and my ability to do things. I'm trying to not let it affect me, but it's starting to, and I worry about what will happen if it continues to progress. I wish there was a cure, but there isn't. In the meantime, I am going to pray, stretch, get massages, and do whatever I can because I have seen people with severe cases, and I just can't imagine being affected that way.

I hope your week is going good. I can't believe tomorrow is Friday!

May 30, 2020

Today was a good day in my world. Though, any day that I am here and doing my thing is a good day.

I am starting to feel a little more motivated about things that I can do to help my business. I have a lot of ideas and today I actually sat down and wrote out my 'to do' list. It's like having a map and over the past two months of not writing it down, I finally feel like I have some direction. That's a really good feeling.

This week I am working on getting my teas out to Sips By. Actually, I will give credit where it is due: my amazing team is working on it. It's quite a big undertaking and I appreciate them working so hard.

I'm also starting to work on some new blends. I have some ideas, so I'm hoping to work on them this weekend and try blending by early next week. I have to get our summer teas ready. I'm excited about them and hope I'm making some good choices for our guests.

Well, it's off to bed for me. It's been a long night between the tearoom and the brewery. I enjoyed every minute of it but now it's time to turn in. Tomorrow, we have guests for tea, and I really want to work on one of my new scones!

Here's to another day in the books.

May 31, 2020

Saturday is my 4th favorite day of the week after Sunday, Monday, and Tuesday. Why you ask? Because after Saturday comes those next three days that I'm off. Honestly though, every day is good, but for some reason I've always liked Saturday.

Today was a good day, but then most of them are good. The shop was open. I got into the kitchen to make some new blueberry lemon scones with a lemon vanilla icing, which came out awesome, and my team was awesome in hosting our guests. It was such a good day that my husband even came by and took me to lunch. Perhaps it's the fact that we had to slow life down a little bit, which I am appreciating, and the ability to break away with him.

Maybe something good did come of the slowdown!

I still haven't gotten used to my shop closing at 4 p.m. every day, especially on a Saturday. I even told Bryan I was bored, and it was too early when I went to the brewery at 4:30 p.m. I contemplated going home, but decided to hang out a little while, and I'm glad I did.

I got to visit some friends on Railroad Square, go to Thai Bistro for dinner with my mom, and then spend some time at the brewery.

The night ended with a great talk with a great woman and friend. You know, in these crazy times it's hard to stay positive. I mean, let's face it; we've all been through the wringer. It's easy to take things super personal and sometimes not see the positive in things. A few weeks ago, I was even feeling down and sad and unmotivated. All I can say is that we need to press on. We need to take a deep breath and take a step back. It's easier said than done, but it can be done. I know my friend will make great decisions and continue to thrive because that's who she is. I will be by her side to help her in any way she needs me. After all, sticking together is all we have. I'm sure she knows I'm talking to her, and I know she will be awesome.

Ok, time for bed. Daytime comes early, so I'm ready to get a little shut eye. Here's to another great day tomorrow.

June 2020

June 1, 2020

So, remember when I said Sunday was one of my favorite days of the week? Well, maybe I should retract that statement.

First, let me say that all is good, there's nothing "wrong" with today, and it wasn't bad. It was just BORING as heck! I mean really!!

For the past eight to ten weeks the brewery was only open limited hours, so I would go in there, sit at the bar and work. Then we'd come home while it was still light, enjoy a nice night together, and go to bed at a decent hour. Now with the brewery being open more hours, that has all become virtually non-existent.

First, I can no longer sit at the bar. I don't feel it is in the interest of my establishment to take up a table when we are on limited capacity and need room for our guests.

Second, the brewery no longer needs my help. The team is back to full strength and no longer needs me filling or sealing growlers. Darn, now I've lost one of my jobs!

Finally, it's really boring to sit there all day. It's one thing to be working; it's another to be just hanging out. Trust me, I love to hang out—just not all day long.

So, what did I actually do today??? Nothing.

Ok, well maybe one thing. I took a photo of the awesome batch of scones I made yesterday. It was so good—blueberry lemon with a vanilla lemon drizzle, OMG! Today was photo day, so I could remember what I did. LOL. I know it's so much!

This afternoon I spent some time at home. I watched a movie and worked on my 'to do' list for the first part of this week. Of course, the list is three pages long, and I could have started it today, but did I? No.

Tomorrow I better be really progressive, so I can knock this list out and be done. Therefore, I'm imaging myself sitting in my upstairs office, unbothered, as I work through the list. Wish me luck, there's a lot to do.

Have a great Monday!

June 2, 2020

As if COVID-19 and its impacts, and now unrest wasn't enough, now we wait through the six-month hurricane season to see how our lovely weather system will wreak havoc on our state. You know, it's kind of funny at this point, that if you aren't just done with the year, this may be the final nail in the coffin.

Today I was able to get quite a bit done in my office for both businesses. I was able to get caught up on bookkeeping, which is something that I truly hate. I don't know why, but since the lockdown started, I have had no interest in doing it. You know, "working too hard can give you a heart attack-ack-ack-ack-ack" LOL! Boy, this song really matches what is going on in my life today.

In all seriousness, I am really working hard on my days off, in my office, to try and push my business forward, specifically the tearoom. I always have so many ideas. I have worked on a few things, but nothing has come to fruition yet because I am still in planning and refining some of my ideas.

I will tell you the one thing that I do miss is someone to throw ideas off and to talk through how to make things happen. One of the things I absolutely loved about working for non-profits and having a board of directors or even when I sat as a board member, was the think tank that was a part of it. I remember trying to come up with new events for Chasco Fiesta and the conversation that was had in the board room—discussing ideas, pros, cons, and then choosing to move forward with certain suggestions. That's one thing that business owners really don't have—a think tank.

Think about it, a business is looking at doing a happy hour...a BOGO sale on beer and wine every Friday from 4 to 6 p.m. That's a great idea but imagine a business sitting with a group of business owners or customers or at least people they trust. Someone says, instead of doing BOGO, what if someone buys a beer or wine, they get 1/2 price appetizers. So, a person comes in and does the BOGO and the wine is $6, they get 2 glasses of wine for $6. But what if it worked the other way? They buy one glass of wine at $6 and get a half-priced appetizer; originally $7.99 at half price would be$3.98. Halfway through the appetizer, they order a second glass of wine. Instead of spending $6 they are spending $15.98. It's not perfect and not everyone will do it, but it has the potential to earn the business a lot more money. Not that this is a perfect example, but where is the group that you can throw these ideas around with? The group that helps you move forward. I totally get the purpose of chambers and business groups and they are awesome. What about those more personal business groups that you are friends with, but they also help each other with business ideas and brainstorming? I need a personal think tank!

Ok, now that I've gone off on a tangent, I'm heading to bed. My brain is fried trying to figure everything out, and I've got a busy day on tap tomorrow. Actually, you will find me in my office, but I have lots of ideas to pare down and hash out.

Wishing you another great day!

June 2, 2020

Today was an average day, as most of them tend to be. I was at my shop by 11 a.m., so a very special woman could pick up some tea. My awesome assistant, Dawne, had everything ready for me before I got there. What a treat it was when she went to pay, and I told her that her daughter had already taken care of it. She was going to meet her daughter for tea and her daughter had paid for their lunch online the day before. This woman was one of the first supporters of my tearoom, and I just love how she lights up when she comes in my place. Her, her husband, daughter, and son-in-law are always so thoughtful and sweet. I am truly blessed to have them and so many others like them in my life.

This afternoon, after a run to the bank that I haven't been to in forever, I came back to work in my office. It was nice because even though I'm not really getting a lot done, I am getting some things off my list, like ordering some new merchandise. Oh, and our "Tea Shirts" came in today. I'm so excited! I'm hoping that with so many of the larger brick and mortar retail establishments announcing closings, that small businesses like mine will be able to fill the niche and see an increase in shoppers in our stores. After all, it's nice to shop online, but it's even nicer to be able to look and touch something you are going to buy. Just remember to only touch after this COVID thing is gone, please!

Tonight was my weekly meet up online with Tea Mastermind. I just love them so much. Despite my internet being spotty today, I had a great time conversing and learning from them.

Tonight, we discussed putting an online shop on Etsy, and also some other marketing ideas. See, this is where that CEO round table would come in handy. Lisa and Dawn: I'm just teasing with you girls but we need to do it! I'm going to start getting my ideas around and walk through them completely, and then it's your turn!

Bryan is at the brewery kegging his IPA. I know a lot of people are going to be really happy on Thursday!! For me, it's a bittersweet reminder that this is how our life is when we own businesses. I truly enjoyed being home each evening, eating dinner and hanging out. Instead, we are back to the old normal of not getting home until after 9 p.m.

or even 10 p.m. some nights and eating dinner at 10 p.m. or later. Trust me, I wasn't happy that everything got shut down, but in some instances, I was happy for the slowdown it gave us.

Well, that about sums up my day. I'm still in my office upstairs of my shop, which is better than sitting home alone. I heard some protesting was going on at City Hall. Someone driving by told me there were about 20 protestors. So, I'm just hanging out working and making sure I stay safe downtown. I pray that someday this will end, and we can all work together, as a team, to rebuild a better place. As a woman-minority, I want to see that happen too.

I hope everyone continues to have good days, and that you are still enjoying my posts. LOL! It has taken a lot of commitment to keep them up, and to keep finding things to talk about. Maybe I should start my own column. I wonder if anyone would read it. LOL.

Good night, everyone!

June 3, 2020

Today was a good day, though I barely got anything done. Do you ever have those days? You know those days—where you always seem to be doing something, but just never get the items on your "to do" list checked off? Yep, the only thing I can say that I actually got done was having a few pots of tea. A huge thank you goes to Dawne for making me a pot when I came in this morning. I could get used to having a pot each morning. LOL.

Today, I connected with a dear previous mentor of mine, Laura. She was the executive director when I worked at our local Main Street, New Port Richey Main Street. When I say she taught me everything I know, I'm not even exaggerating. She took this young person who didn't know a lot and taught me about event planning, media and business. We chatted on messenger today since we both have retail shops, and I am going down to check out her place in a few weeks. I am truly so happy that we reconnected, and I can't wait to see her! I am where I am today because of her encouragement and guidance when I was a young person.

This afternoon I got some new merchandise for my shop—a whole line of Savannah Bee Company items, new 'tea' shirts, and more items are coming this week. I'm still working on getting more things ordered, especially since most of my companies are starting to ship again. That makes me very happy! Now to work on a makeover in my shop to include all of these new things! It's so exciting!!

Tonight, Bryan and I went to dinner at one of our favorite restaurants, El Cerrito Mexican Restaurant. It was so good to be able to go back there. We hadn't been there since the beginning of March, and I really missed it. Bryan missed it so much that he had the 'big' margarita!

Tonight, at dinner we talked about ideas for the tearoom and how to move it forward. I still don't have an answer as to the right direction to go, but I'm working on it. I mean, we are doing well, but I'm always looking for ways to increase businesses. I have a few options, and it was nice to discuss it with Bryan over dinner. I mean, he is 49% owner. LOL.

Overall, I have to say that today was a good day. It was one of those days where you may not get a lot done, you still feel pretty good about where you finish. It doesn't happen often, but today it did.

Here's to another successful day tomorrow, even if I don't get everything done that I feel I should.

June 4, 2020

What another great day! Maybe it is because we are getting more seatings booked in the tearoom. We still aren't close to capacity, but it's been nice having more people around. That could be the reason I am feeling better about my days. Truly, we are social by nature, and I think by being around more people my mood is just better overall.

We are starting to move along with some new things in the tearoom. Today I met with my senior staff to talk through ideas, and we had a great brainstorming session. I am in the process of working through the notes from today to finalize some of the ideas and put them in motion. I'm so excited about that! I can't wait until we finalize everything, so I can share more.

Speaking of the tearoom, I want everyone to know since many of you have asked, the large front window that is broken in our tearoom actually broke several weeks ago. It wasn't caused by any kind of vandalism, but by a day of strong wind. That particular window broke several years ago and with the framing being weak, all it took was some constant wind for it to crack and break again. We will be getting it replaced soon, and I really want to thank you all for your concern. Truly, I know many people were worried that it was broken as an act of violence, but that isn't the case. So far, downtown has been good. We have a very close-knit family in this town, and I know we all look out for each other. I appreciate all of you who stopped in or messaged me to ask and to make sure we were all right.

Tonight was one of our 'new normal' nights. Bryan was at the brewery, and I was at home. I didn't fix dinner until after 9 p.m. and Bryan didn't eat until almost 10:15 p.m. This is exactly what it was like before everything was shut down. I have to say, I'm really not enjoying things going back to the way they were so quickly. I'm sad, because before I never knew what I was missing. Now I miss the calmness and less busy life. I miss Bryan being home with me for dinner, running errands and just hanging out. I guess for now, I will be happy that both of our businesses are closed Monday, Tuesday, and Wednesday evenings, so at least we have that time together at least until the brewery opens more evenings. For now, I will be thankful for the times we do have.

I hope you all are having great days! I am trying to find the good in every day, and to continue to move myself ahead. I hope you are doing the same.

June 6, 2020

TGIF! You know that that means, tomorrow is MY Friday! It's been a good week so far, and I've enjoyed using my time to move some projects ahead. Now I'm even more excited to keep moving forward.

I am working on a new project for my establishment for several evenings a week. It's utilizing the same space the tearoom uses during the day, but then transitioning the space into something different for the evening. It's actually a pretty cool concept, and I'm excited to see if I can pull it off. If so, it would be remarkable, and something that people just wouldn't expect when they currently think of our establishments. Of course, the tearoom will never go away, but having it multi-use would be wonderful.

I haven't given up on my outside area yet either. I'm working on getting the inside area set and running, and then I want to expand into our alley and back patio. For now, I am working on getting the bistro lighting set up. I also want to get some furniture outside to give us a little 'life' on the street. It's truly amazing how noticeable the furniture is in front of the brewery. I used to put tables out at the tearoom, but I'm thinking we need to rethink what we do with the outside seating here. The tables we had were so big and heavy and smaller might be better. These are just more things to work on as we continue to push our business and our town forward. After all, that is why we do what we do.

For the gift shop area, I'm also working on ways to expand our tea to go service. I'm actually looking for any friend who has worked at a coffee shop, as a barista, to help answer some questions. With setting up our tea to go area better, I want to be able to offer things like lattes and such, but I need to learn how the 'big boys' make things. This way we can offer a wider selection to our guests. I haven't found anyone yet, so if you know of someone who will give me some pointers, I would be so grateful!

A few days ago, I got a new iPhone! Anyone who knows me knows how much I absolutely hate changing technology. Lucky for me, Apple makes the transfer simple, so that my new phone screens and apps are exactly the same. I have found that I do at least 50% of my work on my phone, I guess it comes as no surprise that I go through phones regularly. Truly, I am in love with my new phone. It's so much bigger and clearer, and the photos come out great. I'm glad my husband talked me into getting it.

Here's to a great Saturday and a great weekend ahead!

June 7, 2020

Saturday, Saturday, Saturday Night's Alright!

My Saturday night was just like my Saturday, uneventful. It's not that I'm sad, I just don't have much to do other than work and come home. It's more that these days when I come home, I come home to myself. Bryan had a brewing day at the brewery today, which always makes the day last longer. I usually end up eating dinner by myself and going to bed at a decent hour, but by myself. I mean, really, here I am at almost 12:30 a.m. and he's still not home from the brewery. I'm not really upset by that, but more so, I miss the days when we were home together. I will be honest, I don't like going to bed by myself, especially going to sleep when I'm the only one in the house, even though we have an alarm system.

Overall, today was a good day. The tearoom and gift shop were more on the slow side than usual for a Saturday. That's probably because it rained nearly every second of the day, and people didn't feel like coming out, getting soaked and being treated like a duck by Mother Nature. Still, we had a few brave souls, and we appreciate each and every one of them.

With it being a little slower, I was able to continue working on my evening project for the tearoom as well. I am very excited about adding this new component to our already successful business. I think our guests will enjoy it too. The hardest part of creating something new is being able to keep the elegance of our existing establishment, but have our space be seen in a different way, and not just as a tearoom. It will still be elegant, but not as formal, if that makes any sense. We won't have set reservation times and we aren't serving afternoon tea, but it will be beautiful and have good bites and drinks. I really can't wait to be able to share the entire concept with you. I am hoping to be able to do that within the next few weeks.

Since it's supposed to rain most of the day tomorrow, I have some plans to work in my office upstairs to keep ahead of the game as things continue to pick up and get busier for both businesses. I also hope to get some blending done for our teas, and to do some shifting in our gift shop to accommodate additional merchandise that is coming in. I know having the time off during COVID was hard for our motivation, but it is exciting to see new merchandise for our guests, and for things to come back together for our gift shop and tearoom.

I hope everyone stayed dry today, and I hope that despite the rain tomorrow you're able to do something fun. And, hopefully in a few days this rain will be gone, and we will be enjoying our beautiful sunshine State again.

Night!!

June 8, 2020

I don't have much to say about today.

I didn't get up and moving until later than planned. I mean, I was awake and emailing and texting, but I didn't physically get out of bed until almost 10:45 a.m. I know, I know, but in my defense, I didn't go to bed until almost 2:30 a.m. My schedule is so screwed up! I have to get it back on track.

Earlier this afternoon I helped Bryan rearrange the kegs in the cooler at the brewery. We also did inventory, so we can stay on track with keeping our beers on tap. I don't want to jinx it, but it seems like we have a really good system right now. I am just hoping to keep it up.

After helping at the brewery, I came home, turned on the TV, and took a nice long nap. While most people will say I probably needed it, I really do hate naps because afterwards I feel so guilty and lazy. Today I may have needed it, but it also led to my unproductive feelings...because when I say nothing got done, I truly mean nothing got done.

That leads to my next issue...how do I find the motivation to actually get stuff done? There are so many things to do that I am actually feeling overwhelmed by them, and I think that's what led me to take a nap today rather than actually work. I don't know where it went, but I need to find my motivation fast!

Well, another weekend wrapped.

June 8, 2020

Today is day two of my weekly three-day weekend. Really, I don't consider it a weekend, but it's nice to know that I have another day after this one.

It's been hard to get going in the mornings lately. My neck has started having small spasms and it makes it hard to want to get out of bed. Just lying in bed helps the pressure on my neck so I don't seem to fight it as bad. I have found that as the day goes on the spasms gets more frequent. They are small, so most people don't notice, but I notice. Tonight, I thought I would try some of my Valium to see if it would help with the spasm and the pinched nerve in my neck and base of my head. I only took 1/4 of a pill and I'm hoping it helps and doesn't knock me out or make me drowsy tomorrow. If memory serves me right, I usually take 1/2 pill, but I didn't want to start there. I'm hoping this small amount will be enough.

Today, at home, I worked on creating my tea bar. We moved the liquor cabinet contents over to one of our pantries, so now I have a cabinet for my tea and teacups. Now I just have to clean off the countertop, so I can actually make tea out there. I am so excited to have this space. And by doing that, I also cleaned off the kitchen counter so I can start working on videos for my tearoom. Another thing I am so excited about!

Tonight Bryan and I finally made it back to our old stomping ground, Fitzgerald's Irish Tavern. I sure have missed their awesome wings and chicken go Baugh. It's been almost 3 months since we've been there. It was so great! And it's truly like Cheers! We ran into Michelle, Kristi, William and Karie. It was so good seeing all of them, and, of course, great to see our favorite bartenders and servers.

After dinner we stopped by to see our friends at Dented Keg Ale Works. Their place is really coming together, and I can't wait for it to open. It will be great having another brewery in town, especially one that is a friend of ours. So exciting!

So now, the Valium is kicking in and I'm chilling on the couch watching a show we love called 'Uncommon Grounds'. It's about a coffee company owner who travels the world. While I'm in the tea world, it's so interesting to watch his adventures to source coffee. It gives me lots of ideas…just what I need. LOL.

I hope everyone had a good Monday, and the week ahead is prosperous and fun!

June 9, 2020

Today, even though I got up late, I feel like I got some things accomplished.

I started my morning out at the tearoom. I answered emails, contacted vendors, and put the finishing touches on our summer tea samplers. I had most of it done but had to get some things finalized and get our labels together. This week we will be putting them together to have them ready for next week. Yea! And I'm finalizing my plan for reworking our gift shop and for our evening venture. Lots of things are going on!

This afternoon I had a massage. My awesome massage therapist is really working on my neck muscles. While my issue is nerve related, it feels so good to have my neck muscles worked out. It usually feels good for a few days, the muscles being a little less tense. Couple that with getting in for some acupuncture and I'm hoping to continue to have a little relief. Yes, Dr. Maharajh, you are next on my list.

Tonight, after my massage, I worked in my office upstairs. I find I can concentrate and get a lot done when I'm up there. I am working on a few different tea classes and find that being up in my office is the only time I really have a chance to read and work on them. In the tea world, you never stop learning and researching. It's something I love to do, but rarely take time for Now, since the brewery is open again at night and I have some time later in the evening, I can see more late nights in my office. I can actually say I'm looking forward to it. That and I have a bird's eye view of the town with where my office windows overlook...I see some very interesting things.

Being busy this evening, Bryan and I enjoyed a late night dinner at Boulevard Beef & Ale. It was delicious, as always, and I love that they are right next door. Convenient and good is just what I needed! For us it's truly like Cheers—like being at home. We truly are so blessed to live in this town and have such great 'family' all around us. I wouldn't want to live anywhere else!

Now it's time for bed and I'm hoping to get a little shuteye, so I can hit the ground running tomorrow. I have lots of things to work out so I can keep moving forward. Fun times ahead!!

June 11, 2020

Despite not being a morning person, my butt was up at 7:30 a.m. this morning. I'm not really sure why, but I woke up and couldn't go back to sleep. I figured I might as well get up and start my day. And that's what I did, so much so that I even made my infamous biscuits and gravy! Yum! What a way to start my day!

I got into the shop early today and was able to get a few things accomplished, which was great. With trying to get inventory in, I have spent some time with my distributors. I enjoy seeing their new products. Oh, and I had to go pick up new sweet treats from our friends at Mmmm Delicious Cupcakes. We now offer some of their delicious cupcakes, edible cookie dough, cakescicles, and truffles, oh my!!

This afternoon I spent some time at the brewery. It was nice to visit with guests and to work on our upcoming schedules. It's so nice to see things coming back and to talk to our friends. I truly missed all of them and I love having conversations with them. You really don't realize how much you missed them until you see them again. I don't normally spend a lot of time at the brewery, but I have recently because the tearoom is currently open less hours, though not for long. Being at the brewery is a way for Bryan and I to see each other more. I don't see myself being there every night, but maybe a little more frequently than I used to.

Tonight, we got home at 11:00 p.m. and now we are eating dinner. Nothing glamorous when you get home so late, so it's chicken nuggets and mac and cheese. Not the healthiest, but it's easy, and we actually got to eat it before midnight. I mean, there's nothing like eating dinner the next day. LOL!!

So, now that I've gotten to wind down, it's time to head to bed. I'm hoping I can sleep in just a little more tomorrow. I feel like I need it.

I hope your week is going good, Friday is growing ever closer!!

June 11, 2020

So, my routine of getting up early didn't last long. Today I was back to getting up at my normal time. Not that I mind in the least, but I must admit that I did feel a little more accomplished when I was moving earlier. Tomorrow, I have to meet someone at the brewery at 8:30 a.m., so it's going to be another early one, at least for me anyway!

I didn't get much accomplished today, but it still felt productive. I had a very enjoyable tea with my friend Nancy and her friend Judy. It was great to hear what Nancy wants to do and to share ideas with her. You know, in addition to loving my tearoom and tea overall, my next favorite thing is being a business advisor. To provide ideas, talk through ideas and issues, and help a business to increase productivity and income, or even to walk through the steps of creating a new business is just awesome—something I love so deeply! Hey, sounds like a second career! LOL!

So, I thought my mom was going to kill me today. We got in more inventory, and we have everything stacked up everywhere. It's really starting to be a problem. I can see a few late nights in my future as I work to fit all this stuff in. The one great thing, it makes the store really full! I love having a full store.

Tonight, I came home early from my shop. One of the issues of having spasmodic torticollis is that the muscles can have involuntary movements and that happens in my neck a lot. Sometimes if I move just right it will pinch a nerve in my neck and send a shooting pain into my head. There's nothing that can be done and most days I don't have it. But man, today I moved just right, and the muscle caught the nerve, and I thought I was going to cry. That was around 3 p.m., so the whole rest of the day I was dealing with shooting nerve pain. Once the shop closed, I decided to come home and rest with an ice pack. My intention was to go back but even now, lying in bed, I'm still having spasms.

The good thing about coming home early was that I was able to make dinner. Tonight, I made a chicken stroganoff style dinner—you know, just like the beef one but with chicken. I made bow tie pasta to go with it and it was amazing!! So delicious, I think I should write the recipe down and share it. It really was so simple, simple ingredients...and something I can see a lot of people enjoying.

The big question after I make dinner is always whether I should do the dishes, because I absolutely hate dishes! The answer is not only yes, I put them in the dishwasher, but I emptied the clean dishes out first. To be even more productive, I did two loads of laundry. Yes, Dawne, I did linens for the tea room. So even though I didn't get any store work done, I did some house stuff.

Yea!!

Now it's time for bed and I'm tired. I'm excited that tomorrow is Friday. We have a few tables in the tearoom, and at one of our seatings on Saturday, we are at our 50% capacity! That's so exciting to me. It means that our guests are starting to come back.

I hope everyone has a great Friday! XOXO

June 13, 2020

Today was another one of those days where I didn't feel like I got anything done, but it turns out I actually did.

My day started late because I woke up in the middle of the night with a cramp in my knee. I couldn't get it to go away on its own, so I had to get in the shower and let steaming hot water run over the muscle until it finally released. I finally got to bed after 1 a.m., ugh!

Today at the shop we had some amazing guests. Well, every day we have amazing guests and the shop had quite a few people in it, which was really good. Not to mention, we have a lot of new inventory that my mom is in the process of getting out. Funny thing is, I'm going to be rearranging the gift shop this next week, so I wasn't in a rush to get everything out. It should all be out next week, yea!

Tonight, I ran over to the brewery for a little bit. Holy cow was it busy! It's so true that people really missed being out. Our inside was at the new capacity and the outside was 75% full. It was so good to see! I am so happy and totally proud of my husband and his team over there.

Tonight, on my way home from the brewery, I purposely drove down Main Street just to drive through the new stop sign at Main Street and Adams. Scary part was as I approached it, two oncoming cars blatantly ran the sign. After the first one, I honked at the second one. Man, if the city needs to make up revenue, all they need is to set some police up just past that intersection for one day. Oh man! It's a true testament that people don't watch signs or pay attention at all. I can't wait until more streets downtown have stop signs!!

Well, it's off to bed. I've got quite a few things on the schedule tomorrow. Some I'm not looking forward to but know I will get through it.

Here's to a great Saturday ahead!

June 15, 2020

Yesterday I attended a beautiful service for my cousin who passed away a month ago. She was one of the most beautiful souls I ever met in my life. She lit up a room just by walking into it and I am so blessed I had the opportunity to be in her amazing life, even if I only had a short amount of time.

After the service the family held a reception in the church hall. As everyone settled around the hall, I had a thought about the whole thing. It was lovely that everyone was together, minus my cousin, but why don't we get together like that when someone is alive? Surely, it's great to see everyone at weddings and funerals, but what about celebrating each other while we are all still here? I even said to my dad, why don't we do this before someone dies? Now that is something for all of us to think about.

Today I attended an online tea program from Malawi. It's one of the oldest tea producing regions in the world and it was very interesting to hear about their tea and their tea farms. There were about 60 people that attended online. I really enjoyed learning about this region I had never really been introduced to before.

Tonight was family dinner. We didn't get to eat until late since the brewery was open until 7 p.m., but it was still nice. I know we used to get together more than once a week, but I'm glad we are still doing it weekly. Even though it's usual my simple dinners, like tonight's burgers on the grill, it's something and that is what is important.

So, my project for my shop is coming along nicely. I am still searching for the right name and designation for my vision. It's hard to make that decision as it will be something I identify everything I do with my new idea, so it must be good.

I'm excited that tomorrow I am going to visit a friend who has a shop too. I can't wait to see her and see her beautiful space!

I hope everyone has a great Monday and a great start to the week!

June 15, 2020

I was up early for me this morning. I got some stuff mailed out at UPS and then headed down to St. Pete to see a friend's shop. All I can say is wow! I love her shop and how she merchandises everything. What a great space and so many great ideas. Today was the perfect example of how small businesses help other small businesses out.

Laura, I loved spending time with you today and seeing how you merchandise your amazing shop! Now I can't wait to see what I can do with my finds when I head back to my shop tomorrow. I also felt like we had just seen each other last week, like we never lost any time, even though it's been over fifteen years. Laura hasn't changed a bit, she's still amazing and I still feel honored to know her! Next time we must take a photo together!

It ended up being a full day, between St Pete, buying supplies for the tearoom, and going by to pick up more chocolates at William Dean Chocolates. I didn't even get back and unpacked until after 5 p.m.! It was a good day, but man did it tire me out!

I've found with my muscle/nerve disease that I get more tired more quickly. Also, as the day goes on it's harder for me to move my head without pain. It's hard to be motivated to do anything, and sometimes it leads to a little depression. Truly, I try to go all day, but I just can't do it sometimes. I'm not sure what the answer is since there's no cure. So, it was only natural that after such a long day, my neck would be playing issues on me, and I would have to take it easy tonight.

Despite my exhaustion and pain, we did get a new piece of furniture moved into the shop tonight. It's a good thing the piece wasn't too big or heavy though. I think if I ever ask Bryan to move more furniture, he will probably leave me, LOL. Still, I can't wait to see what we come up in my gift shop tomorrow.

Well, overall, it was a good start to the week. Here's hoping it's a good one all the way around!

June 16, 2020

Whew! What a day.

For my day off I sure did a lot of work. It started when I had Bryan help me move a dresser to my shop from my mom's house last night. You see, I had this vision of reworking and redesigning my shop. So, with moving the dresser in, I had to do it today so that the dresser had some place to go. Hence, a whole entire day was spent in the gift shop.

I am honestly so pleased with how things turned out. It's almost like every little star aligned for my vision and things came together so perfectly, as we worked through the store. We shifted merchandise, added merchandise, shifted displays, and ultimately made a shopping space our guests are going to love!

This is something I have wanted to do for a long time, and I'm so glad I finally took the time to do it. I also have to thank my mom and Tara for coming in on our day off and helping and working so hard.

I know that so many of the larger retailers are struggling and we are going to see more decide to liquidate and close. Add that to the fact that there are very few 'all occasion' gift shops left, and you realize it's time for the small business gift and retail to step up and be ready to serve guests looking for gift items. I am that shop and I'm going to be ready. Yea!

Tomorrow, all I have left is to finish the jewelry section and then work on a few odds and ends; just some finishing touches. I also have a few tea projects to finish up, and some business things to attend to.

For now, this tired body is heading to bed. I hope to get some good sleep so I can hit the ground running again tomorrow.

Wishing you sweet dreams, and a restful night!

June 17, 2020

So, what happens when you get your gift shop just the way you want? Today you get twenty-four boxes of inventory that have to be opened and displayed. Yes, I said that right. And the gift shop is already so full! The way I look at it, what are a few more pieces to sell? LOL! I'm so glad my team is a good sport about this stuff. I can't wait to do more—I just need the motivation. Actually, I think what happens when you lock me up and don't let me shop for myself, then I shop with my distributors for my store. Very dangerous, but oh so fun!!!

Other than working in my shop, fulfilling online orders, and doing general stuff, my day was pretty uneventful. I do like days like that, but it also gets me down a little.

Honestly, as much as I am continuing to move forward, I am struggling with it. I can't help but have something the pastor said at my cousin's memorial service constantly run through my head. He talked about when our time is up, when the tomorrows end. We don't know when we won't get another tomorrow. That is so true, but it also got me thinking, what is all of this for? What is the end goal? Where is the motivation? Then it also hit me, I don't really have any goals. I used to have goals for everything, but lately I don't seem to have anything I'm working towards. I mean, I don't have a car, house, vacation or anything that I care about getting. I already have it all, and I'm perfectly happy with where I am in life. I'm learning now that to stay focused and move forward, I need to have a goal and I need to get some motivation!

Tonight, we had a lovely dinner in Tarpon with some friends. Of course we went to BackDraughts! It was wonderful as usual! I just love that we can take friends there and it's consistent!! I love that they still have their outside area on the street. We sat inside, but it was still so good to see they were still utilizing their great space outside.

Well, today is 'hump day' and that means we are full speed ahead to the weekend, yea!! Hope your week is going great!

June 18, 2020

Today was one of those days where I felt I got a lot done, but it didn't feel crazy.

I finally took the time to contact the hotel in Atlanta that we were supposed to stay at when we go to Market next month. Unfortunately, Market was postponed until August, but we also had a non-refundable room, so we might have gotten stuck going just to use the room. With the issues in Atlanta right now, which go beyond just COVID, the hotel understood and let us cancel. I really love that hotel, and I'm hoping things will be good for us to go there in January.

So, we have been having an issue with the dumpster at our shop. All the tenants in the building share one dumpster. Now that business is picking up, it seems to be getting filled a lot more quickly. Last night when we left the shop it was so full you could see it over the enclosure it was in. This morning when we got in, I was excited to see that it was empty.... or so we thought. My mom went out there to throw a box away and came in to tell me the dumpster must have been set on fire. I went out to look and it was 1/2 full of charred wood and everything inside was charred too. Yep, fire! After talking to the landlord, we called the police to file a report.

Dispatch at the police department told me that last night they had a call for a dumpster fire on Nebraska Ave. I told them we were between Nebraska and Missouri, and they told me it was another dumpster at a restaurant down the street that they had to put out last night. Turns out we may have a fire starter in town...everyone keep your eyes open and if you see something, please say something. The police were nice about it. The same officer that came out for my window also came out for this and wrote us up a report. Now our landlord is reviewing the camera footage and I hope they see it. I mean, really!!

After all that, I took a load of stuff out to our shop's storage unit and picked up a few things, thanks to Tara who helped. The shop is looking so nice and it's really coming together just like I envisioned. Just a few more touches in the tearoom areas and we will be good to go! Yea!

Tonight was one of the highlights for me for a long time. I went to my friend Phyllis's house, and she let me help her and James release some of their monarch butterflies. You should see their set up! It's so cool and their yard is looking amazing too! Anyways, I've never really picked up or touched a butterfly, so I was a little nervous to hurt them, but James taught me how to pick them up and let them fly off. It was so neat and something I definitely want to do with them again. I know I don't have the ability to raise them because they require lots of time and care, but I am so happy to support my friends that do. I told them someday I want to come and sit in their yard with some teacups and take some photos. You know, I used to love going to beautiful gardens and photographing the flowers! I should go through and look for some of my old flower photos.

Well, that was my day. Never a dull moment! Hoping everyone is having good adventures too!

June 20, 2020

What a productive day. Today was one of my days where I worked on stuff on my computer almost all day and I actually got stuff done. I paid taxes, worked on my World Tea Academy class, and more.

The tearoom was on the slower side today, but the guests were amazing! The gift shop wasn't too bad either. I've found that since we rearranged our shop, we are getting quite a bit more sales and that is awesome! I walk in now and I love the layout, so that makes me happy too. It's so much easier going to work when you enjoy it!

Tea sales online continue to come in and I'm so thankful. We can always tell when our teas get sent out through the subscription service we use because it creates an influx of orders. That shows it's working, yea!

This afternoon I worked with our wine manufacturer and distributor for both the brewery and the tearoom. I was able to get some menus finalized for our evening venture at the tearoom location, and now it's time to sample and try things. To me, that's always the most fun part—first coming up with the ideas and second trying things out. Now, if my vision can just be pulled off it will be fantastic!

Tonight was a low-key night for me. I got home a little after 8 p.m., fixed dinner, read a little and am now turning into bed. It's a busy day tomorrow in the tearoom. We are at our new capacity at our 12 p.m. seating and that is very exciting. Tomorrow I'm working on blending some teas and decorating too. That's truly my favorite! I have just a few days to make some minor adjustments to our tearoom, and then on to the trial phase of our evening adventure. I can't wait to host a VIP preview the second week of July and open right after. Truly there is no rest for the weary, but this will be a good financial move for us and allow us to breathe a little easier, so that the tearoom doesn't have to worry.

Here's to exciting times ahead, and of course the weekend!

June 20, 2020

This morning, I woke up feeling pretty good. Though I'm not sure how, since I just went to take my medicine tonight and realized I forgot my hormones last night. Maybe the vitamin D helped pick up some of the slack.

Today was a good day at the tearoom. For the first time since reopening, we were at capacity at our 12 p.m. seating. Granted it's only 50%, but I'm so excited that we did it today. My team was amazing, and everyone worked together to make it a success. The gift shop was busy too!

It was our overall busiest day since Mother's Day weekend and boy did we need it.

This afternoon we took down the large curtain between the tea parlor and the tearoom. It needed to be washed, and I adding some teal sheers in with the white to create a little more drama for our evening venture. I can't wait to get it up to see what it looks like!!

Tonight, I got home early, and I did some laundry. I was trying to finish up the home stuff, so I can do my shop laundry. Man, it never ends! I also took a nap while I was waiting for the laundry to dry. It felt good to sleep. It's funny, but every afternoon I just get exhausted. I find that if I can close my eyes for 30-40 minutes, I am good to go and get more done at night.

Now I'm at home and I decided that I wanted to read a good book. Turns out all I have are my history books from college, tea books and business books. Man, I wish I had a good feel-good book. I mean, I remember the summer books I used to read—Devil Wears Parada and that. They were great and just for pleasure reading. You know—those books that you can just enjoy reading and that don't have any educational value—just a good book. I wish I could find some of those! Anyone have a good book to recommend? I have one to start with from a friend who is a writer, Elisa. I can't wait to read her book, but I'd love some other suggestions too. I like 'feel good,' but not cheesy books. I'm not into drama or mystery at all. I know that's kind of limiting. I'm hoping that reading in bed at night will help me sleep better than using my phone until I go to sleep.

I'm looking forward to tomorrow. I have a relaxing day on tap. Doing some tea blending, finishing up my summer tea sampler, and hopefully work on a few recipes for our evening activities. I'm also hoping to set up one room to take some photos for promo! Yea!!

I hope you all have a great and restful Sunday. And, to all the fathers out there, including my dad, Tom, whom I love, I wish you a relaxing day doing exactly what you love. Happy Father's Day!

June 23, 2020

Yesterday I didn't have much to write about that was interesting. I had breakfast at Rose's, went to the brewery, went home and did laundry, took a nap, went to my tea shop to hang new organza curtains—thanks to my awesome husband, went back to the brewery and helped move kegs in the cooler, went home, had dinner and went to bed! That's it in a nutshell, nothing even remotely interesting...

Today, y'all would be so proud of me. I was up before 7:30 a.m., left the house at 8:10 a.m., and didn't get back home until after 7 p.m.! And I was productive all day!

After picking my mom up from her dropping her car off and dropping her at the rental car place, I decided I was going to see how much I could get done today. It turns out quite a bit.

I went right to my shop this morning and made a list of all the things I wanted to accomplish over the next two days. Oddly enough, I was focused enough to get over half my list done.

I spent the morning blending teas—three different ones that we were running out of, and then taking deposits to the bank for the brewery and tearoom. After an afternoon trip to the bank and Office Depot, I worked in my office upstairs. I reconciled both QuickBooks accounts for April and May and brought them current to today. Then I finished and printed our Summer Tea Tasting packets, wrote thank you notes to all the people who ordered tea online this week, and caught up on a lot of emails. I'll tell you, having a list gave me focus to get my stuff done. Now tomorrow, I have just under half of the list left. I'm feeling good that I will be able to get it done, but it's going to need to be another early start.

Tonight, Bryan and I took some quiet time and had a nice dinner at Thai Bistro. We just love the relaxing atmosphere there, and they always do such a great job. Honestly, they have some amazing Thai wings that I just can't seem to live without for very long—so good. After dinner, we came home and had a quiet evening in. We watched a great move, *The Peanut Butter Falcon.* If you haven't seen it, you must. It's truly adorable—just cute and funny. The lead character is a young man with Downs Syndrome, and he is a character. It had a great storyline. I don't know if I enjoyed it more because of my family or what, but it was a great movie.

Now it's time for bed. Tomorrow is another busy day. I'm taking another trip down to St. Pete to see my friend Laura and pick up some more things for my shop, then to Restaurant Depot. Later, I'll work at my shop, have my tea mastermind group at 7 p.m., and possibly take my niece to Vampire Penguin for some shaved custard dessert. I'll be sure to tell you all about it.

For now, have a great night and a great Tuesday!

June 23, 2020

Well, I didn't get up as early as planned. I think it's because I was so tired after yesterday that I really needed the rest. So, I was about an hour behind schedule, but I still made it a good day and moved through my list and goals, yea!!

This morning, my mom and I made another trip down to my friend, Laura's place. Gosh, I just love her place. I especially love that, though time has passed, she is still the same amazing person she was when I worked for her years ago. When I say she taught me everything I know, I'm not exaggerating. She was my role model and still is, and when I worked with her, I tried to absorb everything I could from her. I feel so blessed that she and I worked together—well, really, I worked for her—and I was able to learn so much, it's made me who I am today. While down at her shop I was able to pick up a little more merchandise for our shop, as well as a few other really cool finds!

After leaving her place we made a quick stop at Restaurant Depot to pick up some things for the brewery. Of course, I couldn't have had the list last week when I went there, LOL. It was probably the quickest and least expensive visit ever! Then, we made a quick stop at Vetter Brewing for some grain, so the brewery can keep brewing this weekend. That's definitely a good thing!

We got back to the tearoom around 2:30 p.m., and honestly it was just too hot to move everything out of the truck. I was already overheated for some reason, so I thought I would get to it tonight. I really wanted to get it out of my truck tonight while it was cooler, but for some reason I have been overheating a lot. I know it's hot outside, but my medication has made it even more difficult to be outside, and I get dehydrated and overheated so quickly. Needless to say, all the merchandise is still sitting in the back of my truck. I look forward to unloading it slowly throughout the day tomorrow.

Tonight, I had my Tea Mastermind meeting. It's truly one of the highlights of my week; it inspires me and keeps me motivated to move forward. I have wanted to do some videos for my YouTube page, and I came up with some great ideas of 'episodes' tonight. Being a part of that group also forces me see how wasteful I am with my time. I really need to get focused. I'm hoping I feel good enough tomorrow to be able to really focus and knock out more things on my list.

After my meeting, Bryan and I enjoyed a nice dinner at Boulevard Beef & Ale. We both had Lou's Chicken and it was delicious!! It is definitely one of my new favorites. Of course, we go there for the company too. We just love visiting with them, Lou is the best!!

Well, I just got home from all that and just finished creating signs for our doors requiring all our guests to wear masks when visiting both of our establishments. I can't say I was happy about that, but I do understand the need to keep people safe—agree with it or not. I don't want to close my businesses down again, so we will do what we can while guests are in our establishments to keep them safe. We always have, but this is just one more mandated step. I am just hoping we aren't met with resistance.

Well, that's it for my busy day. Looking forward to tomorrow and getting even more done!!

June 24, 2020

Despite dragging my feet and not feeling like doing much during the day, I'm actually managing to get things done! It's funny, but before and after the shop is open, I tend to get so much done—when the shop is open, not so much.

Today I got lots of orders mailed out, did some errands, and got some paperwork done for the brewery. Then, I decided to bring home my computer to keep working but realized that I left both of my chargers at my shop. So, I guess no working for me since the battery was already dead.

Instead of working, because I couldn't, I decided to buy a movie on Amazon that I used to love watching. It was made back in 2000 and it's called *I Dreamed of Africa*. I just love the whole movie, the adventure, and everything. It makes me sad that right now there aren't many adventures to be had. I wish there were more things to do that are safe. It disappoints me that that I am missing that adventure this year—no Tennessee, no trips, so sad. I guess I will live vicariously through movies that are made in foreign settings, so that maybe I can enjoy a little visual travel.

While I'm thinking about it, I'm also so disappointed in some people right now. It's so disappointing to me how people are acting towards each other and how they say not nice things about others. We are all doing the best we can, but I've never seen people so cutthroat towards each other over all kinds of things. I mean, people who have been friends for upwards of twenty years or longer, people you thought were friends, who supported you and helped you. And now, for whatever reason they are bent on bringing their 'friend' down. They say nasty things about someone's character and wish them ill harm. I am not sure if anyone else is facing this, but it's truly disheartening when, for so long, you thought you knew someone and thought you both had mutual respect for each other. Still, I know the truth about me and my integrity and that's all that matters. It's just sad and disappointing when it happens. Still, knowing someone's true colors and feelings is better than going a whole lifetime being fooled. I mean, are people really that crazy these days?? Boy, oh boy!

Well, as cases of this virus continue to rise, I continue to do all I can to be safe and keep everyone around me safe. I also find myself trying to be more kind to people. I hope my friends are doing the same, and if you need me for anything, just know I am here for you, no matter what, and no strings. We all need each other more than ever and despite any differences in beliefs, I love you all for your kindness and integrity, as that is what true friendships are built on!

Happy Wednesday and here's to a great rest of the week!

June 25, 2020

What a day—good and bad all in one.

My morning started out very slow, and it's because I just didn't feel like getting up. Well, it's not like I didn't want to get up, but that I didn't sleep well. For some reason last night my brain just wouldn't stop. Like dreaming every minute to the point where you feel like you are still awake—yep, that was me!

The shop was great today. Our guests were amazing, as always. If nothing else, they are the bright shining stars in my day these days. Without them it would be hard to be motivated to get up and get moving. This afternoon I hosted my first 'Tea with a Sommelier' since February. We only had a few guests to ensure safety, but it was wonderful sitting down and talking about tea. It's something I truly love and have a passion for, so I know it excites our guests too. I wish I could do that every day!

So after all that at the shop, I went to see my amazing and smart friend, Dr. Lisa for some acupuncture. It was so good to be back. And man did she hit my problem area...but on my way to her place, my truck stalled and said 'low oil pressure' when I pulled in the parking lot. It wouldn't start back up, so I actually had to put my truck in neutral and push it. Holy cow, it's not easy pushing an F150 by myself, but I did it. When I came out from my appointment it started just fine. Now tonight it's sitting at Master Mechanics for Steve to take a look at. It is truly never a dull moment...except for maybe tonight.

So, you know, before this whole pandemic, I used to run around a lot, always busy, and I always said it was good that Bryan was busy with his thing, and me with mine. I loved that life. But then COVID happened, and life slowed way down for us. We were no longer passing in the wind. We were visiting, spending time together, and eating dinner together. We spent more time together from March to May of this year, than we didn't the whole year prior. And selfish me enjoyed it and hoped it would continue. Sadly, our reality from before COVID has returned.

Back are the days that he works in Tampa, where he runs from job to job, where he comes home and eats dinner at 11:30 p.m., and we go to bed at different times. It makes me sad because I haven't quite worked back up to where I was before the shutdown. I just don't have the motivation since there is so much uncertainty. But where does that leave me? It leaves me at home alone at night, eating dinner by myself, and being bored out of mind and lazy. It makes me sad. I used to love my time, but that's before I knew what I was missing. I don't know how to have the best of both worlds, yet but I hope I figure it out soon.

Tomorrow is another day and I hope I make it a great one. I hope I can stay focused and get some of my motivation back. Here's to a good Friday!

June 26, 2020

All I can say is what a day....I really don't think there is any other way to explain it.

The day started off normal, getting to work at a decent time and starting on a few projects. I was finding my flow and getting things wrapped up. Then, bam! The state makes an announcement that bar licenses are being suspended for consumption on premises. Wrench in the day!

Now, I know I wrote yesterday about wanting to spend more time with my husband, how I hated that he was coming home so late, and that we weren't having dinner together, but I didn't want the businesses to have to stop operating. Needless to say, my today was sent in another direction, getting growlers ready and closing off the seating area again. Oh, what fun! Now I feel bad for complaining about being at home alone and bored.

So, with the new situation at the brewery, Bryan is getting home earlier, and we might be able to have dinner together. It's a simple gesture, right?? Apparently not tonight...we got home at 9 p.m., and I called right away to order pizza. All was good and they said it would be about 60 minutes. After an hour and a half, we called, and they told us our pizza and wings were out for delivery and that the driver had 2 orders with him. Ok, great. Another half hour passes, and we call back and get the manager. Turns out our slip was put in the done drawer and was never made. Great! So now it's 11:20 at night and we are sitting in the only drive through that is open this late, waiting to order. So much for enjoying a nice dinner, not at 11 p.m.!

And tomorrow, I'm sure, will be no less entertaining. Gotta love the craziness that is 2020! If I couldn't laugh, I would probably cry (thank goodness for meds)!

This is the story of my life!

June 27, 2020

We had a nice end to the week at the tearoom. Of course, we had amazing guests, and I enjoyed all the stories they shared with us. It was truly so heartwarming.

It was also a sad day at the tearoom as our beloved Michaela leaves us to move to North Carolina. She has been with us for a while, working with us on the weekends. We will miss her but wish her all the best with her new home and new adventure. She definitely leaves a hole that will not easily be filled.

This afternoon, after we closed the tea shop, I went over and spent some time at the brewery. It was slow there today, but then again, why wouldn't it be…especially when you can't serve for people to drink onsite. It wasn't horrible, but you can actually see people are less inclined to come out right now. Not that I blame them at all. I am very hesitant to go anywhere or venture around people right now too. We will see what happens over the next few weeks, as I'm sure our brewery status isn't going to change for a while.

I did have fun playing with flavors at the brewery. We tried to design a mango blonde and a peach blonde. The peach came out okay. It was a little light on the flavor. Now, the mango, on the other hand, came out amazing! I am so glad I could guide Bryan and encourage him to put some more flavor in. It has a great flavor and I hope our guests enjoy it as much as I do.

Tonight, we finally got our pizza that we ordered last night. The company was very nice, and the owner made good on their promise to get us our pizza and wings tonight. All I can say is yum! It was good, even though it was a day late.

Tomorrow is Sunday, my day of rest...not really! I hope to do a little bit of work and come up with a strategy or a game plan for both the tearoom and tea brand. I have some ideas on how to keep things going as we slow down again; I just don't have a cohesive plan. That's the plan, so we see what happens. Oh, and I'll probably take it easy tomorrow. My neck is completely killing me. It hurts to look in any direction but forward. I'm hoping I can get my strategy started and not let my neck get the best of me.

Have a great rest of the weekend. You still have half of it left!!

June 28, 2020

Happy Sunday! I hope everyone had an enjoyable and relaxing day—hopefully one without stress and anxiety.

I had a nice day...Bryan and I slept in and then enjoyed a late breakfast at Rose's Bistro. I just love their breakfasts, and todays was perfect, even though we ate it at lunch time, LOL.

Today was the first day I adventured out. I have been staying very close to home, just going to my shop, the brewery and very few little errands. It's not that I'm afraid, I just feel limiting interaction with people keeps me at a lower risk for anything. I tend to do this during regular flu season.

This afternoon I went with my mom over to Pier 1 in Trinity, just to see if they had anything I couldn't life without, and at a great price. The only thing I found was some baskets that were a steal that we can use to put together baskets in our gift shop. I bought quite a few of them for us to have on hand. Other than that, I didn't really find anything that I couldn't live without. Funny but looking at their prices, they are still quite high for even being on sale. I figure I'll check back in another few weeks to see where they are at.

Next was a trip to Publix. Truly, nothing exciting there, just picking up our normal groceries that I get once every few weeks. I was amazed how packed the store was and how shelves are still somewhat empty. I don't think people are panic buying, but I think they are keeping more on hand at home these days.

This afternoon I met Deidra and Ava at Vampire Penguin to try out the desserts I have been hearing so much about. I was not disappointed. Actually, it was delicious, and I can actually eat it. Sometimes ice cream messes with my stomach and this was so light that I had no issues. I enjoyed cookies and cream shaved cream (whatever they call it) with Oreo cookie crumbles, chocolate sauce, and whipped cream.

After that, I went back to the house and worked on my blending class at the World Tea Academy. I only had a few minor assignments to turn in and a few discussion boards to do. As much as I know about blending, especially winning at the Global Tea Championship for my blended green tea, I was still able to learn a few new things. Next class I will take is Blending 2. I'm excited about it because one of my tea industry friends authored the class and I can't wait to see what he says. I love that if I have any questions,

I can just call him. I'm so excited, and it's so hard to know that it doesn't start until after July 4th.

Tonight was a quiet night at home. Didn't I say I wanted more of those?? Bryan cooked chicken on the grill and we watched a movie together. It was nice and I'm thankful for every moment like this because before I know it, the craziness of everyday life will be back again.

Here's to the start of another week of 'what next' and 'you've got to be kidding me.' Oh, the stories we will all be able to tell in the future!

June 29, 2020

I don't believe in 'days off' anymore. Just because my business is closed for a day doesn't mean the work stops. Don't get me wrong, I do take downtime, but there is truly never an end in sight for the amount of work that needs to be done.

As you probably guessed it, I worked most of the day. Honestly, I kind of find it therapeutic to be in my shop by myself and get some work done. It gives me time to focus on what I need to catch up on without distraction. I mean, today I paid bills and settled books for both companies, filed receipts for the past three months, filled bags of tea, filled online orders, and did some store errands. Sure, there were a lot of little things I got done in between all of that, but it felt good to be getting organized again.

Tonight, we had to get our house ready for the new refrigerator coming tomorrow. We had to move furniture and detach furniture from the wall to make room for the new unit to come in. Funny, when we pulled the one cabinet in the kitchen off the wall, we realized how long it has been in that spot because apparently the last time we painted, we painted around it. Lol, I had forgotten it has been there that long. We also threw away three big garbage bags of bad stuff in the fridge. Who knew leftovers could pile so high! I swear this new fridge is going to be empty!!!

Tonight, Bryan and I went to Thai Bistro for dinner. You know they are good people when we sit down, and the lady comes over and nicely hands me back my little hand sanitizer I had left on the table the week before. I thought my sanitizer was a goner after I realized I left it behind. They joked with me about it, but I thought it was so sweet! We need more people like them in this world.

Dinner was wonderful, as usual. I just love going there. It always feels so welcoming and like home. And I really like the flavors of Thai food, and I'm glad my husband does too! If you haven't tried them yet, you should. They do a tremendous take-out business, but nothing beats going in, sitting down and relaxing there. If any of my friends haven't been and want to go, let me know and I will be very happy to meet you there. Ahem, you know who you are!

For now, it's off to bed. I've got a busy day on tap tomorrow...not really, more just waiting for the fridge to come, and then a few things to get done at the tearoom.

I hope your week is starting off good. Make it a great one!

June 30, 2020

Okay, so if someone would have told me a few months ago that we would still be at this for me to be writing for ninety-nine days, and for sure now day one hundred tomorrow, I would have said they were crazy. There is no way, in this day and age, we should be dealing with this craziness for so long. Boy, was I wrong!

So, here we go...

Today is the day we got our new refrigerator. After a lot of back and forth, we decided we didn't want to keep coming home not knowing if the unit was working or if our food was going bad. Since we are rarely home, it could go a long time without us knowing. So, I bit the bullet and bought a fridge. Now, if anyone knows our house and our kitchen, we have a very small space to fit this fridge. Finding one that fit was a feat in itself. Imagine my anxiety today, delivery day, stressing over whether I got one that would fit. Yes, stress as in anxiety. It was horrible and I could barely breathe until they slid it into place. Well, I'm happy to say it fits perfectly with an inch to spare. The height is a little shorter than our previous fridge, so overall it's smaller. That's truly okay, this time we aren't filling it with anything extra and we are going to keep it very limited with leftovers. Sure, I say that now. Just know I'm going to try.

Bryan stayed home today to help make sure everything with the refrigerator went well. He also decided to brew since he would have the day off. It's good that he did since we need to keep fresh beer on tap. Today he brewed the Red. I love brew days because it means lunch. Today we had Heros. Of course, it was awesome, and I love that they are local right in downtown. If you haven't checked them out yet, you should. I like every sandwich I've ever gotten there. I love how they really take pride in what they make, using fresh, great ingredients. Yum! It made my lunchtime great today. Well, that, and I got to see my hubby.

I did get some work done at my shop today. I have a few projects that I still haven't gotten to, but I will, in time. And Travis came and hung two new chandeliers in the additional tearoom area. They are looking so nice! Next up will be the front windows. I just have to get some more cable. Then that part of our updating will be done, and I will be able to work on something else.

Tonight, I had Tea Mastermind with my tea leader friends. I would be lying if I said things weren't tough right now and that it's hard to continue to stay motivated when things seem to change daily. That group keeps me grounded and helps me stay motivated and focused. I am truly so blessed to have them as a support system. I find them invaluable. They have some really good, simple ideas too. They all are especially uplifting to each other when we are facing these difficult times. So wonderful!!

Tomorrow is one hundred days that I've been writing, and so far, the tearoom has a good amount of people with tea reservations. I'm glad about that. It's nowhere near where we need to be, but it's a start. Anything these days is good!!

July 2020

July 1, 2020

Day 100!

Woohoo! Actually, I don't know if I should be happy that I have stuck with my daily post this long, or if I should be sad that I've done it for 100 days because life still isn't back to normal. Well, since I'm at it, I might as well keep going, right?!

Today was a busy day for me. It started out with cleaning up our tearoom annex area. Yesterday we installed beautiful chandeliers in there and we had moved furniture, so I cleaned that area up and got it ready for guests.

I met with Evelyene and Gilles at my shop. They are one of the French companies we work with and purchase from for our gift shop. We have carried their perfumes and small heart soaps before, and they sell really well. We also added their room fragrance dispensers and incense sticks, all brought in from France. Today they brought a new line in that includes hand lotion, body lotion, and bath gel soap. They are all made by a company in Provence, France, that is owned by a former Miss France. Of course, I had to sample the different lotions and they are wonderful. We decided to add some of these new items to our shop, in limited quantity, and we have already sold some. I'm so excited to bring higher quality and beautiful products to our shop!!

This afternoon I had lunch with my friend Diane from Nature Coaster. I always love having lunch with her. Not only is she wonderful to work with for marketing my businesses to counties north of mine, but she is a great businesswoman. She's someone I can talk to about business, and she doesn't judge, she helps me solve the issue or gives me ideas. You truly need friends to bounce ideas off of, who aren't in your area or do what you do. I so enjoy our visits; it always ends up being like a 'gal's lunch' and not a work meeting. That's what I absolutely love about her, and other friends I have tea with. We end up being just like the guests that visit the tearoom— visiting and having a really nice time!

Tonight, Bryan and I enjoyed a date night dinner at Carrabba's Italian Grill. I hadn't been there since February, and I have missed it. It was just like I remembered, and our server, Kelly, was wonderful. Of course, how could she not be, she has the perfect name, LOL! While there, I saw some blasts from my past! Kara, it was so good to see you, Kaitlyn and Sarah! The gals are just beautiful, and it was such an honor to watch them grow up at the church. I am sending you prayers at the loss of your furry friend, and I wish Kaitlyn a Happy Birthday! It truly warmed my heart that you stopped at my table. Don't let those girls ever tell you not to say 'hi' or bother me if you see me. It's never a bother, I love seeing you guys, and all the guys and gals that I had the opportunity to help spiritually mold while I worked at the church. It truly fills my heart!

After dinner was another trip to Vampire Penguin for me, and a first for Bryan and my mom. They both loved it. It was great watching Bryan's face as his brain tried to figure out what he was tasting since the texture is different. It's something you've never had so it's hard to describe. All I know is that I really like it and I can enjoy it without being too heavy on my stomach.

Well, it's time to lie down. I have found that my neck nerve doesn't hurt as much when my head is on my pillow, as there isn't as much motion. Tonight, I'm going to start reading a new book—something for pleasure, not learning. I am very excited about it.

So, tomorrow day one hundred and one, or day one...I haven't decided yet, lol.

July 2, 2020

Starting the next one hundred days, so let's see if I can keep this going some more!

This morning, I woke up early. It was nice, but I actually got up before Bryan today, and he still had to go to work in Tampa. So, while he was getting around, I stayed in bed and played on my phone. It was nice, I find I get a lot done in the morning when I'm in bed working on my phone. That and my head spasms aren't so bad that I can actually look at the screen without jerking and moving to keep it in focus.

Today was a good day in the tearoom. Yet, I don't think I did anything productive today. I walked around the tearoom and gift shop, and did a few little things like make labels, and that's about it. I'm sure I did more, but none of it was worth really remembering.

One thing I did do was work on our 4th of July sales. We are going to do some grab and go teas, our purple lemonade, and a Liberty Lemonade with hibiscus (red) and the blue pea flower (blue—for color only). Both came out beautifully and they tasted great too. I can't wait to have these for our guests! Next up...maybe Bubble Tea??? I'm working on ways to make these teas in our shop, hoping to make room up front in our register area. It would be so cool!

After work today, I took Ava and Deidra, Josie and Tara, and Ryker and Dawne to Vampire Penguin. Truly, where else better can you take three five- to six-year-olds to get to know each other? Ice cream sounded like a great idea, and it was. I just thought it was important for them to be with some little kids their own age, to visit and talk to since they haven't been in school for so long. From what I could tell, they had a fun time and I'm hoping I can get them back together again soon.

Tonight, I came home and rested before getting on the computer and scheduling our social media for my shop for the next few days, over the holiday. Our work never ends! So now I'm getting ready to head to bed. I hope it's going to be a busy two days, and I want to be ready!

July 3, 2020

It's another day where I don't feel like I'm getting ahead, but I'm getting somewhere.

I received word today that I passed my World Tea Academy class, Blending Part 1. This month I take the second part of the course. I'm excited about it because, even though I understand blending and flavors, there's always something I can learn to improve my craft. I also especially love that some of my industry friends helped write the course, so I reached out to them while I was working on the class, and they provided me even more insight. It's wonderful!

Our shop was quite a bit busier with guests shopping today. They love our sweet treats from Mmmm Delicious Cupcakes. I love that we offer their desserts in our shop. I'm looking forward to selling lots tomorrow for the 4th. Actually, I'm excited about being here tomorrow. Normally we are in Tennessee this week each year. While I miss Tennessee, I'm glad to be home. I can't wait to offer some awesome iced teas and lemonades for people downtown. So exciting!

Today we sent out two big boxes of tea for a subscription service we participate in. That makes four boxes or two thousand bags of tea in the past two weeks. It's good because we are becoming very consistent on receiving tea orders. That is helping our business a lot. I'm also working on some campaigns for our tea brand that I hope to roll out in the next two weeks. Finally, it seems like everything is coming together.

So, this week I am missing Tennessee very bad. I know Bryan and I spent a day up there in November, but it truly feels like I haven't been there in forever. I miss my home away from home. We are still hopeful to get up there, maybe over Labor Day weekend. With as hot as it has been, the only thing I want to do is go down to Little River and lay in the ice-cold water. It's like my body is craving that refreshing water. So, here's hoping that in September we are in a much better spot to go up there.

Well, off to bed I go. I have to go to work early to make some fresh iced tea, and welcome guests for the ride and roll golf cart and bicycle parade in downtown. I'm so excited that we have been able to find a way to bring out community spirit and keep everyone safely apart. Now if the weather will just hold out!

July 4, 2020

Happy 4th of July!

Today we celebrate the independence of the United States from British rule. It's a day to celebrate our country and its amazing history, diversity and our future.

Today, our celebration was so much different than it was in the past. There were no large gatherings, no family picnics, and no mass fireworks for people to enjoy. However, there was no less of a celebration of what this day represents. It was just different. For example, instead of fireworks, our local community came together to bring the spirit of our country to our residents and businesses. We had a golf cart and bicycle parade. People decorated, people came downtown to watch, and the shops were open. It was like 'small town America' and it was perfect! People were out walking the streets, saying 'hello,' and keeping their distance. I want to give kudos to everyone who worked on this amazing event, pulling off something for us to celebrate our community and nation in a fun and safe way. I really hope this becomes an annual event! I have some photos and a short video on my Facebook profile for you to enjoy.

The shop stayed pretty busy today with our 4th of July specials. I think the Liberty Lemonade and the Purple Lemonade were the big hits and that makes me very excited. I actually want to keep those on the 'to go' menu all the time. I just have to figure out how to do that. I am just so thankful for all of the love our shop and business is continuously shown by so many. We are truly grateful.

The brewery did pretty good today too. It's so great that we continue to be busy even when our guests can't consume on premises, but restaurants can allow for consumption on premises because of their restaurant license. Though it is true we stay busier when both bars and restaurants can't allow consumption, I don't wish that on the restaurants because it affects the tearoom and my friends. However, I will say I am concerned because virus cases are going up and I wonder what the governor is going to limit next…after this weekend we will know more, I'm sure.

Tonight, Bryan and I enjoyed a low-key night together. I am truly thankful for the invites we had from friends to go out and celebrate with, but tonight we cooked chili dogs and mac and cheese and just chilled. Then we rode down to Key Vista Park to watch the sunset, even though the clouds kept it hidden. It was nice to be out, and the weather was amazing. Then, after a quick stop for some snow at Vampire Penguin, we headed home to watch a movie. Since we had down time so early tonight, I'm already ready for bed.

I'm looking forward to a great day tomorrow, a Sunday Funday!! Hope yours is too!

July 6, 2020

Today was a good and productive day. Of course it started with Rose's Bistro for breakfast. It was wonderful as usual. I love the omelet I get there! And surprisingly enough, we were there early enough that I actually had time to spend at my shop before going over to the brewery. I think it's because Bryan was excited to have the day to play with his smoker and I was covering the brewery. He was up and showered before me, crazy!!

With my extra time, I was able to print off labels for another 2 mail outs for the tearoom for postcards I had done, and for another round of teas to go to our subscription partners at Sips By. Thanks to Tara, who is part of our team at the tearoom, we are on schedule to get our teas out just in time, which is great so we can start getting sales in. I think this week we will be able to get another one thousand tea bags out. Isn't that just crazy? Oh, and there's some other things going on with our tea. I am working on finishing up a campaign for our tea brand that I will start to implement in the next two weeks. Oh, and that bubble tea thing…I have some samples of popping boba coming in this week. Yes Leah, one of the popping boba is lychee! While we can't do the tapioca or milk teas right now, we can certainly add some boba. I mean, how delicious would it be with strawberry boba in our fresh made lemonade? Just saying…

Tonight, the moms and I enjoyed the fruits of Bryan's labor. His smoked ribs were wonderful! It's been so long since we used the smoker that I forgot how much I liked it. That along with Bernice's famous corn bake, some mac and cheese I froze from Arlisa's Events, dessert from Vampire Penguin, and watching the trilogy of Jurassic Park, made it a great evening.

I'm excited and nervous for this coming week. I am nervous that all of the increases in the virus numbers are going to have the state limiting or even closing restaurant dining rooms again. It's very scary to think about it, but watching how things are going, it has me concerned about what the next step will be. Still, I'm heading to buy my supplies for the week, hoping and praying that we at least stay where we are. It's hard to spend the money when you don't know what each day will hold. Still, I know we will beat this thing and I know it's going to be ok, somehow.

I hope everyone has a great Monday! I mean hey, week one of July (a partial week) and nothing else wacky has happened. Can we keep it that way through the week?? Let's make it a great one!

July 6, 2020

I'm happy to say that this Monday was a pretty good. Hopefully you had that kind of day too. I'm tired of every day being crazy and I'm glad that this Monday was somewhat calm.

My day started with a trip to Largo to get our weekly groceries for the tearoom. All went well there; it was actually very quiet, and I think I'm going to plan to do some shopping there on Monday mornings again. We weren't running into people, carts and craziness. Perhaps after almost five years, I've figured out the best time to go.

When I got back, my mom and I enjoyed lunch at El Cerrito Mexican Restaurant. We usually end up there for dinner, but after going down to Largo, it just sounded so good, and it was. The off and on weather today made it a perfect day for their tortilla soup. Man, I wish I could make that at home. I need to work on that. Pinterest, here I come for a recipe!

This afternoon I didn't do much of anything. I got some postcards ready to be mailed out and I read the first week material for my tea class. I have been looking forward to this class. It's my second one about blending and it was written by a friend of mine in the industry. Hopefully it will provide some insight to some more blending for me. I've had a hard time concentrating on coming up with new blend ideas. I think my creative juices have been stifled a little lately and I need to get them back, but it's hard.

Tonight was a low-key night for us. I picked up a pork tenderloin in Largo, so Bryan cooked it on the grill. It was delicious! It's so nice to be able to do some cooking at home. It's not that eating out doesn't taste good, but home cooking is so much better for us, and honestly it does taste better too. Now Bryan has lunch leftovers for two days. And yes, the fridge has very few leftovers because we are working really hard to keep it cleaned out. So far, we are a week in and doing really good! If you saw our fridge before, you would know exactly what I mean, and how hard it has been for us to keep it empty, LOL.

Bryan and I made a big decision today for our future. Today, we found a space to park our camper, in Tennessee. The reality is we have this beautiful camper we never use here. Every time we go away, we spend time in Tennessee. Now, we have decided it is time to move our camper to our favorite place so when we visit, we will no longer need to rent a cabin. Instead, we will be able to go to our own place. For now, we are renting a place for it to be stored on the same property where we camp, and over time we will look to get our own piece of property up there. It was a tough decision since we are all the way down here in Florida, but it's the right one. We have always said that we would like to have a home both here and there, so we are moving toward that goal. I've only been going there for thirty-four years so it feels like my second home. For now, we will be staying in the Townsend area, at the base of the Smoky Mountains. Someday we would like to get some property in Wears Valley or Walden Creek. That's been my dream since I was a kid and I'm excited and nervous about this at the same time. One thing I look forward to is more time in the mountains, yeah. I can't wait to share more as we finalize the details and schedule our trip to take our camper up there.

So now it's time to start to wind down. Looking forward to a productive day tomorrow and a great rest of the week! I hope your Tuesday is good too!

July 7, 2020

Today was a productive day...well, maybe the first part. Of course, they all start out pretty much the same. I begrudgingly get up and shower, do my make-up and hair, and get dressed. Truly it's like everyone else, except I totally dread it...well, not all of it. I just dread doing my hair. One of the worst things with my disease is fighting my head and getting my arms to do what I need to do to get my hair up. It's something I never thought I would have trouble with but the longer my hair grows, the harder to get it in a ponytail. It leaves little to be desired for my hair and doing anything cool. I just need someone to come to my house every morning and put it up for me. Anyone??? LOL!

That makes me think...I need a maid. Someone who comes in and cleans the house, fixes dinner, and does the laundry. Is there such a person that helps you keep things organized and going, and makes sure you eat? I know when I was younger it was my mom but I'm way too old for that now, and my mom does enough already. Seriously, I see someone like this in my future.

Ok, back to my day...I stopped at my shop and got some things situated. I talked with Jacob from the City about the 4th of July event, ran to the bank, went to Home Depot to get a part to fix the toilet in the gift shop, dropped a box at storage, grabbed lunch at Chick-fil-A, and was back at my store all before 1 p.m. This afternoon I got a few packages ready for mailing and did a few things for my marketing plan. Then, we worked on recipes for our boba tea. Right now, I have strawberry, blueberry, passion fruit, and mango green tea and lychee popping boba. I have strawberry popping boba coming tomorrow, and passion fruit and mango will be in next week. We are working on our menu for 'to go' teas, boba, and more, and I can't wait to release it later this week! So exciting!!

Tonight was my weekly Tea Mastermind meeting. It is truly a highlight and I have so many ideas for things I can make to add to my gift shop. I am so excited about it. I just need to take a minute to step back and pick one or two things that I can concentrate on first. Still, it feels good to be motivated and excited. Not that I'm not every day, but I'm excited about trying a few new things.

Tonight, I helped Bryan at the brewery. Actually, I hindered more than I helped. We were trying to make a chocolate and peanut butter porter, but everything we did didn't seem to work out. So, we ended up with more of our delicious porter and I am going back to the drawing board. I wish it would have worked out, but man, with that robust malt it's hard. I'm going to try again though. I just need to sit back down and figure it out.

Now it's time for bed. I'm excited about tomorrow!! Not for any particular reason, but more so that I am looking forward to doing some more work and moving us forward. Yea!! Have a great Wednesday!

July 9, 2020

Today was just a weird day, I just can't explain it. I woke up just fine, but from the moment I got up, I could tell the day was going to be off. There was nothing wrong, just a strange feeling.

I got to my shop, and everything was good. Dawne was taking care of the tearoom, and I was listening to the council meeting from Tuesday night, trying to catch up on all that was going on downtown.

Today, Tara worked so hard to get so many of our tea bags made for our subscription service. She worked like a machine and got four hundred and seventy-five bags made today. I can't believe she stuffed that many, and man am I excited to be able to get them out, so that we can move on to other projects. I opened probably three hundred bags for her, and my fingers are sore tonight. I have got to toughen up so I can do more tomorrow.

I made a decision about my work. During the days I am going to be available in the tearoom and gift shop for my team, and I can do my computer and general business stuff before we open and after we close each day. I think that will allow me to be more productive and to better support my team all the way around.

This afternoon Travis came by the tearoom and helped hang some more chandeliers. Finally, I feel like we are getting some finishing touches done and making the shop look great. Only a few more things and our little updating will be done!

Tonight, I ran to JoAnn Fabrics to look at a few things. I don't know if it is because of the closure or what, but their store was low on inventory. Not material and that, but where did their wedding section go? And so many shelves had minimal stuff on it. I was kind of surprised, though I haven't really been out shopping in a while.

For dinner, Bryan and I enjoyed a nice time at El Cerrito. I know, I know... it's my second time there this week. But it was so good, and he didn't get to go with me on Monday. Of course, he had to have the big margarita, but luckily, he has learned how to drink it. The first time he got it, he drank it slowly that after we were done eating it took another twenty minutes for him to finish the drink. God forbid that we leave anything in the glass, LOL. So tonight, he started on it the minute he got it and had it finished after dinner. Funny though, the gentleman behind us ordered one and didn't realize how big it was, so Bryan offered him a tip to get through it—drink at least half before dinner comes or you'll be too full to finish it. LOL, I love his tricks!

Tonight, we booked our spot for camping in Tennessee. It's still a few weeks away, but I am so excited to be able to get the camper up there, so we have a place to go! I just know we are going to love it and that this is really going to offer us a break when we need it. As if running two successful businesses wasn't enough, this pandemic has played a number on my health, both mentally and physically. I am looking forward to being able to escape, even if just for two or three days.

Well, off to bed I go. I hope I wake up tomorrow and feel a little better, not so off. I don't know if it's the stress, the weather, or what, but I don't like feeling 'off.' It's time for rest to see if I can get back on track tomorrow. Night all!!

July 9, 2020

Finally, I had a somewhat normal day. It wasn't great, but it was one those days where things kind of just flowed. I felt like I got things done and was able to concentrate a little bit.

The shop had a nice flow today as did the tearoom. Honestly, it was almost like a normal day. I know, I know, nothing is ever normal anymore, but today it sure felt like it.

We also got some amazing news today about a great recognition that we received. Truly an honor and I am so completely blessed. I can't wait to share more, but right now just know that good things are and continue happening, and I think everyone is going to be excited too.

Tonight, I was on a conference call with Tea Lifestyle magazine. I have to work on an article or two over the next few weeks and get writing. My problem is that I have a hard time coming up with topics to write about. Not to mention this is fall themed, and with as hot as it is outside, it's hard to even think about Fall. So, if anyone has any ideas of things I should write on that pertains to the tea world and Fall, please let me know!

All in all, it was your typical day, as usual. Now tomorrow...tomorrow should be an interesting one! Can't wait for that one to unfold and share it with you!!

July 10, 2020

A Friday like no other, and for once that's okay!

My morning started off early. Now, for those of you who know me, you know early may not be early to most people, but anything before 10 a.m. is early to me. So, be shocked when I tell you I was in the shower and getting around to start my day by 7:45…in the a.m.!

My first stop of the day, after running to my shop, was a meeting at City Hall. Today, I was the designated representative for our brewery since Bryan was working in Tampa. The city asked us to come in, along with 2 other bars that are on Railroad Square. They wanted to talk about the 'wet zone' where people could consume alcoholic beverages after they purchased them from us. Long and short of it, the city is going to let that area be used for consumption. However, currently, we are opting not to use it. The area isn't completely easy to access for us as it's through our back door and an exterior door, and we aren't able to ensure social distancing and patrol the area. It doesn't mean we won't in the future, but right now it just doesn't make sense. I wish the other two places all the best and hope they have success with it, and maybe we will look to utilize the space in the future.

Today was a good day at the shop. While we weren't overly busy, I did manage to get some creative things done. I don't know if it was me getting up earlier or drinking tea early or what, but I didn't really slow down today.

This afternoon I sat in on a conference hosted by Jacob from the city. He had some great comments and points about social media, and I actually took a whole page of notes. I will be reviewing them this weekend to make sure I am taking full advantage of my social media when I work on my schedule for this coming week.

Tonight was low key. I'm working on a few little projects, so that kept me busy until Bryan got home from the brewery. Have I said how nice it is having him home and able to spend more time with me? I like this slow down again. I know it's a little scary, but I am going to enjoy every minute of it until some sort of normalcy returns...

Well, off to read my book, For the Love of Cities. So far, I am about 50 pages in, and I have realized I am a co-creator. I love how it talks about people's love for their city!

Night all! I hope you have a great Saturday!!

July 12, 2020

Today was one of those days that, from the minute I got out of bed and knocked things over in the bathroom, I was sure my whole day was going to be thrown off. Luckily for me, it wasn't.

The tearoom was filled with quite a few reservations today. Nothing crazy and we stayed under capacity, but we had multiple tables at each seating. It was so nice to hear people laughing and talking in our tearoom. Also, the gift shop did well today. I'm a glad we bulked up on our inventory, so we have lots of gifts and unique items for our guests. While it wasn't like a pre-COVID Saturday, it was more like a pre-COVID weekday. It felt good!

This afternoon, when the brewery slowed down a little bit, Bryan came to the tea shop, and we had fun working on our bubble tea. Actually, it's popping boba. Over the past week or so I have been working on our fruit tea recipes that will go with this venture. I am confident that I finally have the right formulations. Next up, we will be making room in the gift shop checkout area to accommodate us making these teas. But today, I made five at one time for trial and Bryan and the brewery team loved them. Yea, something fun and exciting!!

Tonight, we went to dinner at Thai Bistro. It was us, the moms, and our friend John and his wife, Connie. It was their first time eating there and they loved it. I'm so glad! It's like a little hidden treasure, and it's local. So yummy!

So, tomorrow is day one of three off, but of course I have lots going on! I am going to make a new scone recipe and a few other fun things! Yea! Looking forward to a fun and relaxing day doing some things I want to do.

July 12, 2020

Last night I didn't sleep well. In fact, I haven't been sleeping well for the past few nights. That has made me very tired during the day. I'm not sure why I'm not sleeping well. I know that over the past few nights, if I lay on my right side, the nerves in my neck get pinched and my left hand goes numb. There's nothing worse than a numb hand in the middle of the night.

This morning, I got up at a decent hour and to my surprise, I didn't drop or knock anything over. That's always a good sign that my balance is pretty good, and that's an indication of how my day may go.

We started our morning at Rose's Bistro for breakfast. Of course, it was delicious as always. I do enjoy a good breakfast, especially on Sundays.

After breakfast, I decided to play in my shop kitchen. Today was an experiment with some lavender white chocolate scones. This was a first-time recipe, so it was a little trial and error. The first try came out great! I also created and drizzled vanilla glaze over them. The goal with this recipe was to figure out the measurements and then package the ingredients in a jar for people to make at home. It turns out that it worked, and now I have this recipe and one more. It's wonderful and I can't wait to get them packaged up so our guests can make scones at home!

I want to give a huge 'thank you' to those of my friends that tried the recipe today. I appreciate knowing I'm on the right track!

This afternoon, after baking, I fixed myself a blooming tea, thanks to Dawne, and hoped on a conference with the US League of Tea Growers. It was so wonderful to see some familiar faces and hear about an update on the tea industry and talk about growing tea. It was a great conversation, and I took lots of notes. I also have some interesting ideas, but I always take some time and think about how to make my ideas work. Honestly, one of the best parts was being with people in the tea industry, and sharing all our ideas, it's great. It's also one of the reasons that I love my Tuesday evening meet ups too.

Tonight, we had dinner with the moms. We did take out from BackDraughts Pizza in Tarpon. Since we can't eat there, the next best thing was take-out. We enjoyed our pizza at home and watched *Ford vs Ferrari*. What a good movie! I have a whole new love for Carroll Shelby! What a visionary and a focused man. Matt Damon played such a great role! If you haven't seen it, I encourage you to.

Ok, off to bed soon! Even though I didn't do a whole bunch of stuff, I'm still kind of tired.

Here's to another good start to the week tomorrow!

July 13, 2020

I think I have accepted that I am not a morning person. More than that, I'm not even an early afternoon person. I try, I really do. But I really need to face that reality and stop beating myself up for it.

This morning, I got up and around in the 9 o'clock hour and got to my shop in the 10 o'clock hour. In all fairness, it was about 10:30 a.m., I didn't wait until the last minute. It was so hard to focus this morning. I mean, I had things to do, but I just either didn't want to do them or I couldn't get motivated. Hey, at least I'm realizing it. It took everything I had not to go home and take a nap in the afternoon.

Now, this afternoon was a completely different story. It was almost 4 p.m. and suddenly everything kicked into high gear. I got a ton of stuff done and even launched a new online retail shop for our tea brand. I worked at it until 7:30 p.m. and I could have stayed longer. I'm always amazed at how much I can get done late in the day and how much of a waste the first 2/3 of my day is.

I was able to take some photographs today of my latest scone creation and some of our delicious tea. I did my website like I mentioned before and got some things finished up.

Tonight, we had a quiet night in. We grilled out some hotdogs and vegged out. Truly, I think this is the slowest day I've had in a long time. Hopefully, I will find some more motivation for getting things done tomorrow.

Hope you have a great Tuesday!!

July 15, 2020

Of course, I didn't get up too early, but I had to be up and at my shop before 11 a.m. Why, you ask? I had an interview scheduled to talk about my tea business. It was so great to sit down and talk about my business and what I love about what I do. In the daily grind I tend to forget about why I love to do what I do. Also, I have so many ideas on how to expand on what I do. It was such an honor to promote being on Florida's Sports Coast. After all, they are the reason I got the interview. I just hope I did them justice, and I think I did because I was called a 'rock star' afterwards.

This afternoon, I sat in on a video conference with Specialty Tea Institute where we discussed the history of tea in the US. With as much research as I have done, I still always enjoy hearing it again, and having the opportunity to learn more. I think if I ever stop learning I'll die, LOL.

Tonight was my weekly call with the Tea Mastermind group. I guess you can see my day was all about tea, LOL. Tonight, we helped one of our team members get more comfortable with a podcast she is doing next week. I remember my first interview and how nervous I was. I am glad that we were able to tell her what we have done, to help her out and not be so nervous. I know she will do great!

Tonight, Bryan and I had dinner at home. He fixed boneless ribs, and they were awesome. I should send him to the store more often because he came home with burgers for tomorrow night too. I do enjoy eating at home, so that will be three days in a row. I wonder what we can fix for Thursday.

Well, wishing you a great hump day tomorrow! I know mine is going to be great!

July 16, 2020

I'm totally of the mindset that there are no bad days. Even my worst day can't compare to other people's good days, or even for not having a day at all. Sure, things may not go the way I want, but it could always be much worse. I never ask how much worse it could be because I feel like then I'm only providing fate a challenge.

This thought on my day got me thinking, what was the worst day of my life? While I was devastated to lose someone close to me, multiple times, while I struggled with things and had days that seemed unfair, these weren't my worst. See, despite these days being hard for me, I consider my worst days simply those that I wouldn't want to relive again. In my life there have only been two of those days. I won't say what they were, but they are days when I wasn't involved in what happened, but rather a witness. One resulted in a loss of life, the other a near loss. And after thinking about them and praying for all involved, I think about how blessed I am to be living this life.

Yes, things are crazy right now. No, we don't know what is going to happen tomorrow. We don't know if our businesses will survive. We don't know when things will go back to the normal we knew. However, we have a life, and my days, despite being hard, are still better than some people's best days. How lucky am I? How lucky are we?

Today wasn't a good day or a bad day, it was just a day. The tearoom had several tables, and I spent time working on errands and a few other little things. I got a few things done that I needed to...things like errands to UPS, Office Depot and Minuteman Press.

Then I had acupuncture this afternoon. Thanks Dr. Lisa Maharajh from Maharajh Acupuncture and Herb Shop, for helping my muscles release the toxic junk! I know I look like a leopard from the cupping session, but in a few days my muscles will be feeling much better. I was afraid to take a picture of it; I didn't want to scare anyone.

Tonight was the highlight of my day as I spent some time catching up with a friend I haven't seen much since March. She has kept her distance from everyone to keep healthy and I've truly missed her. Tonight, we talked and laughed in the tea parlor. She sat at one table, me at the other. It was great, and if that's how I have to see my friends I say— bring it on!

This evening, Bryan was going to grill some burgers, but the radar looked horrible, so we decided on a delivery from Morty's Pizza instead. The dinners we got were wonderful. And, in true New Port Richey fashion, the storm dissipated just as it got to us. Of course, we could have grilled out, LOL. So instead, we will enjoy burgers tomorrow.

I hope everyone's hump day was good. On to the homestretch for the week and full speed to the weekend!

July 16, 2020

What started off as slow, turned out to be an odd but satisfying day.

This morning my team and I started out with tea. I love when we start days off that way. We sat and talked about upcoming events and activities, and worked through some ideas that we can do to help draw guests in. To be honest, it's a struggle today with COVID numbers going up and people being scared. We did come up with a few ideas and I'm excited to see how they turn out.

Around lunch time Dawne and I took a platter of tea sandwiches over to the police department. I really just wanted to do something nice for them because I see them out all the time working really hard. I hope they enjoyed it and I look forward to doing something nice for them again in the future.

This afternoon I enjoyed tea with my friend Dawn. We caught up about her vacation and life in general. It was so nice to just catch up with a friend. I swear, time flies when she and I get together. I truly enjoyed it.

My friend John from Heros stopped in too. We sampled some more cheese that we are working on for our evening project. Of course, it's always amazing to try cheese and work toward what we are creating in our space. I am excited about this next venture.

Tonight, Dawn called, and we met her and her husband, Jim, for dinner. We went to a little hidden gem in Tarpon called Bayou Bistro. It was tiny, but don't let the size fool you. I had a chicken sandwich, which was seasoned and cooked to perfection. However, their seafood, fresh off the boat, is their highlight. Bryan had their special, blackened snapper with crab and hollandaise sauce with a side of rice pilaf and zucchini. He said it was absolutely amazing. We both are looking forward to trying more food there in the future.

Tomorrow we are working on tea blending in the shop. We have a lot to blend, and I can't wait to try some new things! It's time already to start working on Fall teas. My fun never ends.

Hoping the week has been well to all my friends! Here's to one more day before the weekend.

July 18, 2020

Today was a really nice day, for the most part.

It was a really slow day in our shop and tearoom. Even in normal times we have slow days, but I think I feel it more since we have been going through this pandemic. Even though I am a smart businessperson, operating on 40% of normal revenue doesn't last forever. I'm doing everything I can think of, and slow days are a part of game, but I really hope things pick up soon.

Today my amazing team all worked together to help me blend up some of our teas that we blend in house. They were awesome. I gave them a little lesson on blending and taught them how to read my recipes and they went to town. It was so wonderful because I was able to get some other things done. We also had an instruction on how to make tea with the popping boba that we are going to start offering on August 1st. I'm so excited about that!

Tonight was a lazy night. Bryan was at the brewery, and I was home alone. I think my lack of energy has been from the drain and stress of dealing with our businesses. I come home every day and know what I need to do, but then don't do anything. It's horrible and I end up feeling guilty. Now, I know I deserve some downtime and I'm good with that, but I am truly being lazy, almost like depressed.

The one good thing that came out of tonight is I finally watched *Bohemian Rhapsody*. What a good movie. I forgot how much I love Queen's music and that it is so uplifting. Maybe we all just need to go out into the street and sing 'We Are the Champions' or 'We Will Rock You'. I don't know about you, but I know that would make me feel a lot better. Do I have any takers?

Well, tomorrow is Saturday and I'm looking forward to seeing some guests in the tearoom. At least we will end the week on a high note!

July 18, 2020

After the week I had, and trust me, it was a decent week overall, I am still glad to see Saturday night. That means it's time for me to regroup and get ready for next week. I often find taking one day to reevaluate, one day to execute, and one day to unwind, is the perfect mix for me to ready my business and myself to stay strong. So, tomorrow is a day I hope to feel good to be able to work on executing a few different things, yes!

Today, the tearoom had quite a few guests. It was wonderful hearing their laughter and seeing their smiling faces. It truly warms my heart! We had some guests in the gift shop. Some of our regulars stopped in and it was so good to catch up with them. They all seem to be doing well and they were so happy to catch up with us and see we were still here. It definitely was a good day!

One of my visits was from my friend Michelle from Chocolates by Michelle. She has always been so supportive of me and my place. Did you know that she was the first person who bought a gift from my gift shop when we had the tiny three table tearoom back in 2016? In fact, I still have the first $1 bill she signed and gave me. It's framed by my register. She is doing meals now, Meals by Michelle, and I can't wait to order some this week for dinner! I love it when others cook for me.

For those who have asked about the brewery, it continues to hold its own. It does really stink that they aren't able to serve guests, but you make do with the hand you have been dealt. We just appreciate everyone's continued support over there and we know we will get through these crazy times. I'm just so proud of my husband for sticking to our plan and doing what is best for our business, our team and our patrons. I mean, anyone who knows him knows how badly he would love to open for everyone to enjoy, but he is really trying to and is being responsible. Perhaps my integrity has rubbed off on him after all this time.

Tonight, we enjoyed some delicious Thai food from Thai Bistro and then dessert at Vampire Penguin. It was nice, as always. I truly enjoy our Saturday evenings out. We don't go out often during the week, so I especially enjoy this time. Now we are just relaxing at home, enjoying a show with Gordon Ramsey, and just taking a break.

I'm looking forward to tomorrow. I'm not sure if it's a day of rest or reorganizing. I think I'll decide in the morning.

I hope you all are having a great weekend so far!

July 19, 2020

Today started off great, enjoying some delicious breakfast with Bryan and the moms at Grandma Sally's Restaurant. I always enjoy going to breakfast on Sunday morning. It has become a weekly tradition for us.

After breakfast I went over to my shop. I didn't do much, just checked on a few things. I decided my day would be comprised of going to Citrus Park mall and getting some bubble tea. While I have the popping boba and tea down, I want to work on the tapioca and milk teas. So, I thought I would go get a tea and watch how they make it. Turns out they were out of vanilla (my favorite), and tapioca. Actually, all they had for boba was passion fruit and mango, the ones that I have at my shop. Needless to say, I left empty handed. Ugh!! I'm hoping to run to an Asian grocery store in Palm Harbor in the next two days to see what they have.

After that disappointment, I came home and decided I didn't want to do anything else. The trip down and back, along with the walking just wore me out today. I didn't sleep well at all last night. My brain ran nonstop, and I didn't feel like I slept at all, so I wasn't in the mood to do a lot more than my little journey. I did read through a special Tea Time Magazine publication, and I read a medicinal tea book. It's more of a reference book, but I read the first thirty pages about tea and medicine. Even though I didn't do work on my computer, I felt like I got something done.

Tonight was a lazy night at home. It's just barely 10 p.m. and I'm bored out of my mind. The problem with being home so early is that I end up with more time on my hands that's not filled with a specific project. That stinks because then I end up being lazy. I can imagine tonight I'll be going to bed early. Maybe I can get up earlier tomorrow and get a few things done. Here's hoping I actually get some sleep tonight.

I hope everyone had a nice weekend and that you have a great start to the week.

July 20, 2020

Today was a good day…I can't say I did much, but maybe that's what made it good.

I spent a little time in my shop this morning, working on social media and cleaning up our register area. I am making room for Boba tea. Yes, it's coming on August 1st. I needed more room to be able to make them, so I took out the Kegerator—it's heading back to my house and I'm sure my husband is thrilled it will be back in the kitchen, maybe.

I'm sure you are getting bored of hearing about my non-existent, non-exciting days. Honestly, on my days off, I find myself to be a little bored. Not that I don't have a ton of things to do to keep me busy, but sometimes I just feel so unmotivated. I find that's more of my issue because I have time on my hands with the extra day off. Don't get me wrong, I enjoy not being pressured, but I also find that it leads to procrastination—something that I often rather regret.

The other reason for my procrastination today was my neck. Over the last two days I have had a pinched nerve in the back of my neck. It makes my ability to turn my head to the left virtually impossible. The nerve and muscle are swollen, and CBD and Advil haven't helped one bit. It's funny but when I tilt my head to the left, it's a cold tense feeling, and it makes it difficult for me to sit and hold my head up. Since I use my hand to hold my head up, the pressure it puts to hold it in that direction causes the muscle to contract and push back, which hurts worse. I just can't win. It was feeling better last week after acupuncture and cupping. Maybe this week I will have to go for a massage.

Tonight, Bryan and I enjoyed dinner at Hooters. It was nice eating there, out in the open air. It was also good seeing the staff and managers, especially Lo. He is always so nice to us, and he made sure to check on Bryan and see how our businesses were doing. It truly felt like being back to normal, in a weird, not normal way, if you know what I mean. We also talked about some ideas for the brewery and things we can do to help move us back to an open establishment. Apparently, there is a way, and we are exploring it. The best part is that we will be able to do it relatively easy. Tomorrow, we submit an application and talk with the state. The best part, it doesn't require becoming a restaurant, like some other breweries are doing. Stay tuned, as this may happen in the next two to three weeks, since we will be away next week. Bryan is very excited.

Well, off to bed for me. I'm tired after all my researching and reading. I'm ready for a good day tomorrow. I have a few things on my list to get done, and some running around to do. Fun things are happening...stay tuned.

I hope the week continues to go well for you! The week seem to be getting a little better, finally. Maybe it's because I've stopped asking, 'what's next?'

July 21, 2020

My Sunday! I'm not always sure how to feel about my Sunday. I'm happy to have the day off, but I also get the Sunday night blues. Even though I love my business and what I do, I can't help but have some dread over the week ahead.

This week is even harder because I am looking forward to taking the trailer to Tennessee. I wish it was Saturday and we were on our way to have a break. I haven't been away for a true break since last year and I'm so ready. The stress has been wearing on me and I've had an increase in panic attacks lately. Between that and the pain I have in my neck and head, it's been a pretty rough couple of days.

For some reason I have this muscle in my neck that wants to squeeze my nerve. Sometimes I move just right, and it shoots pain where I can hardly move. The last two nights, I took 1/2 a Valium to try and help me stay calm and help the pain. Then today I felt like I was in a little cloud. I couldn't focus and I was tired. No meds for me tonight. Even though I don't feel drugged, I don't like not feeling sharp and on my game. I hope I'm making the right decision. No, I don't like being a medicine head!

Well, I'm looking forward to tomorrow. I have a few meetings and I'm very excited about our guests tomorrow. It's no joke that it's been slow, so I'm excited that it looks like this week is already going to be better. I'm really looking forward to being a little more focused tomorrow.

Here's to a great, short, but productive week!

July 23, 2020

This morning started off pretty well. I got up, and despite my neck giving me grief from the start, my morning started off like usual. I went through my normal routine, but today when I checked my sugar it was quite a bit lower than it has been over the last few months. Now, it's still not good but at least for today it was moving in the right direction. It may be different tomorrow since I ate dinner late tonight.

My tearoom day started off with tea with my friend Nancy. She owns a great business in Dunedin, and we got together to talk business. It's always nice to visit and shoot ideas around with other business owners. Right now, they are the only ones who really know what we are going through. We are all struggling in the same boat and it's scary. Still, I'm excited for her to be thinking outside of the box and for her to have some new adventures with what she has. It's very exciting to see a business owner transform, grow, and live their dream.

With as much advising and idea generating as I do, I wish I could someday open a coaching or a consulting business to help current and potential business owners and entrepreneurs. It's too bad that I love what I do now too much, and I don't have the time to devote to it, but it would be pretty cool. Maybe a side job here or there, but I wouldn't know where to start to get paid for such services.

After Nancy left, I visited with my guests and friends in the tearoom. Thank you to Laura for making the trip up to New Port Richey. I know it's a drive, but your support really does mean the world to me. There's so much that you taught me so long ago that I absorbed and use almost every day. Truly, it was so great seeing you and your gals enjoying the tearoom today!

You know, I did the math and today, 60% of our guests were from outside our county—how awesome! That tells me people are willing to venture a little bit to places they feel safe. Maybe I should do a little video about our safety precautions and what we are doing, so everyone knows. I always feel safer dining in a smaller establishment, so maybe it's time to share! Fun idea!

Tonight, I worked on our newsletter. It's coming along nicely and I'm hoping to finish it up tomorrow. I have a few photos to do before then, some boba tea photos specifically. The best part is after I take the photos, then I can enjoy drinking them. Boy, it's a rough job!

I know it seems like all is going well and believe me I know how lucky I am compared to many others, but it's still a daily struggle. I have anxiety and stress and some days I handle it well and other days not so much. Add to my normal stress, the stress to get ready to move this camper, and my stress is through the roof. Once I get to Tennessee, I will be able to relax, but for right now it's the stress of getting packed and making sure we have everything that has me anxious. Perhaps that's why I'm still up at 12:30 a.m. writing this.

So, I'm going to turn in. Hopefully I will get some sleep and that tomorrow will be a good day for all of us too!

July 24, 2020

I'm sorry I didn't write about my day yesterday. It's not that I didn't want to, I just physically couldn't. My neck pain and pinched nerve were so bad when I got home last night that I actually stood in the kitchen and cried because I couldn't move. I have not been in this much pain since I had a pinched nerve ten years ago. I can't even describe the pain, the muscle pulsating and the nerve shooting pain into the top of my head. This, ladies and gentlemen, is a side effect of spasmodic torticollis. It is quite debilitating, and it will come and go, but for the last two days and now for the next week or two this is what I will deal with.

Today when I woke up, I felt slightly better than yesterday. Today I was able to get out of bed myself. I got up and took some medicine, sat on the couch to rest, and then got around and headed to my shop. Thank goodness for my mom helping me so I did not have to drive. She picked me up and ran me to my massage appointment, did our business banking, went to Office Depot, and Bed Bath and Beyond, and this afternoon she took me on a few more errands. She didn't have to do that and really after all these years, I feel bad that she is taking care of me.

My shop had a pretty good day today. We had a nice number of people come in the shop and the tearoom had guests. We have had guests every day this week, so it's been good. We've had a few people in shopping which is always so nice, too.

Today, despite not being able to move well, I got quite a bit of work done. It did make me feel a little better to be productive.

Tonight was a take it easy night. I didn't do much of anything just because the last thing I want to do is strain my neck. I've been alternating ice and heat like I'm supposed to. I also cleaned out my purse so it's not as heavy, and so I don't add extra pressure or weight to my shoulders. I know it's the little things!

Well, off to bed I go. I hope I sleep better tonight, and that tomorrow is a step in the right direction.

Hoping everyone has a great Saturday!

July 25, 2020

Today was a good day. My neck continues its course, but it's not getting worse and I'm able to function a little, which is a good thing. Luckily today I didn't have to do a lot, so I can continue to rest.

Before heading out to take our trailer to its new home in Tennessee, I did go into work. I had some tea orders to send out and a few loose ends to tie up before I left. I got them done pretty quickly, which was good. However, I'm glad I stayed a little bit because right around 12 p.m. the gift shop got busy. It was Tara's first time handling the front on her own and I kind of threw her in without any training. Good thing for us, she has been a part of the tea team for six weeks or so, so she does know quite a bit. She's a great fit to our team and I'm so happy to have her at our place.

Of course, Dawne has assured me that the tearoom will be great while I'm gone. I am sure it will be better than great because she knows all of the ins and outs. I'm so thankful she's part of our team, so I can run away once in a while—trust me, it's not often—and I have no worries.

This afternoon we hooked up the trailer and headed out to take it to its new home. I'm very excited about where it's going to be because it's going to be in my favorite place. The best part so far—it has ridden so nice. It's like we don't even feel the trailer on the back of the truck. For a heavy big trailer that's a really good thing. Tomorrow, we have four hours to go and we will be there! Yea!

We had a great time on our ride today. John from Heros got us some awesome sandwiches to enjoy on the road. They were perfect, and we enjoyed them for lunch and dinner. Oh, and John, the chips were awesome!! Great flavor, not too crunchy, just right!

Today we sang to some of the classics and favorites. You can't possibly go on a road trip without singing American Pie! Sorry Bryan had to endure my horrible singing voice. At one point we laughed so hard, and it was so good to hear the moms laughing like kids in the back seat, without the 'she's touching me' crap! So much fun and something I will remember and cherish forever.

Well, time for bed! I have to get my beauty rest to be ready for tomorrow's adventure! Have a great and relaxing Sunday!

July 27, 2020

Well, with spotty internet it looks like I'll be writing these posts in the mornings for the next few days.

We arrived safely in Tennessee, and I am excited to say that our camper is now in its new home. The campsites are nice here, though when we stay in the national park we are used to a little more room between sites. Everyone here is so nice and I'm glad Bryan found this place.

Unpacking and hooking up wasn't too bad. Old habits come back quickly, so we actually remembered what to do even though we haven't used our camper in over two years.

Last night we enjoyed a fresh cooked meal at a little mom and pop restaurant. It was a welcome change from road food. And then we took a short drive through the national park. It was about fifteen degrees cooler there, so we rolled down the windows and enjoyed the fresh air. Then we came back and sat outside for a while and just enjoyed the downtime.

One thing that is so weird here is there are so many people without masks. I don't mind and we are still wearing ours and being careful, but it's just so strange. In talking to some locals, they are just so over everything like the rest of us. Here in the mountains where they tend not to have as many issues, they are going about normal life. Yes, the businesses are being cautious, but it's nice to feel like things are somewhat normal. Still, we are doing our part to stay healthy and being outside has really done us good.

I'm looking forward to some adventures today. Stay tuned!

July 28, 2020

It was a good and relaxing day for the most part. We went to one of our favorite restaurants for breakfast. You know those small-town hidden gems. We eat there when we are in town, and it never disappoints. Breakfast was delicious and I'm looking forward to visiting there again this trip.

Today we went into Elkmont. It's a campground in the national park. We took a short walk up Little River trail and checked out one of the restored cabins. It's beautiful. Then we drove through and stopped at the town. It's within Elkmont and it is a line of cabins that families used to own before their land leases ran out. I've been following the project for over 20 years. The National Park received funding a few years ago to start re-stabilizing these beauties. While we were up there, the parks maintenance workers were working on a few of the cabins, which are looking so good. We talked to one of them and he was a nice, truly excited about his work, and thinks the whole world has gone crazy too! I am so excited to see the restoration project well underway.

We also took a trip through Roaring Fork Motor Nature Trail. It's a drive through trail and it's always so pretty up there in the woods. We take it almost every time we come to town just to get away.

Lunch was at our friends at Gatlinburg Brewing Company. We love stopping there. They have great pizza and wings, perfect for their awesome beer. We were there a while, enjoying the ability to drink a beer in a brewery since ours in Florida are closed.

On the way back out of town we stopped at a new distillery with whiskey, vodka and moonshine. Of course, Bryan did a tasting. He said it was really good and we picked up a few bottles to bring home. We also ran into a bubble tea place in town. I had to try it since we are getting ready to start that at my shop. I watched their every move and it's very similar to ours. The only problem, one too many scoops of vanilla in the milk tea made it almost frothy and milkshake like and their popping boba would not fit through the straw. Their popping boba was also much thicker and wouldn't pop. I'm glad I found the company I did for ours because I liked our better.

Well, today is our Cades Cove Day. We will be heading out there this afternoon. We decided to have a cookout in their picnic area and enjoy the day breathing fresh air and being in nature. I'm really looking forward to being out there.

July 29, 2020

What a great day! There's nothing like waking up in your favorite place, knowing you still have a few days there.

We had an amazing breakfast at our favorite place, Riverstone. You know, I am extremely picky about my sausage gravy, but theirs is made in house and it's delicious. I made sure to enjoy a real southern treat of biscuits and gravy. Yum!!

We spent the day in Cades Cove, driving around the loop and just being out in nature. We saw a deer and a bear that was cooling in one of the little streams in the center of the cove.

While we were out there, we had a cookout in the picnic area. Bryan cooked hamburgers and hotdogs on a charcoal grill. I forget how much I enjoy doing that. We just sat and relaxed and enjoyed the smell of the grill and the beautiful trees.

You know one thing I noticed while being up here is how nice everyone is. The majority of people here are from other places. We've seen plates from Oklahoma, Illinois, Pennsylvania, Kansas, and all over, so you can't say it's the locals. Many people say they are here because they just needed to get away from the craziness and needed a normal vacation. People are polite in the stores, they let each other in traffic, waving and smiling afterwards. They smile and say 'hello' even if they have a mask on. This year I have seen more families than I have in the last thirty-four years coming here, stopping to picnic, play and enjoy being together. While I can't say all of this didn't happen in the past, this is certainly happening way more than before.

So here it is, the silver lining to all of this craziness over these last four months is rediscovering what our ancestors knew, and we have forgotten: life isn't about the run here, run there activities. It's not about working the most or making the most money. It's realizing the importance of slowing down and spending time with each other. It's the quality over quantity and I, for one, am so happy to see that other people from all over the country see it too!

So now I ask you, when was the last time you slowed down? When did you stop thinking this pandemic was a nuisance and inconvenience and start thinking it was an opportunity?

Have a great day!

July 29, 2020

Today was a good day despite it being our last day here. I always get sentimental on the last day because I look forward to being home, but I'm also sad to be leaving this beautiful place.

This morning, we had a delicious breakfast at one of our other favorite breakfast places, Elvira's. It's down in Wears Valley and they have the best hash brown casserole. I always forget they have it and then I always remember how much I enjoy it.

On our way into town, we did a little shopping at some of the general stores. I found a beautiful purse that I already moved my stuff into. It was time…I shouldn't be wearing crossbody purses because it pulls on my neck, but they are so convenient. I can't wait to carry this new purse and see about getting them in my shop. They are so adorable and some of the purchases go to animal charities.

Today was the day I was looking forward to the most—Salt Room Day!! I absolutely love the salt room and believe in the benefits of Halo Therapy. If you haven't tried it, look it up. It can help with allergies, sinus, respiratory and other issues. This was my second time visiting this particular salt room. It's so relaxing, and I always feel so much better and I sleep great. I found another salt spa in Wesley Chapel, and I am going to look into going there soon. In the meantime, I have also booked our next appointment here for when we come back in September.

After the salt room we went and had lunch at The Fox and Parrot English Pub. It's one of our favorite places to go when we are in town and it's off the beaten path. Today we talked with the owner there and just enjoyed hanging out.

Tonight, when we got back to the camper, we went into the river. Oh my gosh, it was so refreshing! It truly made me feel better. I'm hoping that when we come up in September, that it will still be nice and warm enough that we can go back in the river one more time before the weather turns cold. Now we are having a fire and are chilling before heading to bed.

It's weird to be leaving our camper here and it's weird to be leaving stuff in our camper for our trip in a few weeks. Don't get me wrong, I love it, but it's just strange. I guess it's good to get this feeling over with, so that when we have a house here it won't be so strange.

The next time I write, I will be back at home. I'm looking forward to sleeping in my own bed in Florida!

July 30, 2020

I am glad to say that we have arrived safely at home. Considering the magnitude of our trip and all we had to accomplish, plus fun stuff, the fact that we made it the whole trip without any real incidents was an amazing feat in itself.

This morning, we got up, packed and headed out, leaving our beloved camper in its new home in Tennessee. We hugged it before we left and told it we would be back in five weeks. I could tell the camper was happy because it worked perfectly. Now we will use it more, and it will be stored with other camper friends when we aren't there. It's a happy situation for all!

The ride home was good. We only had one minor hold-up and even that wasn't long. Other than that, we made decent time.

Something interesting about this trip, my anxiety and little panic attacks lessened as the time went on. I have been getting these for several months now, but by yesterday I think I was down to one a day, and none so far today. Geez, I wonder why? LOL.

Also, on my way home I realized that the muscles in my neck weren't cracking as much from calcium deposits. The sharp pain and nerve in my neck that I cried over last week were virtually gone. Though I couldn't turn my head to the left long without holding it, I was able to look left and focus for a few seconds before my head turned back to straight and slightly right. As I tried to turn my head left there wasn't the sharp pain or pressure and tension like before.

I attribute this slight, and probably temporary, improvement to a few things. My stress level, anxiety, and worry level are down. I went down to the river last night and laid in the ice-cold water, I let it run over my head and neck and cool my entire body. Also, I started these CBD patches I got from Maharajh Acupuncture & Herb Shoppe. I did the first patch for two days and then none for a day, and the second patch I started today. The one today was only on for a few hours because I put it on when I was hot and sweaty. It slipped off my neck area and made a mess while we were traveling, so I took it off. Tomorrow, I have to stop by their shop and grab another one. Any one of those things or the combination could be helping.

Whatever it is, I actually feel-good today. I feel a little more normal, and I can't wait to face tomorrow, which I usually dread because of the pain.

So, here's to a short vacation that was good for my health. And, to more short trips to keep me healthy and feeling good in the future!

July 31, 2020

I have so much to be grateful for! While we were away, my amazing team of two took care of everything! I think I might start calling them the dynamic duo. They were awesome and I walked back in today like I had been there the whole time. Things that needed to be done were done, guests were happy, and all was right with The White Heron world. Thank you Dawne and Tara for making my get away possible. Ya'll did such a good job that I'm going to run away again soon!

It was nice being back at my shop. Of course, I have quite a few things to get caught up on and that is expected. For the most part, I had a list and worked through it and got almost everything done.

I will say this though, the stress on my body returned immediately. My neck cramped today and for a good portion of my day my chin was basically tied to my shoulder. The interesting thing about that is I could tell I was starting to have issues during different conversations. It is very apparent that certain things trigger the nerves in my brain. I do really good and then a conversation or person comes up and it seems to cause instant tension and pain. Maybe part of this is me being able to identify those triggers. Here hoping that's the case, so maybe I can work to control it a little more.

Tomorrow is a big day in our gift shop area. We are starting to sell boba tea. It's very exciting and I hope a lot of people come in to buy some. We've done a lot of research and worked really hard, so I'm excited about this one! I must admit, I am looking forward to trying some more combinations myself, especially since I will be the one making them tomorrow.

It's off the bed for me. I need my rest for what is sure to be a busy day tomorrow!

August 2020

August 1, 2020

I don't know why, but I thought yesterday was Saturday so this morning I was so discombobulated. I woke up thinking it was Sunday and then I finally realized I had to get up and moving.

This morning at my shop, I worked to finish up our boba items. We got everything set up and ready. Some of our friends were the first in to grab up some of our newest offering. Honestly, we had so many of our friends stop in, it was awesome! I am so humbled by how many of my friends stopped in and tried our boba tea. I am so blessed, and I thank each one of you.

The gift shop stayed quite busy today, which was good because the tearoom was slower. It's funny, but it has been going in waves with the tearoom.

So, I've got some other things up my sleeves for that. I'm trying to be inventive and come up with some new ideas. I'm looking forward to a few days off to get my head going again.

Tonight we had a nice dinner with our friends, John and Connie at Thai Bistro. Their food was great as usual. Now we are just hanging at home watching some TV and I did a little work. Tomorrow, I have to go to Restaurant Depot. That's always a daunting trip…

I hope everyone had a great Saturday, and that tomorrow is peaceful and restful!

August 2, 2020

You know, I don't know what it is about being on vacation verses being at home, but I could get up very early while away whereas here I can't seem to get up. I think every day on vacation I was up before 7:30 a.m., most days by 7 a.m. Here at home, I'm lucky if I can get up before 9 a.m. What is that about???

Well, today, once I finally got up, we enjoyed breakfast at Rose's Bistro. Turns out our friends, Michelle and Travis were having breakfast there too, with their kids. They had come downtown for breakfast and boba tea, but we are closed today. However, after breakfast we went over to the tearoom, and I made them some boba. Travis is always helping us out and doing things for our businesses and us, so it was a way for us to show our appreciation. I just loved seeing their daughter run around my shop too. She is growing up so fast and she's so adorable. I remember when Ava used to run around my store before she got older. Is it possible that I have become a lot more tolerant of kids in my older age? I like to think that I have more empathy and understanding these days. I really try not to let things upset me or bring me down. That's my choice and I work really hard at it. I know Michelle was worried about Em running around and didn't want her to break anything, but not me. I wasn't worried. I think her wanting to explore is so fascinating and it was fun watching her.

Today Bryan and I ran down to Restaurant Depot. We had to get some things for the tearoom. Since we haven't been too busy, I haven't had to run down there very often, but today I stocked up so I'm hoping I don't have to go down for a few more weeks. Though I'm sure it would be nice to be so busy that I have to go again soon.

I also stopped in to see my friends at William Dean Chocolates. I had to grab some chocolates for our mini cupcakes. Fortunately, they had them, so we are restocked now.

This afternoon I chilled at home. My neck has been better since yesterday and I'm trying to take it easy, so I don't relapse. Today I had a little pain and a little pinched nerve, but it was manageable, and it didn't get worse through the evening. During my chill time, I read and had a movie on in the background. It was nice and I appreciated the time.

Tonight, Bryan took me to dinner. We originally planned to cook on the grill, but he was craving wings, so we went to Hooters. We had our waitress from a few weeks ago and man is she awesome. As we were sitting down, she came over with the beer Bryan drinks and my soda. It was awesome that out of everyone she has seen there, she remembers us. I know they are a larger restaurant, but I love the hometown atmosphere there. The managers recognize us and talk to us, and it makes us feel special. It's so nice!

Tomorrow, I don't have a lot going on. I have things to do for my shop, but other than that I'm going to start laying out my week and trying to figure out a new strategic plan for my business's future. That is something I have been dreading doing, but it's time for some solid plans. I've been following my plan, but now it's time to readjust for the current day.

Here's to a great week at ahead for all of us!

August 4, 2020

I didn't write about yesterday because honestly, there was nothing to write about. I truly did nothing…well, I went to the bank and got Chick-Fil-A for lunch. Oh, and Bryan grilled out an awesome pork tenderloin on the grill. But honestly, that's not really enough to write about.

Today was much of the same…I don't know how, but I am so much more productive on the days that I work. Maybe it's because I have to be somewhere. Also, it seemed like I got so much more done when my business was open five days a week instead of our current four-day schedule. I'm not complaining about the time off, but truly, I wish I didn't have it.

Now I know what would have happened to me five years ago if I hadn't decided to open a business that keeps me busy. I can't imagine waking up every day and not having some place to go or something to do. Without having some purpose, I think I would truly be lazy and crazy.

So, that begs me to ask myself a question—how do I stay motivated on my days off? How do I keep going and push forward when I'm doing all I can, and customers aren't quick to come back? How do I come up with more ideas and do more things to bring in more traffic to my tearoom?

I saw a picture today on one of the Facebook restaurant pages and the restaurant was empty. In fact, the poster said it was empty every day at lunch. So that begs me to ask, how do we get people back out??? I know that I'm not the only one in this boat...restaurants can't survive on 50% capacity, and they certainly can't survive on 15% of customers daily compared to normal times.

I won't lie and say that it hasn't been hard. We are trying very hard to keep pushing forward. It's getting disheartening knowing we are doing everything we can and only some guests return. We are so grateful for our guests that have come in, but I just don't know how to get more of our guests to come back. My brain is fried trying to come up with ideas—my emotions are shot after continuing to give it my all, and my motivation to keep moving forward and coming up with ideas and strategies is about worn out.

Tonight, I'm hoping for a good night sleep, so that tomorrow I feel a little more revived and optimistic.

August 5, 2020

Today was the day that didn't turn out any way that I expected. It wasn't bad, just not like I had planned.

The tearoom and gift shop had some guests today and both did nicely. We sold boba tea, chocolates, hot and iced teas, and gifts. The tearoom had guests at both seatings. Our phone also rang a lot, but I imagine that's because our newsletter just went out and it always reminds everyone to call and come for tea. It's definitely a good thing. It's still only about 40% of normal, but I'm grateful for that.

I decided to work late tonight to get some extra things done, like marketing stuff. So, Bryan met me at the tearoom after work. He came in and it was so fun to watch him ranting about bars and breweries being closed. He doesn't want to go through the process of making a restaurant in the brewery so he can open, but it also feels like the state isn't going to let breweries and bars open until after Labor Day. He asked if we should sue the state and went on and on. He's just so upset! He truly sounded like a vested business owner, talking things out loud, using logic and reason. I had to sit back and smile because he sounded like me—reason and business in one. I'm so proud!!

After listening to him and watching him pace the floor, he informed me that not only was he upset, but he was also hangry. I decided he needed a good drink and a nice meal so off we went to enjoy a nice dinner at Carrabba's Italian Grill. I missed my friend Boris. Our dinner was perfect and just what we needed. We were able to talk about lots of things and after it all, I think we finally came up with a few ideas for the brewery. I even checked with a business we work with, and they thought we came up with some awesome ideas. We just have to see if people will want them. If not, I don't know what we will do.

That also doesn't solve the problem of the tearoom and its struggle, but these days I just have to take one issue at a time, and today was the day to deal with the brewery issue. Fingers crossed!

I hope everyone had a great Wednesday! We are heading to the homestretch of the week. Let's all do what we can to make it a good one!

August 6, 2020

It seems like as the week goes on, the days tend to run along a little better. Maybe the first part of the week is hard because I'm off for a few days and my motivation is low, but as I work, I get more efficient and get more things done. I don't know why that is.

I'm still not able to get up at a decent time in the morning. For some reason, I just end up lying in bed and snoozing for an hour! But, once I get up and have my "coffee," aka a shower, I'm usually ready to go. It's just getting the engine started that's the hard part. I also realized today that I didn't take my Vitamin D last Friday. Thank you to my good friend for reminding me to take it tomorrow! One whole week without Vitamin D while I'm so deficient certainly isn't helping my situation.

Today was a good day in the tearoom and gift shop. It didn't equate to a lot of income, but it's not always about that. It's about our guests in the tearoom and introducing new people to all our shop and tearoom have to offer. In that, it was a successful day.

I had a great lunch today! I actually had tea in the tearoom with my friend Elisa. We laughed and enjoyed sharing stories. I really enjoyed being in the tearoom and spending some time doing what my guests do every day. Sometimes I forget how nice it is—what we do. It makes it even better that I got to spend that quality time with such an amazing and caring woman!

After tea, I was working on some other business things, and we had two different sets of guests come in and enjoy our Happy Hour. It was so cool! It's something we just started and I'm going to push more because it allows people to come in and get a small sandwich and tea without a reservation. Granted it's not as grand as the Afternoon Tea, but it's still nice. Honestly, I'm excited guests came in for it. So cool! And boba tea is going really good too! Yea!

This afternoon my friend Michelle stopped in to see me with her friend Cindy. We talked about business and how things are going. We are all in similar boats right now and that's the scary part, but it's forcing us to think outside the box, which is good because it keeps us fresh and relevant.

After the shop closed I went upstairs to my office and got a lot more work done. Through this whole pandemic and closure, I haven't been very good at keeping up with general business stuff, so tonight I laid everything out on my desk and started working through each pile. By the time Bryan came up after his live video at the brewery, I was finishing paying the last few bills. When I left, files were put away and bills were paid. I actually feel good about buckling down. Now to be more productive tomorrow!

Tonight, Bryan and I enjoyed dinner at our favorite Mexican restaurant, El Cerrito. I absolutely love their tortilla soup, so I was excited to enjoy a nice big bowl. In fact, I wish I would go there and get soup more often or maybe I should take it home. It doesn't have to be winter, I just love soup!

Well, I'm heading for bed. I am looking forward to a great day tomorrow, starting with tour of the Hacienda bright and early at 9 a.m. Since you all know me, you know how this is early for me, LOL! Have a great Friday!

August 7, 2020

Today started off nice and early for me, like I said it would. I was up before 8 a.m., and arrived at the Hacienda ten minutes early, after dropping my work stuff at the shop. Go Me!

The tour through the Hacienda was nice and very hot with no A/C and a mask on. It was so great to see this former beauty being restored. I can tell from the structural side that they are doing it right. I'm sure someone else would have come in and just patched and opened it. So it gives me a lot of faith that, while taking longer than expected, it will be done right and will last for a long time.

After getting back to my shop and cooling off, I worked on quite a few general business things. It was nothing really important or to speak about. A lot of our days as business owners are dealing with monotonous type of things. Today was one of those.

This afternoon I enjoyed sitting in on a conversation with the city about branding with our businesses. It was good and I love that we are working towards a common identity for our town. I have some ideas on how I can use it as we promote our businesses.

Tonight, I hung out at the tearoom and spent a few hours visiting my amazing friend, Helen. I haven't seen her much, though we text a lot, because she has been good about not being around people so she can stay healthy. We chatted for hours, and I miss the days when we could go out to dinner and do that. For now, the tearoom will do though.

Well, tomorrow is Saturday! It's my Friday and I'm excited to have a great day. The tearoom has quite a few reservations, almost like a normal day. I'm looking forward to it as it's been too long!

August 8, 2020

Well, last night I didn't get to bed until 1 a.m. and honestly, I didn't sleep that good, so today it was hard to get up. I knew I had to get into the shop and get a few things done before we opened. I was at the shop by 9:30 a.m., with linens and other things I needed to bring in.

Of course, I ate dinner late last night and then went to bed, so my stomach was a little achy, so I started my day with peppermint tea. It definitely helped that I was able to take a few minutes this morning and enjoy my tea, so I could feel better and get back to work.

The shop was up and down today with guests. Sometimes it was full, sometimes it was empty. It's like the new normal.

It's a good thing the tearoom was pretty full. Probably the fullest it had been since March. It was almost like a normal day, pre-COVID. Even though we had a few little snafus, just silly stuff, it was a pretty good day. It was one of those days that after one of the seatings you just shake your head and say, "well, we made it through." All good, but I was tired and didn't feel like doing much, so it may have just been me too. Still, I am so honored and blessed by so many amazing guests. It's so great seeing everyone who continues to stop in and support us, my friends included.

For lunch we all enjoyed the delicious shredded chicken BBQ from Heros. It was something new they tried today, and the sandwiches turned out delicious! I could see them adding these new creations to the menu and me enjoying them a lot. And it worked out perfect because I have been thinking of making some BBQ chicken. Now I don't have to.

I spent a little bit of time at the brewery tonight. We have some ideas on things we can do to open and events we can offer, but we still haven't made any final decisions on anything. There are so many aspects that have to be considered…there is truly no right or easy choice on how to proceed. It's actually a little scary because we don't want to make the wrong decision.

Tonight we decided to run down to Tarpon Springs for dinner. We enjoyed eating at Johnny's Tap house. It was delicious. I really enjoy the fried mac and cheese. It's one of my favorite things there. I also enjoyed a delicious BBQ chicken flatbread. Yea, I didn't get enough BBQ chicken yet today, LOL. It was Bryan's first time eating there and he really enjoyed it too. Our server, Molly, was so nice. It was a great experience and I can't wait to go back. I wish we had a restaurant like this closer to home, but it's a good thing that Tarpon Springs isn't that far.

Well, off to rest. I'm looking forward to an online class tomorrow with a tea and cheese pairing. I'm so excited to take it, as I would love to offer a similar class at my tearoom someday.

I hope you are having a great weekend! Enjoy your Sunday!

August 9, 2020

Today started like any other day, except for having a major leg cramp when I got out of bed, and a pinched nerve in my right shoulder because I slept weirdly. I'm thankful when things go decent in the morning, for the most part, because I feel like if I struggle first thing that the day will be a struggle too.

I got to my tea room by 10:30 a.m., so that I could be ready for a tea and cheese pairing event online. I was really looking forward to it because I love pairings and I love both tea and cheese. I actually really enjoyed sampling the cheese with the tea, some of the cheeses went together really well with the tea and I was slightly surprised. I can tell that I am going to be craving some of these pairings in the future. In fact, I imagine myself fixing a nice cup of kukicha with some alpine Cabot cheese tomorrow. OMG, I think that pairing was my absolute favorite!!

This afternoon I worked on pairings for the brewery using our wine and beer. We are going to be offering two events through the brewery at my tearoom. One is going to be a pairing with a flight of beer and one with a flight of wine. I'm so excited about this because it allows me to use my pairing abilities and offer it with complimentary samples of beer or wine to see how they go together. It's very exciting! It's going to be very limited capacity and I'm hoping it's a way for the brewery to make some money since it's been really hard for the past few months.

Tonight, Bryan and I enjoyed a delicious dinner at Tarpon Tavern—OMG, what a good place. I also love that since they are limited inside they have added seating outside on the side walk. It's so cool! I would even love to see something like this in our downtown restaurants. I especially love that they put the seats right against the street with the walking path between the tables and the bushes or building. They even put a fence up, and they are tapping into the power on a light pole to have hanging bistro lighting. How progressive!!

The food for dinner was so good. I enjoyed their burger sliders. OMG, the fact that they come with grilled onions, which I love so much, and a garlic aioli, made them so flavorful. After our chicken tender appetizer, I was so full that I only ate one slider. I can't wait to enjoy the other two as my leftovers tomorrow!

Well, here's to another nice weekend in the books. Tomorrow I have a lot to do for my shop and also a new opportunity I'm exploring. You know me, always doing new things.

Let's make it a great week!

August 11, 2020

This morning, I was extremely lazy. I had to get up while Bryan was still home so he could take one of the medicine patches off my shoulder. It has been helping the muscle to relax a little. I thought I would get up after that, but decided to lie in bed and snooze a while longer.

When I finally got up and around, I headed to my upstairs office to get some work done. I find up there, as much as I would rather be downstairs, I tend to concentrate more and get more things done. So, up the stairs I went.

Today I was able to balance the checkbooks, finalize the pairings on the upcoming beer flight and wine flight sampling nights, and meet with John from Heros to go over our needs for some food. I'm looking forward to getting these events going! I also wrote letters, worked on our brewery reopening plan, and got some general work done.

This afternoon I went on an adventure, business hunting. All I can say at this point is that it was an interesting day and I'm curious to see the future. Fun stuff! Then, because the weather was looking really bad, I came home to relax. My neck can only take so much these days and when it starts hurting I'm done. So, I came home and relaxed and waited for the rain that never came here.

Tonight, Bryan and I enjoyed dinner together and talked a lot about business. He's still feeling frustrated about being closed and I can't say I blame him. We just keep talking about it and hopefully we will see things change soon. I do have a little plan, but just like before, this is a fluid situation and we have to constantly be thinking and adjusting. Most people would probably think it's fun to come up with things, but my brain is totally fried at this point.

So, my goal tomorrow is not to be as lazy as I was this morning. It's to get up and moving and get more things done. Wish me luck, as you know I'm not a morning person.

August 12, 2020

OMG, I almost forgot to write this tonight...I am lying in bed going through all these things in my head that I needed to do tomorrow, and it hit me—I still had to post about my day.

Today didn't start any earlier than yesterday. Actually, it started later...oops. I guess that really shows that if I don't have something to get up for, it's just easier to lie in bed. That and once I get up, I start dealing with head bobble issues and that is no fun. Sometimes, I just feel like it would be easier to stay in bed.

My midday started with a few things at my shop, and then a delicious lunch with my mom at Herschel's Scratch Kitchen. I am so excited they are open. Today I enjoyed one of my favorite meals, Fried Chicken Benedict. I'm not usually a fan of eggs, but this combination is so amazing that I ate it at 1 p.m. I'm looking forward to going again soon.

After lunch my mom and I had a meeting to check out a potential business opportunity downtown. While I think we have found the perfect place for what we want to do, I now have to come up with all of the ideas and plans so that we can get it in to the city to see about a grant. Unfortunately, with the other two businesses going, the only way this will work is with some support and grants. My tearoom was fortunate to have a little help in the way of grants when we opened, but we did the brewery completely on our own. Between those two we've exhausted quite a bit of resources and I'm not willing to risk the safety net, so on this new business, I will have to do some grant writing. Still, I know the idea has a ton of merit and that it would be a draw like the tearoom and that businesses downtown would benefit. Now I just have to get to work.

Tonight, I had my weekly call with our Tea Mastermind group and I just love it. It lifts me up so much and keeps me motivated to move forward. I always get so excited to talk to them and share ideas. It's truly a blessing in my week. I have so many amazing opportunities in my tea business and they keep me motivated and moving forward, though I need to do better at being focused.

After my call, Bryan and I had a nice quiet evening at home. We ordered take out and watched a funny movie, while I also worked on scheduling Facebook posts for my shop for the week.

Now it's time for sleep because it's already tomorrow. Well, maybe just one more game of Sudoku and then bed. Night all!

August 12, 2020

Today was a late start to my day. Though, at this point I'm sure you already know that. I actually enjoyed lying in bed, relaxing, and listening to the thunder in the distance. Like most days, I waited for the rain, and today it actually came, though it seemed like it took forever.

I got to the tearoom and my team was already busy at work. I'm so glad I have them and that know exactly what to do. I'm so blessed.

I enjoyed visiting with my guests in the tearoom today. I especially love when I get to talk tea with them. And I love when guests come in and ask about tea. I have studied and read and done so much research and tasting, that I love when I can share what I've learned, and to help someone feel better. Truly, I light up and love it so much! I wish I could do more of it!

Today I had my team sit down and try two different teas and three different cheeses. It was fun to let them try things and share their opinions. Of course, I am partial to certain pairings, but I love that they got to try them and make their own pairing opinions. So now, I think it's time to make up a pairing sheet and have a tea and cheese pairing night. Of course, that's after we do the beer and cheese pairing for the brewery in two weeks. Fun stuff!!

Today I also finished the reopening plan for the brewery. I asked Bryan to send it to the governor and the secretary of DBPR (Department of Business and Professional Regulations for the State of Florida – they handle all different business licenses). I know that they have not talked about reopening breweries and bars yet, but I thought that maybe if we presented them with a comprehensive plan, that they would see we are serious about safety and consider allowing us to reopen. I mean, it worked for Disney…it never hurts to try!

Tonight we enjoyed a nice dinner at Back Draughts Pizza in Tarpon Springs. Of course, it's always so good. We had an opportunity to talk about our next adventure. I'm a little apprehensive just because it's more to handle, and I worry about stretching myself to thin and becoming a 'jack of all trades' and a 'master of none.' I really like being a master of tea! I worry about losing that because I have to focus on other things. I would just be devastated if I had to take more time away from my tearoom, but I also really want to do this next venture. It would be so wonderful!

Well, after all that, I'm heading to bed. I have another big day on tap tomorrow. And I vow to get up earlier than today!

August 13, 2020

Well, today started a little earlier but not much. I mean, to be fair I was working by 8:30 a.m., from bed. Perhaps the biggest downfall to modern technology is my social media and emails are on my phone so I can lie in bed, where my neck is most comfortable and get work done.

I got to the tearoom today and everyone was just having off days. You know when you have an off day, but now imagine it with your whole staff. Granted it's only three other people but that still throws everything off. I mean, we got through it, but I couldn't help but wonder if we were in an alternate universe or if it was a full moon. Turns out today's just one of those days.

I did have a bright spot in my day, having lunch with my amazing and caring friend, Elisa. She brought me a macaron kitty stuffed animal. I have to take a picture of it to show it off. It goes perfectly with the travel cup with macarons on it that she gave me. She's always so thoughtful and I am so glad that God brought her into my life a year ago. I am truly blessed to know her and so many others. If nothing else, my business has brought some amazing people into my life that I wouldn't have met otherwise, I find myself feeling so blessed so many times throughout my day.

We had so many amazing people in the tearoom today; quite a few regulars and some newbies. I loved seeing my friend Laura and her husband Frank. He's an Englishman, so I always get nervous because the English are very picky about their tea. He said he loved it, so that made me feel really good. Of course, I had warned him that we do tea American Style, LOL.

It truly warms my heart when I see friends and also my guests that have visited us for years. I am so honored that they know us and trust that we are doing everything to keep them safe. Truly, the benefits of a small business, we can do more and keep everyone safe, and that makes my heart happy.

Tonight, I worked on a business review of my potential new venture. It took me all afternoon, but I buckled down and did it. I think it came out really nice. Now to submit it to the city to see if we can do it in the location we want. Fingers crossed!

I also got the form done for Bryan's beer and cheese pairing event. I'm just not sure when I want to do it though. I'm thinking maybe in a week or so. I have almost everything together for it...I just need to work out a few more logistics and then post it online for people to buy tickets. The hardest part is we have limited seats, and I have a feeling tickets will sell fast.

After a short visit to the brewery and making an easy meal at home for dinner, I think I'm going to go and read a little. It's one of my all-time favorite things to do and I rarely take the time. I'm hoping by putting the phone down that I may be able to sleep better tonight and get up and moving at a more decent hour. Wish me luck.

Have a great Friday everyone!

August 15, 2020

Well, today I did better. I was out of bed before 9 a.m. and at my shop before 10 a.m.! Not that it's an accomplishment, but for me it was and I'm happy about that.

This morning I got to my shop and asked my amazing neighbor, Rose from Rose's Bistro Off Main for a slice of tomato for one of our vegetarians that was coming in. I only needed one little slice and she was so great that walked me down a tomato. I just love that I have amazing neighbors like her and Lou at Boulevard Beef & Ale. It always seems we are helping each other out and it's wonderful. They are the neighbors we all dream about at home, being able to walk over and ask for a cup of sugar and they are always happy to help. Truly, I'm so lucky!

Today I worked on a few projects for the tearoom and the new venture. I finished my business overview and sent it to the city for zoning approval. Before I lease any space, I want to make sure the business is allowed to go in that space. Then I ran over to the city to look at past plans filed with the city of the building I'm looking at that were previously denied. I wanted to see what the plans were, so

I will know what I have to do to get it where I need it. While I was there my awesome friend who works in city hall came to see me and see what I was up to in the development department. Also, while I was there, the great zoning guy who has been helping me came out and told me that zoning was approved for the business I want to put in. Yea! They really made the process so easy and I'm looking forward to moving forward. The next step for me is to meet with the landlord and talk about the numbers, get my contractor in there, get Bryan to do the layout, and start putting my grant applications together for the city. Boy, now the work really begins!

Then, after all that, I met with John at Heros to finalize the items we need for Bryan's upcoming beer and cheese pairing. We are going to do a sampling tomorrow to make sure we got it right and then the event will be scheduled. I'm looking forward to hosting it! And honestly, I'm really looking forward to trying things out tomorrow!

I returned to my tearoom and finished up a few projects there. I had some notecards printed by Minuteman Press using some of my tea photos, so I was putting them in ten packs with two of each of the five designs. I love that we have some of our own stuff for our guests. They are so cute!!

Tonight, we joined John and Connie at El Cerrito for dinner. I always love going out with them for dinner. It's nice to have another couple to go out with where we can all talk and just have a good time. I've often said that as business owners, while we know lots of people, we don't seem to have a lot of close friends that we hang out with. We tend to keep business and personal separate. I'm looking forward to enjoying another dinner with them again soon.

Well, after all that, it's time to hit the bed. My neck is absolutely killing me. The nerve is so pinched that it's pulsating in my head making me want to cry. I'm hoping that after a good night's sleep, I will feel good to tackle a busy day tomorrow.

Have a great Saturday everyone!!

August 16, 2020

Well, I'm happy to say that this morning I was up even earlier than I was any other day this week. I haven't figured out if it's because it's my Friday or if it's because I took my vitamin D yesterday, which always makes me feel a little more alive. Regardless, I was up and got to the shop at a very decent time. Yea me!

The shop was steady today...it seems like that has been happening more lately. The tearoom continues to book guests too. Albeit nowhere near where it was, but the gift shop has seen an uptick. I'm not sure, but I would venture to guess that guests feel safe because our spaces aren't too crowded, and we have the ability to keep people safe more than larger places. That, and we've had quite a few more people now that we have boba tea. Overall, with all we have going on, it was a good week.

Today the brewery did well too. It utilized a wet zone designated by the city to allow guests to enjoy 'to go' beers. It worked really well from what we saw, as guests would enjoy a drink and then move on. Unfortunately, it's not the same as being open, but it did help and the guests were more than gracious and understanding about helping us keep everyone safe. Hopefully we demonstrated that we can do this in a safe way and that city will allow it to continue.

Tonight I did a trial run of a cheese and beer pairing with my family and Tara, over at the brewery. I plated up cheese and meats from Heros and had them sample different ones with four of our core beers. All I can say is, wow! I nailed it and I'm so excited about that; now to schedule it up. It's going to be a beer and cheese pairing by the brewery, held at my tearoom. We are going to supply complimentary flights for each guest with our predetermined beers, and provide them a plate with all the cheese and meats. Then we are going to give them the pairing information and let them enjoy the evening. Each guest will also get a coupon for a 32 oz growler to pick up when they visit the brewery next time. I am so excited about this since I'm able to use my knowledge of flavors to build a really nice and unique experience. Next up will be a wine and dessert pairing. Oh my!

After all that today, I'm heading off to bed. I have to be up early tomorrow. Bryan and I have an adventurous day ahead! Have a great Sunday!

August 16, 2020

Today was an ideal day. Truly! It started off nice and early and is just now ending.

This morning, I got up nice and early. Well, by early I mean before 8 a.m. and we were actually on time to meet John and Connie, my mom and Bernice for breakfast at Herschel's. I absolutely love their breakfast, so I'm so glad that they are open downtown. I think I will be frequenting them quite a bit. Of course, the company was awesome too. Just a great group, we laughed and had a great time!

After breakfast, Bryan and I headed over to St. Augustine to pick up some growlers and our new 'Two Year Anniversary' pint glasses on Monday. Oh and to get some neck gaiters with our brewery logo on them. So, since we have to pick them up we thought we would run away for the night to be ready to grab things in the morning. It also gives us a break away, even if it's just for the night.

I was able to book a room at Casa Monica Resort & Spa, a Marriott hotel, in a building that was built in 1888. It's so beautiful! Under normal circumstances we would never be able to afford to stay here, but I was able to get a one-night package that was the price of a normal hotel in the area.

All I can say is, you know it's going to be a great hotel when they ask you if you would like a complimentary glass of champagne as you are checking in. Umm, yes! They gave us two glasses and two small bottles of champagne to enjoy in the room. Add that to the champagne and chocolate covered strawberries that were left in our room when we got back this afternoon and it's pretty wonderful! I'm so glad I've gotten to stay here at least once!

This afternoon, Bryan and I had an appointment to enjoy a session at an area's salt cave. We walked through town and stopped a few places on the way. The salt cave was a part of a spa and it was really interesting. Unlike the salt rooms that I have visited in the past, this one is an actual cave that regenerates salt. The other rooms I've visited have a generator that brings salt into the room so you breathe it in. Not that you don't breathe it in when you are in the cave, it's just not as concentrated. While I enjoyed this experience, I wish the salt had been a little stronger. Though I will say, I am glad that I went today because I'm learning what would work in the place I want to build, and I'm seeing what I want to do—my vision is becoming a little more clear.

After the salt room we walked around town and made our way back to the hotel. St. Augustine had some tourists, but it's nice to be here when it's not so crazy. We decided to drop our stuff at the hotel after some shopping and walk to a brewery that's down the street from the hotel.

When we got to the brewery the guy working recognized Bryan's 'beer is essential' shirt and they started talking about our printer, Skinny Lizard. The guy tells us that Chris, the owner of Skinny Lizard, is out back in their yard enjoying a beer. Low and behold, we go out there and he's sitting with some friends. They invited us to join them, so we sat and chatted. Turns out the couple he was sitting with had been to our brewery last October during bike fest. What a small world. We had a nice visit, it is funny how being so far away we ran into Chris and someone who had been to our place; so cool.

Tonight we enjoyed dinner at Nonna's Trattoria, a little Italian place we ate at, street side, two summers ago. Tonight we sat streetside and it was just as amazing as we remember. Truly the best Italian I have had since I was here last. I took some photos of where we were sitting and enjoying dinner. I love al fresco dining! I just wish we had more of that by us. I would definitely enjoy eating out more.

Overall, it was a great day. I was looking forward to today for a while and I'm so glad we stayed here, tried the salt cave, and had an amazing dinner.

I'm looking forward to getting our stuff from Skinny Lizard tomorrow and heading back home. No rest for the weary, but I'm glad I have some downtime tomorrow while we travel.

Hoping you have a great Monday and a great week!

August 18, 2020

You know, I never remember how exhausting traveling is until I'm doing it...

This morning, we woke up in the beautiful Casa Monica Resort & Spa. I slept great and woke with no neck pain. Even though I still found it hard to move, it was nice to be pain free for a while.

Since we had a hotel package, we decided to enjoy breakfast in the hotel's restaurant. Of course, like everything else, it was divine. The food was perfect and the portions were great. It was just enough to get us going.

Once we checked out, we headed over to Skinny Lizard to pick up our latest growlers, some neck gaiters with our logo, and some very special glasses. I can't say anything about the glasses until the brewery shares it. We managed to fit all the boxes in the back seat. We didn't want them getting wet on the way home. Thank goodness we did that because boy did it rain!

The ride home was nice. I always say it takes much longer to get there than it does to come home. We hit some rain at I-75 but other than that the trip was uneventful. Once we got home and unloaded our new items, we decided to take the moms with us out to dinner.

Tonight, it was Johnny's Taphouse in downtown Tarpon Springs. We went down there to watch the end of the hockey game and talk about our potential new venture. Now comes the hard part with it…budget and necessities, and whether or not to go forward. This is always the critical juncture and the part that makes me physically nauseous. I don't know why, but I've had the same thing happen when I was at this point with the tearoom, when I bought Karen's shop, and before the final decision to open the brewery. It is probably because the point of no return is ahead and that scares the heck out of me. To me, due diligence is always easy, it's pulling the trigger, and that part is coming up very soon, not so easy. Yikes!

After Johnny's, we stopped at Orange Cycle Creamery. I just love their creamery and even brought some home with me. Then we stopped at Brighter Days Brewing Company, so Bryan could see the guys there and grab some beer for home. It was good seeing some family. Yes, my family is involved in that brewery. 'Hi' Staci , the brewery is beautiful! So glad we got to see Aaron today. Next time I'll stop in when you are there! They have a beautiful place and I know once things get going again they are going to be really busy. I'm so excited for them.

After all that, we came home to relax and I fell asleep. All the running really wore me out. So now I'm headed to bed for real. I'm looking forward to a good day tomorrow. I am still having some allergies, so I've scheduled a visit at a new salt room in Spring Hill tomorrow. Also I have lots to do for my shop to be ready for the week. I'm hoping to get some good sleep, so I can tackle all that I need. I just need to get my energy back.

Here's to a great Tuesday!

August 18, 2020

Well, today didn't go as planned, at least this morning anyway. I just couldn't get out of bed. It's funny, sometimes I can get up and sometimes I just can't seem to get going. I stayed in bed until 10 a.m., but I did some emailing and other work starting around 9:30 a.m. I don't think it's depression, but more just being overwhelmed with all we have been facing and trying to deal with it. It's also trying to determine what to do, events and promotions, and what to wait on because of all the uncertainty. It's so hard to be focused and motivated.

Today I did go to Spring Hill with my mom. We went to a new salt room. I was so excited they use a salt generator in their room instead of a cave that regenerates. The place we went was so beautiful, and they offer all kinds of modalities for wellness. Truly, it was beautiful! And Betsie, the front desk clerk was so wonderful and gave us a tour.

Tonight, I enjoyed our weekly Tea Mastermind gathering. We talked about some ways to put our best foot forward and ensure we are doing our best every day. I know I try, but I haven't been giving it my best. Probably because of all of the uncertainty, but still…staying motivated or even wanting to try has been hard. I've lost my mojo. That's why I'm so thankful for that group I'm in every Tuesday. They really help me process and think, and to try to refocus. I just hope it gets me out of this funk.

So, here's to a more productive Wednesday for me. Fingers crossed!

August 20, 2020

I decided to write this early in the day, as I forgot last night, and I actually had a few minutes to do it before it got too late.

Yesterday was a good day in the tearoom. We stayed busy with reservations, and we even had three tables for our new Happy Hour, yea! It was great running around and feeling like it was business as usual for one of only a handful of times since March. I don't expect it to be long lived, but I am ok with that for now.

Other than that, my day was uneventful. Well, except for securing a spot for my new business. Now, for those who worry about me and my health, don't. This new business is nowhere near as demanding as the other two and I'm actually designing it for my health. I'm very excited about it and now it's time to get my thinking cap on for design. It's my absolute favorite thing to do, so I'm hoping that I find the inspiration I need to make this place as amazing as the other two have been.

Now on to today...

Today was a good day too. Other than my neck causing me constant grief, I have been really good. I know everyone has their challenges and that's what makes me keep going even though there are times I want to just lay my head down and stop. Well, I actually did that—put my head down and stopped. Around 5 p.m. I was sitting in our parlor area with an ice pack on my neck and I put my head down and was out until a large clasp of thunder woke me up around 5:45 p.m. I never do that, but I guess today my neck said enough. So, of course, now I find myself wide awake when I should be winding down, typical!

Today I met with the building inspector at the new unit. I wanted to make sure everything that was currently in the building as 'existing' was good to go. Turns out all I need is a structural engineer to certify the walls are good to go and I'm good to go! Holy cow, something not so difficult!

Then it will be time to lay out the new place, and we should be good to start very minor construction in the next few weeks. It's time to get my friends Tamara and Ken involved!

You know, I can't believe this is happening! I said I would never do another business and here I am. Every time I remember why, but here I am. The truth is that I love creating these beautiful spaces. I want my town to be beautiful. I want people who visit our town to think it's beautiful. So if that means I have to open up a whole bunch of businesses around town to make it the gem that it is, I will. My undying love for my City…I'll do whatever it takes—this could be my campaign slogan, just kidding!

So, I guess you could say all was good today…though I did hear that my favorite tearoom, the one that my mom and I first had tea at, is closing. After twenty-three years the owner has decided to retire, and I'm heartbroken. After visiting her tearoom in Tampa, I decided to start on this adventure. I am truly grateful to The Royal Tearoom and Gift Shoppe for their inspiration and love of tea. I know times have been hard and it just breaks my heart that they are closing. I had so hoped to visit them for tea, but they weren't serving in their tearoom when the closures happened. I even messaged them a few weeks back about having tea. I wish their owner, Denise, all the best in retirement and thank her for hosting such a fabulous tea that it made me want to do the same.

Such as life, time moves us on, and I must be moving on too. I'll move on to home, or dinner, or someplace other than sitting in my tearoom parlor on my computer working.

I wish everyone a good night and look forward to a fun Friday tomorrow! BTW, can someone please make me an afternoon tea tray emoji???

August 23, 2020

I'm always amazed when I run into friends out in the community, and we get to talking and they tell me they read my posts. Not that I didn't expect anyone to read it and that I would only be writing for myself, but if no one else reads this, at least I would still know where I am and what I was doing on this day in history. So, for all of you who read about my days, I hope it makes you smile, I hope I sometimes make you laugh, and I hope you know how truly blessed I feel to be able to share a part of me with you.

So, on to my days!

Friday was a good day, as are most. I believe that when I get up in the morning, no matter how late, I always make the conscious decision to do whatever I can to make it a good day. I'm glad to know I'm not the only late riser (ahem, Bonnie). Of course, some days you can't help because things just go wrong, but they can still be good.

I don't remember anything that stuck out in my mind as being overly impressive on Friday, other than when I came home I was content with how the day went. It was rather slow on the tearoom side, but that happens after two really busy days and when it's the week before school starting. I managed to get some work done for all three businesses, which is becoming a juggling act, but so far so good.

The brewery did well on Friday night with its 'to go' area. We still haven't promoted it, but people are smart and they are finding it. We are so grateful to be given the opportunity to utilize the front wet zone.

What will be even greater is when we email the state this week to get feedback about our opening plan to see if they will allow us to open. I'm not sure if I mentioned it here before or not, but we wrote and submitted a fifteen-page reopening plan to the state for approval, just like Disney and Universal did. I thought since they had a state approved plan, why shouldn't we? I know it was a long shot, but we want the state to know we are committed and serious about safety. Monday we touch base to see if they will let us open. Fingers crossed.

Now on to today...it wasn't going to be a busy day in the tearoom, but I prayed the gift shop would do well. And today my prayers were answered. The shop stayed busy and people were buying gifts and all kinds of cute things. It made for a really nice day.

We also met some amazing guests. We truly are blessed to have some great people walk through our door. It's like we made friends today and that's exactly why we do what we do.

You know, I just don't think there is enough kindness in our world right now and I love when guests come in and we are our friendly selves, and they warm up and chat with us. There just isn't enough of that these days. How blessed am I that I get to do this every day!

We did get a major project started today. My mom started working on cleaning my office. Oh boy was it a mess! Truly, there's just no other way to describe it. She's such a trooper, asking me what things are, throwing stuff away, making piles. She is going to get me organized at work and at home, one way or another.

Tomorrow should be a relaxing day. We have breakfast plans and then afternoon plans. Somewhere in there I plan to do dishes, laundry, and pick up some things around the house...oh, and measure our new business space and work on the website. A gal's work is never done!

Wishing you a beautiful and relaxing Sunday.

August 23, 2020

Can someone please tell me why on the days that I don't need to be up early for anything major, that I can wake up early and get out of bed and rolling with limited issues?!?

Please, someone explain it to me because that's exactly what happens every Sunday, it seems.

This morning, I started the day off with a great breakfast at Herschel's. Of course, I never change what I get, so today it was once again the fried chicken Benedict. Yum! It's the perfect way to start the day. Normally eggs make me feel a little nauseous and no good, but the poached egg served with a biscuit makes them taste good to me. Joining us this morning for breakfast were the moms. We call them the moms because it is both my mom and Bryan's mom. It was good having them at breakfast so we could chat about our new venture. Since they are a big part of our support and encouragement system we like to tell them what we are up to.

After breakfast, we ran over to the new unit to take some more exact measurements. We need to get a layout done of the existing unit, so that we can do a layout of what we are going to build, and get a permit and get moving. Whew! From what Bryan told me, we can get moving pretty quickly, and that is a good thing because I really want to get this open right away.

After measuring things at the new place, we spent some time at Home Depot. We looked at paint swatches, light fixtures, doors and tons of other things. I always forget, as we start putting these businesses together, that there is so much, especially little things that are needed to get the business up and running. It is fun putting it together, but there is so much!

This afternoon Bryan and I were so excited to be guests on the Lucky Booty Cycle Boats private tour with our friends John and Connie and their family. We were celebrating John's birthday and it was a lot of fun. To answer the burning question, yes I cycled! But I'll also be honest that I wasn't very good at it. If they were waiting for me to take them any place, I doubt we would have gotten past Sims Park heading north on the river. In the end, the boat ride was nice and the company was even better! We can't wait for them to get final approval for tours so we can go out with them again! We had a great time just relaxing and hanging out, something we never get to do. It was nice just being normal and not worrying about things for a few hours.

Well, tomorrow is the first day of school for the kids and teachers. While I don't have kids and I'm not a teacher, I wish everyone starting school tomorrow a great start to an amazing year. I know it's not traditional like it has been in the past, but I know the kids and teachers are going to make it the best they can and I'm excited for them. After all, life is nothing without knowledge and knowledge is power.

Let's all make it a great Monday!

August 25, 2020

What a productive day, for getting up after 9:30 a.m. Once I got myself out of bed, I got around quickly and got to my shop to start my day—not that I had much planned.

The first task of the day was to head to storage and get our Fall merchandise, then a personal errand, a stop in to Pier 1 to see if they had anything good on sale, and Chick-fil-A for lunch. I know it doesn't seem like a lot but in my defense, our Fall merchandise took up the entire back of my truck. I think there were at least seven totes of items. Fun!

While my mom and I enjoyed our Chick-fil-A in the parlor of the tearoom, we talked about our new venture. We have been working on our new venture for a while now, but we had not really sat down and talked about budgets, lay out projections, and that kind of important stuff. You know, always the most fun part of any idea is figuring out the nitty gritty of your idea...and either killing it or choosing to go forward on a chance. Today, after crunching the numbers and looking at everything we decided that we think we can really make it work, so we are going to continue moving forward.

The decision makes me excited and nauseous at the same time. I'm excited and scared, and also worried about all of the things that I have to do to get this going. I'm sure anyone looking at me would think I'm crazy, especially starting another business in this craziest of times. I also always forget all the work that has to go into getting a business up and running, until I get the brilliant idea of opening another one. What am I thinking??? Help! I think I've lost my mind!

Tonight, we celebrated my dad's birthday. It was so nice to get together for dinner with my family to celebrate him. It's been a long time since we have been together. We were only missing by brother, Steven, and his family. Still, I know time is short and I would love to plan to get together and have dinner with them more often. We always laugh and have a nice time.

Well, off to bed to get ready for tomorrow. I'm not really sure what the day holds for me. I still have to make my 'to do' list and I'm kind of afraid to make it as it's going to be so long.

I hope you all had a great start to the week and that tomorrow is a great day!

August 25, 2020

Another productive day but I don't feel like I moved forward very much. I was so proud to be up and out of my house before 10:30 a.m., and it was a non-work day.

This morning, until late midday, I worked upstairs in my office. I reconciled the checkbooks for both companies, and got finances caught up. That's pretty important, you know—to know where you are at.

Then I went downstairs and moved some things around in our middle room to create a permanent workspace area to package tea. I felt bad having to apologize to our guests when we walked them into the tearoom because of all of the things we had out and all of the projects we were working on. So the other day, my mom suggested that I create a space just to work. For the past few days I thought about how to lay it out and today I moved things around. We will see how it works out over the next few days, but I already feel better about having our parlor area looking more together.

After all that, I pinched the nerve in my mid back/shoulder blade area. I couldn't move my head without pinching the nerve and feeling shooting pain. The worst part was that it's the opposite side of my neck issue, so moving around was oh so fun. I decided around 5 p.m. that it was time to go home and ice my shoulder and back. I'm glad I did because any movement was causing pain.

I hate having to lie down early. Truly it makes me feel lazy, no matter what I accomplished earlier. The good news is the meds have kicked in and this evening I'm feeling better.

Now I'm getting ready to say goodnight as I'm watching a rerun on Shark Tank. There's a guy pitching genetic testing for DNA for research testing. He's talking about how there will be a pandemic someday and how having people help with studies will help figure it out. The Sharks were asking him about his comment about a pandemic and he talked about different strands of diseases and how people's bodies respond differently. He was selling them his company that works with DNA and testing for colleges, research studies, and someday, drug companies. I found it ironic as I was watching, so I checked, and it originally aired in November 2017. How crazy!

Anyways, now that I've seen that I'm heading to bed. I've got a busy day tomorrow with lots to do to keep moving forward, even though I feel like I'm still always taking two steps back.

August 26, 2020

Well, I don't have much to say about today...it was a day, much like any others. Getting up is hard to do. Not because I don't want to, but I know what awaits me getting up and getting ready for the day. All I can say is that it only took me three tries to get my hair in a ponytail. Granted, that may not seem like a lot, but when your neck is spasming constantly, it can take a while—and look pretty funky, LOL.

The shop wasn't too busy today, but we did have a steady flow of guests visiting. That was good because the tearoom was on the slower side. I'm not too worried about that though...it's the first week of school and it always tends to be a little slower for a few weeks while teachers and students get settled. I forget about it every year.

I did have a beautiful surprise today at the gift shop with an amazing couple coming to visit me. I was so happy to see my friend, David and his wife, Midge. I can't believe that I have known them for so many years. No matter what, they have always been so supportive of what I do in the community—from buying photos that I showed at an art gallery eighteen years ago to having tea in my tearoom. Through these crazy times they make me feel so loved and I am so completely blessed that they think of me still today. I enjoyed visiting with them even though it was brief. I look forward to the day when I can spend some more time with them when COVID isn't such a concern. I wish that day would hurry up and get here!

Tonight, our awesome friend, Travis, came over and got my last two chandeliers up in the tearoom windows. Now I just have two more to order and put in the parlor and we will have the two dining rooms done. Yea! Also, he changed the air filters in our three 3 A/C units. It's really high on the ladder, so I don't dare climb that high with my neck. I'm so thankful that we have friends we can come help with these tasks.

Well, it's time to head to bed. Tomorrow I have quite a few projects to get finished with the new business. We are also making another scone mix for guests to take home to make. The new mix is Triple Chocolate Chip, yum!!

I hope everyone's week is going good and that you are moving swiftly to the weekend!

August 28, 2020

Today was a good day. It only took me two tries to get my hair up in its ponytail. Thank you, Esther, for offering to help and when I get to the point I can't do it, you are my gal!

The shop was good today. We didn't have any reservations in house, but we did have to-go teas, which we were thankful for. We also had some decent foot traffic today too, and quite a few people that toured the tearoom. While it's still slow, it's so nice to see people.

For the past few days, or longer, I have been struggling with moving forward with our newest project. It's not that I don't think it would work; it's the concern of taking on a new project while we have two businesses that are not back to their normal capacity. It's very scary taking a risk and taking the safety net we have had around our two businesses away to do something else.

For days, I prayed and asked for guidance to make the right decision to be able to offer something great for our community, but not to risk what we have. I mean, let's be realistic, we know there is a risk when you do anything, but particularly at this time, should we do it? I have continued to pray for a sign or something to show me what to do.

Anyone who knows me and Bryan, knows we work very hard and we take a lot of pride in doing the right thing. Sometimes, when things are tough, it can be easy to cave and not do the right thing. Despite it being hard, I always look internally and pray and ask myself what is the right thing to do, even if it's extremely hard.

Well, today, my prayers were answered, all of the hard work and making the right calls paid off and proved to me that when you are a good person, good things happen. I can't go into specifics, but let's just say that I am feeling much better about taking the risk of a new journey because our current businesses will not be at risk. Both businesses are healthy and, despite being down nearly 40% from this same time last year, they have the vitality now to remain strong for a long time. I am truly blessed.

In a few more days I will be able to share more about our new venture. Just know that right now, I am secure in my decision that my tearoom and Bryan's brewery are strong and here for the duration, and that something new and fun lies ahead. Thank you God!

Wishing you all a wonderful Friday and a great weekend ahead!!

August 28, 2020

It was a good day overall indeed. I got up at my normal time, around 9:30 a.m., and got around to head into work. I knew it was going to be a decent day when I got my hair up on the first try. I know it's sad that's how I gauge my day, but if you really knew how hard it was to even get my hands and arms going in the right direction with my head, one time should give me a gold medal!

The shop was slower today, but we knew that going in. We did have quite a few guests in the gift shop and that was really good. We needed it and it was good to meet new people.

One of the things that we continue to hear every day from people visiting is they can't believe how the area has changed and how it's so cute downtown. It always makes my heart melt when I hear that. For sure that wasn't the case five years ago when we were starting our business. It's been really great to see things transition and to be a part of that. I love that people are impressed by what they see and that they love our downtown.

Tonight I had dinner with my friend and my mom at Thai Bistro. As always, it was so good and I just love that we have such a gem in downtown. Yum. We sat for two and a half hours and talked. Then we walked down to look in the window of my new place. I can't wait until we officially have it! Then I can really start working on getting things done so we can get open. It is so exciting!

I really can't wait to share what we have going on—share our name, a logo and design ideas. I am beyond excited! Don't worry, the announcement is coming soon. Once we sign paperwork on our location and finish our corporation paperwork, then I will share the specifics.

Well, tomorrow is going to be a busy day and I'm exhausted tonight so I'm heading to bed early.

Tomorrow the tearoom is completely full, not for real, but for our new capacity. It's going to be a busy day but I'm ready to have a day like that. Yea!!

Wishing you all a great weekend!!

August 29, 2020

What a day! Whew! I don't think I've had a day as busy as this for a few months, and as exhausting as it is, it feels so good.

This morning, I was up and at my shop by 9:30 a.m. My goal was to be in early enough to help Dawne in the kitchen to get ready for our day. We ended up having thirty-two guests in the tearoom and nine take outs today. While that may not seem like a lot, it's a great Saturday compared to what we have had over the past few months, and it seems like we have been starting to see a steady increase. I hope it continues.

Now, it's time to find a helper for the tearoom kitchen on Saturdays. Unfortunately, it's a position to wash dishes and help plate food, and eventually make food. It's literally only eight hours a week, but man, after today, having someone those eight hours is going to be a blessing to us.

After we closed the shop today, we went and did a thing...we signed the lease on a new space downtown for our new project. I am so excited about it that I can't wait to get it going! Only a few more days until we submit plans to the city for permits and then we will be on our way to a new addition in town.

You know, I have been through project development and business development twice now and each time I feel nauseous when we officially sign on the dotted line. In addition to those two projects, I also felt nauseous when I purchased the gift shop four years ago. It's not a bad thing; it's more like a gut check. It's the fear of the unknown with the project that's ahead. With this project, I feel confident that it's the right decision and that I know how to make it work. I'm truly excited about it and I can't wait to share it with you soon.

Tonight, I enjoyed dinner with my mom. It was her birthday and because we worked so hard today neither of us had made plans for anything this evening. I know it was a low-key evening, but to be honest, I kind of like it that way. I mean, we spend so much time together, but we don't. Not sure if that makes sense or not. I enjoy these little times when it's just her and I. I know it wasn't a big year, but every year is important, and I just am so blessed to be able to celebrate with her. Love you mom!

On that note, I want to thank all of you for your continued support, encouragement and love. I do this for you and for our community, so that we may all have a beautiful place we call home.

Wishing you a restful and relaxing Sunday!

August 30, 2020

What a rainy, lazy day! I woke up this morning and thought it was still night or very early morning and it was really 8:30 a.m.! I guess that wasn't too late for me since I went to bed at 2 a.m. It was nice sleeping in a little, though. To be honest, I could have slept a lot longer with the cloudy and rainy weather.

Well, I pulled myself out of bed and got around. Bryan was ahead of me today because he had to get to the brewery and start brewing early.

My mom and I enjoyed breakfast at Rose's Bistro. It was yummy and a perfect start to our day. Then, we were off to Restaurant Depot. We hadn't been there to get stuff for the tearoom for a few weeks so we had quite the list. Honestly though, it wasn't nearly as bad as I thought it was going to be. Of course, when we got back to unload our groceries, it was pouring down rain. I only got a little wet and it was okay. I'm just glad it wasn't raining harder.

For lunch today we ordered from Herschel's. It was good and I'm so glad they are right across from the brewery. It's very convenient! We enjoyed lunch at the brewery while Bryan and Tara brewed. We are really low on our IPA so Bryan wanted to make sure we didn't run out. Got to keep the beer flowing!

After lunch, I went home to relax until we took my mother-in-law, Bernice, to dinner for her birthday. I was wiped from the weather, so I was looking forward to just chilling. Of course I get home, disarm the house, and go to turn the lights on and nothing. A power outage! I'm glad I have lots of battery candles around the house, and the cloudy and rainy weather kept it nice and cool inside. It was just dark enough that I could take a nice nap. Fortunately, the power came back on about twenty minutes after I got home, but I still took a nice long nap. Truly, I must have been exhausted because I was out for a few hours.

Tonight we took the moms to dinner. Today was Bernice's birthday and yesterday was my mom's so taking them to dinner together was really nice. It's kind of like a yearly tradition.

Now it's time to head to bed. Despite my nap today, I'm still completely exhausted. I hope to sleep good tonight as I have so much to do these days and I'm going to be using my brain a lot. It's time to get the rest while I can.

Tomorrow is the start of a new week and new opportunities. May it be a great week for all of us!

August 31, 2020

Today kind of went as planned. I truly planned on getting up at a decent time, but I must have hit stop instead of snooze on my alarm because the next thing I knew, it was 9:45 a.m. and I was just rolling out of bed. I'm not going to say it didn't feel good sleeping in because it did, but it put me behind on my day. Thank goodness it was a day the tearoom was closed.

My truck is up getting detailed today and tomorrow, so I am without my own transportation. I'm glad my mom works for me. She was off today so she could run me to my shop and other places I needed to go.

Yes, I am finally getting my truck detailed. It's been years and I'm sure my wonderful husband is tired of being reminded that I backed into our fence one too many times. That's why I took it to my trusted body shop to make it pretty again. No longer will I come out to my truck and see a huge area with white PVC. I just wonder what they are going to find under my seats. Maybe they will find my SunPass that I haven't been able to find in months! Please, fingers crossed!

So today, I got quite a bit done to get our businesses caught up. I got lots of bills paid and lots of correspondence done. Now tomorrow will be spent working on the new business and our marketing of the tearoom and brewery. I'm also working on getting us set for the beer and cheese pairing on Wednesday. I'm actually really excited about it. I worked really hard on these pairings and I kind of wish I was able to enjoy it myself. Those lucky ducks attending!!

Today, Jenny came and painted our front window for the Fall. It looks so awesome. I always tell her a general idea of what I'm thinking and she creates something absolutely amazing. Today's window is perfect, and I can't wait for our guests to see her beautiful creation.

Tomorrow I start really hacking away at our new business. There is so much to do...website, social media, checking the status of our corporation, and the list goes on and on. I can't wait to share it with you soon, now that you know where it will be located!

Well, it's time to relax a little before bed. I have a few things to get done tomorrow so I want to be able to get up at a decent hour and start my day.

Here's hoping you have a great Tuesday!

September 2020

September 1, 2020

Well, today did not turn out at all as I planned. Then again, I've always heard that if you want God to laugh, tell him your plans. Boy, today must have been one comedy after another.

You know, it's strange because the day started out so good. I was up at a decent time, around, and getting lots of work done. I was on my A game. My mom even ran me around to different stores that I needed to go to, since my truck was being detailed. Then more luck, at JoAnn Fabrics I found a material to recover chairs in the same pattern that I had used before, perfect. Truly.

Now, it's not that my day was bad after all that. Trust me—I know there are people that have such bad days that they would wish for one of mine because it would be a good day. I know, and I'm not ungrateful in any way.

I received some bad news—my "safety net" disappeared. Here I am trying to keep 2 businesses viable, which, let's face it, is no easy task normally, but these days is becoming exceedingly difficult. Now I'm left wondering how to keep it going when I am truly pulling out all my tricks and thinking the safety net was there to open another business. I just have no words.

The struggle is real and as good as we are as business owners, even the seasoned of us struggle sometimes. That's where I'm at...struggling for ideas, struggling for ways to drive traffic, and struggling to find ways to bring guests back, to help them not be afraid to go out to eat... struggle, struggle, struggle! I'm so exhausted, just completely tired of it. And for the first time since I started my tearoom, I don't know the future of it. I'm sure it will always be here because I refuse to fail, but these days that confidence is different. It's hard to face realities of how difficult it is to run a business, especially retail and restaurant, and if the big boys can fall, so can the little ones.

So tonight I go to bed, not telling God what I want to do tomorrow, but praying that tomorrow will be a good day and that I will be shown some sort of sign of the path ahead—that things will turn, not just for me, but all of us and that there is a bright future ahead. God willing!

September 3, 2020

After yesterday I figured I needed to do something to push myself forward. I am not a quitter, and despite how far down I may think I am, I'm not at the bottom.

This morning I was up before 7:45 a.m. and was at my shop by 8:50 a.m.! My husband was shocked I was up before he left for work, and my mom was surprised I texted her before 8 a.m.

I didn't have a reason to get to my shop early, only to help get things ready for today. It was going to be a long one since we had tea seatings at 12 p.m. and then we were hosting a beer and cheese pairing for the brewery tonight. I know I ask a lot of my team when we do these events, but we also know how important it is for us to keep people coming back and having fun. And honestly, it was a lot of fun being in the kitchen, though I do tend to make a mess.

The shop was really good today. I will say this—people are generally in really good moods when they come in. For so long we didn't see each other that it seems today people are happy to be out and about, while staying safe of course. It's definitely a good thing for them and us, being around people.

Tonight we hosted an event at the tearoom, soon to be known in the evenings as The Riviera Room at The White Heron. We changed out the linens and created a whole new feel for the evening event. More classic and modern, but more upscale, we hosted a beer and cheese pairing for our partner, Cotee River Brewing. The event was sold out, by today's capacity standards, and I really think everyone had a great time.

For me, it was the first time hosting an event that I paired beer and food together. I have been working on learning pairings for a while, but this was the first time I designed it for an event and guests. I had tested the pairings a few weeks ago, and had some family try it too to make sure I was on the right path. Those reactions were good, so I was hopeful it was going to be the same at the event. Honestly, it came out so much better than I had anticipated. The guests loved it and everyone seemed to have a really nice time. If you couple that with the pairings being really good, I consider it a win.

As a foodie that is very picky, tonight I was extremely proud. I may not like a lot of food types, but I am great at putting flavors together, which is something I have loved doing for a long time. I'm glad I could finally share that part of me with others. So now the pressure is on to be able to do some more foodie events with beer, wine and tea. I am excited about it, but it's not like it happens overnight. I really have to sit down and compare flavor profiles, then sample, and then create an entire meal so to speak. But, I'm up for the challenge.

Now, the next thing for me is to build my PR and outreach, so we can get some promotion on the cool things we are doing. I feel press releases coming on…it is time to get my A game back!

Here's to another great day tomorrow, and to some much-needed motivation for me. I hope I can get up early again tomorrow. Wish me luck!

September 3, 2020

So, I didn't start out as on my game as I did on Wednesday, but it definitely wasn't as bad as last week.

For some reason after the beer and cheese pairing I just couldn't sleep. I couldn't get my body to relax and it kept fighting to release my muscles. I eventually fell asleep only to be woken up at 2:45 a.m. by a severe knee and calf cramp that I couldn't shake. Twenty-five minutes standing in the shower with extremely hot water pounding on it and I was able to make my way back to bed and sleep for a few more hours. I woke at 6:45, 7:15 and 7:45 a.m. and finally got out of bed by 8:15 a.m. I did my usual 'get around' routine and even did laundry before heading into the tearoom. It was a good morning.

Today the shop was really nice. I got to have tea with my friend Elisa. I got to see my friends Pat and Pat for tea. Even one of our first customers, Renee and her mom came in for tea. Renee and I talked and she asked me to consult with her about business. She said that she thinks I'm a great business woman and very thorough and thought out in my decisions. She would love to sit with me and have me teach her about business, as a client. WOW! I was so honored. I told her I always wanted to write a book about small business ownership. She suggested that as I consult with her, I write things down so I can put my book together at the same time. I'm so excited because this is something I have talked about doing for a long time!

In addition to all that, my friend Michelle came in with her friend Cindy and got boba, and we talked about working together for an upcoming chocolate pairing. I can't wait to start working on that!! So many fun and rewarding projects, how did I get so lucky!

And, now I have to get back with my friend KC about another project that I put on the back burner. That one I'm even more excited about, if that's even possible!

After all that, I came home around 5:30 p.m., after dealing with other business stuff...and my neck was just shot. I've had this pinched nerve acting up the last few days and every now and then the muscle spasms pinch the nerve and send a cold shot up my head. After dealing with that and everything else, I decided I was done. I came home and vegged and read a book. It was nice, but my reading time is never long enough.

Out of nowhere, around 9:15 p.m., I had a horrible panic attack. I haven't had one of those in a long time. It came on all of the sudden. Panic breathing, tense muscles, stomach ache...I sat down, did some slow breathing, and played a game of Sudoku on my phone to not think about it. It passed in about ten minutes, but those ten minutes were like crazy time. Now I remember why I'm thankful I don't get them often anymore.

Bryan was awesome today. He went to Walgreens on his way home for a few things we needed, then to the brewery, then home for dinner, and after all that we put a cover on the bed of the pickup, for traveling. I'm so glad we did it at night because it was so hot that we were drenched. As we were finishing up, he pinched his finger in one of the grips and it has already turned his nail purple. Poor guy! I guess the only silver lining, other than that we got it installed right the first time, is that we weren't trying to do it in the heat of the day. We surely wouldn't have made it.

Now that we have cooled off, it's time for bed. Here's to a better night's sleep than last night and to a fun Friday ahead.

September 4, 2020

Well, old habits die hard.... I woke up at 5 a.m. and by the time I got back to sleep it was almost 7 a.m.! Needless to say I didn't get up until later, around 9 a.m.! Of course I knew all was good, so I got around and headed into my shop.

I'm trying to finish up a few things and tie up a few loose ends before I head out for a few days. I had to pay a few bills and renew some licenses, so that I didn't have to rush when I got back. It was nice to get caught up, for the most part.

We had the most amazing guests again today. Honestly, it's so fun and warms my heart so much when I hear them laughing and sharing stories in the tearoom. I can't even explain it.

Of course two of the women I look up to so much in my life, Trish and Mary Ellen, came in for tea today. I'm so happy they let me crash their teatime for a little bit. I spent so much time with these women over the years that it was like being home to me.

This afternoon I got to enjoy tea with another amazing woman, Kolby. I love that we can talk about ideas, and I can hear how she is doing with all her projects. Whenever she and I get together, time slips by and before we know it, two hours have passed! I love when that happens. I mean really, can you imagine if we could all talk and do business over tea…we would get so much done and probably be much nicer to each other. She gave me some great ideas too! I'm really excited about our future!

Tonight I came home to lots of laundry. That's always fun. Also Bryan had asked me to make a few different snacks to take with us on our trip, so I did. I made oyster crackers and this other pretzel thing with cayenne and garlic and lemon pepper. Now, in the oven is Rice Chex mix snack with cinnamon sugar. Oh my gosh, does the house smell amazing! I love making stuff like this!

Well, time to finish up laundry and head to bed. Tomorrow we get to do it all again, and despite the craziness that is life, I'm glad!

Hoping everyone has a great Saturday!

September 6, 2020

Well, I was up a lot later than I anticipated last night, so getting up this morning was a bit of a chore. You would think that the opportunity to go away for a few days would make me feel like a kid at Christmas, but that just didn't work when I was so tired.

Before I headed into work, I got a lot done this morning—laundry, packing, and the usual getting ready for the day. For this non-morning person that's quite a feat and something even I was proud of.

I had to make a run down to my friend, Jenn's shop, Mmmm Delicious Cupcakes. I had to pick up some cookies and cream cakesicles for the shop. We also filled her in on our successful two-year anniversary promo for the brewery that we got cupcakes for. I can tell she knows her business well. When we were talking about which cupcake flavor our guests chose more than any other, she guessed it right on. Oh, in case you are wondering, it was peanut butter and jelly!

I also stopped at her next-door neighbor's place, Corey's, and ordered a cookies and cream cheesecake to pick up next week and picked up two little cakes to take with me on our trip. Yummy!

The tearoom hosted several tea parties today and the gift shop remained quite steady. Today's big take was boba tea. While small in price compared to other items, it was the third most sold item today behind the tearoom and some miscellaneous stuff. It has brought in a lot of new and excited guests and is giving us more exposure. I'm glad we decided to order it and I look forward to offering more options soon.

With the shop being so busy, we didn't get to head out for our trip until almost 4:15 p.m. Well, that's the time we started loading up the truck and the moms. LOL! We actually left town around 5:00 p.m. So far the trip has been good and we've made some great time. Traffic was relatively light, and we made it north of Atlanta in six and a half hours. I know that sounds crazy, but we only had to stop for bathrooms once and we didn't have to stop for gas at all. We will fill up tomorrow and that will get us the rest of the way and then some. We have been getting twenty mpg! This is so much better than the last trip when we pulled the camper.

I will say I am looking forward to seeing our camper tomorrow. It sat next to our house for six years and I saw it every day. When we left it in Tennessee in July, I was slightly sad, but it's made me excited to get back up here sooner.

Though, we've already had our first oops. I need to start a list of questions that I need to ask Bryan before we leave to come up here. Here's a sample of what I need to ask... "do you have the keys to the camper?" Truly I'm not kidding. Oh and this isn't the first time someone has forgotten them. Well, it's the first with this camper. Thank goodness we left a spare set with our campground host; otherwise the start of this trip would be epic. LOL!

I'm also looking forward to a little break from my messy and unorganized home and office. While it's true I won't stop working, I will at least be in a different setting and that helps refresh me. Also, I brought some tea things to photograph while I'm here, so that's exciting too because it's one of my favorite things to do.

Well, off to bed so we can get up and get to our camper home at a decent time. I'm hoping everyone has a relaxing Sunday and I can't wait to share my adventures with you while I'm away.

September 7, 2020

We arrived safely in Tennessee. After a four-hour drive, we arrived at our destination, and our camper was set up and ready to go. It was the simplest set up ever! All Bryan had to do was hit a button to put the awning out and hook up the sewer line. No sweating for an hour to set us up. Why didn't we do this years ago??

On our way up we stopped at a few shops. Honestly, with it being Labor Day weekend and the last weekend people are really vacationing for the summer, every place was packed. I can't wait until Tuesday when all of these people go home! LOL! Being in a tourist town is crazy and I like when it's quiet. It's kind of like at home when all of the winter visitors come down; we tend not to go out as much. Maybe it's just me, but I love the peace and quiet more than the over-packed, waiting for thirty minutes to get a table times.

Other than our drive, we didn't do much today. We hung out at the campground, had a fire, and just relaxed. It was a perfect day!

Now that we are here, we will have lots of fun adventures and I can't wait to share them with you!

September 7, 2020

I woke up this morning in my favorite place away from home—the mountains of Tennessee. It was a brisk, cool morning and the mist was absolutely beautiful on the mountains.

We started our day with breakfast at one of our favorite places, Riverstone Restaurant. While we were waiting for a table, I decided to go through my purse to make sure I had a mask. I found one of my scarf masks and Bryan decided to try it on. Talk about hilarious!

Then, we did some shopping at some of the cute stores in Townsend. We came across this little coffee shop, Dancing Bean Coffee Shop. We enjoyed a flowering tea, boba tea, some macarons, some fall flavored drinks, and an apple cinnamon scone. Amie, the manager was awesome! We chatted about tea, and she gave me a contact for some awesome designer desserts. I just love a small town!!

Tonight, we cooked hamburgers and hotdogs at the Cades Cove picnic area. It was absolutely delicious! I really love when we cook on the grill in the woods. Everything always seems to taste better!

After dinner, we went out and enjoyed a ride through the cove. It was absolutely beautiful out there. The temperature was in the low 70s and no humidity. We rode around for a while and saw a bear in a tree; people were everywhere, and the poor bear couldn't get down. We also saw two coyotes and an absolutely beautiful hawk that almost flew into our truck. It was so cool to see the coyotes!! I've heard them being up in the mountains before, but I haven't seen them in years.

Tonight, we are ending with a campfire, and I am so happy to be relaxed and enjoying this trip. It's not that I haven't enjoyed other trips, but I am truly trying to relax and it's working so far.

I hope everyone had a great and restful Labor Day and that you are ready to face the week ahead!

September 8, 2020

Why do I love vacations? Because I can relax and do things I wouldn't normally do when real life gets in the way.

Today we visited our favorite salt room in the area for halotherapy. We make it a point to visit it every time we are in town. Our visit was wonderful, as usual. I can breathe so much better now. I always find I have a little sinus congestion when I go back and forth between the humidity of Florida and the coolness of Tennessee. I just love how the salt works for me and I can't wait to have a salt room closer to us.

After halotherapy, we went to see our friend's new location of his brewery, Gatlinburg Brewing Company. They opened a second location and we hadn't had a chance to see it, so today was the day. The place is really nice and they have a great set up to make a lot more beer. Bryan chatted with Stewart, their brewer, for a while and I think they are going to try to work on a collaboration beer when Bryan and I are back here in November. That would be really great!

After our visit, we headed over to The Island in Pigeon Forge, where we enjoyed some nice beverages at Yee Haw Brewing, before going on their huge Ferris wheel. That was quite an experience! It was very high and reminded me of being on the sky lift at Disney. Though I think this thing went higher, it was a lot of fun to relax and see the area from a different perspective. We walked around their outside mall and then enjoyed dinner at Paula Dean's restaurant. The food was very good and served family-style. I think my favorite was the fried chicken and mashed potatoes, yum! The best was when Bryan was eating and asked us if our forks were as big as his and why he got a bigger one. Then we told him he stole the serving fork from one of the entrees. The couple next to us thought it was hysterical too. LOL!

Oh and my favorite part of dinner, teaching the server about tea. They serve Earl Grey by Tazo, but when I asked he had no clue, so I told him about it and turns out he is a tea lover! I wish I could talk tea all day every day!! How do I get that job?

Tonight, we are relaxing night by the fire and I'm getting ready to fix me a cup of apple and chamomile tea that I picked up. I hope it's a good and relaxing one! If so, I may have to try to blend up my own at home.

Tomorrow will be another fun day as I have some more adventures planned. This has been a good trip and I miss home, but being here makes me wonder if living up here would be as nice of a lifestyle, or better than what I have at home. Not that I want to move, but being here just brings me a sense of calm and peace, different than what I have with my rat race. Hmm...

September 9, 2020

Today we decided to do something a little different, something I haven't done in a few years since we have been renting cabins instead of camping—go hiking. Though I wouldn't consider this a real hike, it was more like a nice walk through the woods. You know it's a stroll when I wear a comfy dress and crock sandals. Regardless, it was a nice walk, some uphill, 2.25 miles up and 2.25 miles back, and at the top, a small waterfall.

It's a hike I've probably done more than half a dozen times, but this is the first time I walked that far with my cervical dystonia. I can't say it was so easy, but I did better than I thought. I did use a hiking stick, although I actually hate using them, and it helped with my balance. My neck and vision did good, but there were times my head was completely sideways and I'm sure if anyone else on the trial noticed, they would wonder what the heck I was doing. With all that, I ended up going to the waterfall two times—once with mom and then we met Bryan on our way back down and I walked with him up as he was only .25 miles away and I wanted him to see it.

I felt good hiking and wished I could have taken about thirty minutes to sit on a rock by the river and meditate. That's something I am going to do in the future for sure. I do look forward to doing some other small hikes now that I know I can. The only thing that will prevent me now is if the hike has a trail that is narrow, because with my balance I tend to be all over the trail, or if it's a longer trail where I have to carry a backpack. Unfortunately, with my neck, I can't carry backpacks or purses that rest on my shoulder as that puts pressure on my muscles. Maybe I can find some other short easy hikes to do. If Bryan wants to do some harder ones he is going to have to find a hiking buddy.

After hiking we came back to town and enjoyed some lunch and stopped at one of our favorite shops, Harper Brothers. They are so nice in there and we love that we have gotten to know them. I always find the coolest things there!

Honestly, I have had a fun time shopping up here. I got a beautiful clear glass painted tea pot and two cups, a cup with a saucer that had a bee on it and mesh steeper in it, and a beautiful pink floral cup. What can I say—I'm a sucker for pretty cups and pots. I would buy more, but honestly, I think Bryan would kill me about putting more stuff in the truck to come home. So every time I come I'll look for that little cute piece or two to bring home and build my collection.

Tonight is our last night here and it was a low-key night for us. We packed up the things we could and got them in the truck. Now we are enjoying a nice fire and are going to cook some hotdogs on sticks. It's the last night so we have to make the most of it. Though we will be back here in November and that's only two months away, it seems like forever, and I will miss my second home tremendously.

I'm looking forward to heading home tomorrow. I have some things to work on during our ride home—lots of events to get on my calendar. Also, I have some more pairings to work on with tea, and dessert things to work on. Fun stuff!!

I hope your week is going well. I'm looking forward to getting back to work when I get home, and to seeing everyone! I love being away and consider this my second home. I love spending time here and now that our big camper is here it truly is a second home. But I'm looking forward to seeing Sam and sleeping in my own bed tomorrow night.

Have a great Thursday!

September 10, 2020

The last day of vacation is always the saddest for me. I know we have a long drive home, but that's not what gets me—it's leaving a place I love so dearly—a place where I feel at peace and at home. We will be back there in less than two months but right now it seems like forever!

I will say it was so nice just putting our stuff in the truck and driving away. The first time we did it I was a little sad, but this time I felt much better. Probably because it was so easy to pull up and see our baby sitting there ready for us and knowing that our place takes good care of it while we are away. Truly, it's like family and I'm so grateful that my husband found this place. In fact, we talked about why we would ever consider even getting a house when we could just keep doing this for years and not pay property taxes or anything…you know, I like this idea for now!

The ride home was uneventful. Smooth sailing the whole way. There was very little traffic in Atlanta and people were just moving along. The truck bed cover worked great and it made traveling so much easier.

On the way home I rested. My neck is hurting a little today, so I really didn't move around much. I don't think it was from my hike yesterday. I think it was from sleeping on my side last night. I woke up and realized I was on my side and my nerve was pinched down my arm and my hand was numb. So I'm sure that's part of my issue today. In reality, I feel good otherwise…that little hike (stroll to most) did me really good and I'm looking forward to another one in November, though it will be much cooler.

One thing that did happen on our way home was that we got the news that our brewery can open next week. Granted capacity will be cut and we will have to continue to work hard to keep everyone safe, but that's what we've been doing all along whenever anyone visits. Safety has always been our biggest priority. We can officially open next Monday, but we are going to work on our reopening plan tomorrow evening so we can open strategically and keep everyone safe. This has been a long road. I'm so proud of my husband for staying true to himself and his business model and having faith that he was doing what was best for his business. Now, he is excited to get back to work and get open for his guests. Yea! No rest for the weary. BTW, the weary is me!

I got laundry started, albeit, it's tearoom linen that I didn't get to before I left. Now we are just chilling. I'm looking forward to getting back to my tearoom tomorrow. I have missed it!

A reminder that tomorrow is Patriot's Day. I encourage you to take some time to reflect and remember those amazing people we lost nineteen years ago tomorrow. And, for them and so many more, let's live a beautiful life to honor those who are no longer here. Oh, and if you see a first responder, smile if you don't have a mask on, and thank them for their sacrifices to keep us safe. I don't know about you, but I have the utmost respect for anyone who runs toward danger while others run for safety.

Wishing you all a nice Friday!

September 12, 2020

Did you ever have a day that just does you in? While it wasn't any one major thing, but lots of little things, adding up enough to make me want to call it quits today. In fact, I've been in bed since 9:30 p.m., hoping to just end the darn day.

I thought all was good, and got up and welcomed the day in my usual way. From the moment I got up, my neck was sore. The nerve and muscles were not cooperating and I had this constant ache that never went away, and only intensified throughout the day.

Still, I got around for work and heading in to the tearoom. It was just Dawne and me today. Although we didn't have a ton of reservations, we did have some amazing groups scheduled.

When I got in, I went in the back to see if Dawne needed any help. She was busy working and almost done with all the prep for the day. She had to make our Devonshire Cream, so she got everything ready and turned on the big mixer and it didn't go. The engine was running but the paddle would only go so far and stop. If I pushed on it, it would go around once and stop again. Something in the motor broke and it wouldn't spin. Great! That thing was very expensive and granted we have used it almost every day for 3-1/2 years, it just isn't in the budget to replace it. Especially as we continue to try and navigate COVID and the lasting negative economic impact it has left us with this year.

We finally got the Devonshire made with a hand mixer that only has one beater that will snap into the unit. Yes it was that kind of day. So I went and put the sign out front only to find a homeless drunk guy asleep in my alcove by the tearoom door. Now, before you get judgmental, this guy truly is a drunk that wanders town. He is very confrontational and not nice. So I called the police department, told them of the situation, and asked them to send an officer to just move him along. Good thing that ended without incident.

The tearoom and gift shop ran like clockwork today and our guest were awesome. For being a slower day we had a really good day—almost a normal weekday. Not quite a normal weekend, but it's better than what we had a few months ago.

After we closed, we started putting together stuff for the beer and cheese pairing we are hosting tomorrow only to find out the ham that we had sliced for it was used by accident for our tearoom guests. It wasn't the end of the world because we have some amazing ham in our tearoom, but this was meant specifically for the tasting. I had to change all the paperwork to make sure we had the right flavors on there. It was just another thing to do.

After all that, it was time to go to the brewery to lay out its reopening plan. We sat down and laid out the brewing plan to make sure we keep all of our taps full, and also determined what days and times we would be open. Things always work better when we have a plan so it was important to get that done.

I was at the brewery until about 8:30 p.m. I went to leave and found that someone had hit the mirror on my truck—just after I got it detailed and so pretty. Really? Like, that was the icing on the cake for me.

It ends up that today is going to be an expensive day between the mirror and the mixers. Ugh! I'm truly done!

I hope tomorrow is a nice and simple day. I really need that after today, when it seemed like lots of little things going wrong.

I hope you have a great Sunday!

September 15, 2020

I am so sorry that I have missed my posts for the past few days. I really don't have any excuse other than I have been extremely exhausted. By the time I go to write, it's all I can do to try and keep my eyes open. I'm not sure if it's the weather, the pressure I'm under, or a combination that has made me just beyond exhausted and barely able to function.

Sunday was a nice and relaxing day. It started with a beer pairing for the brewery that we held at my tea shop.

We had a great little group of guests. The party of three came from an hour away because they have always wanted to try our beer. It was a nice time, and I'm glad that we decided to host these events so that it could provide our guests the opportunity to try some beer and food together to show how the combination can change the flavors of both. Next up, I'm working on a wine and chocolate pairing to host during the holiday season. Oh, and of course, a tea and cheese pairing as well. That one I'm really looking forward to.

Monday was a good day. I virtually attended the Salt Therapy Association's annual conference. I learned quite a bit about halotherapy (the true name for salt therapy), and why it is beneficial to us. I also learned a lot about the importance of breathing well. How it can affect your health, sleep, etc. James Nestor wrote a great book that came out in May called *Breathe, The New Science of a Lost Art*. He looked at free divers and their capacity to control their body with limited breath and breath held for extensive periods of time. He examined skulls from thousands of years ago. The interesting thing is examining the skulls, their teeth are perfectly straight (no braces, etc.). And why was that? They breathe differently than us, through their noses versus mouth. It's something that has been changing for thousands of years and it was interesting how over time we change. Also, if you look at other animals in the animal kingdom today they have perfectly straight teeth—notice a chimp smiling or a dolphin. It's because their breathing hasn't changed. So interesting! Of course I have to research more! That got me thinking, how much do I breathe through my nose verses mouth. I know I'm weird, but I have been consciously breathing through my nose. Holy cow, it's hard because I really do breathe through my mouth a lot. So now I'm interested in breathing and how we breathe and the benefits of different types of breath. Great! Another book to read!

Not that you wanted to know all that, but that's just a snippet of why my brain has been so fried and I've been so tired...way too much thinking, LOL.

I'm working on a few things for the shop today and then I am taking some time for me. This week is shaping up to be a good one for the tearoom and I know I am going to need every ounce of energy I have.

I hope all of you are having a good week. I promise to get back on my schedule so you can read about my days daily! I honestly enjoy writing about them because writing brings me peace!

Until tomorrow...

September 16, 2020

It was a slow start to my morning. I've been having spasms in my neck quite a bit lately, so getting around and starting my day wasn't so easy. I tried to get my hair up and my head wouldn't stop shaking. I look like I'm telling someone no and shaking my head that way vigorously. Today it started with fighting with my hair and moved to my hands and arms not wanting to work. It's a never ending battle, but at least it doesn't hurt. It's just really annoying.

Today was a good day at my shop. It was a little on the slower side, but our guests were amazing. I stopped in to visit them and I love that they are having a nice time. While it's smaller groups than normal it's wonderful to hear them laugh and visit.

This afternoon I finally sat down and wrote out my 'to do' list for tomorrow. It's something I haven't been doing lately and I need to have structure again, so I can be more effective. It's just in my nature, so I feel good that tomorrow I have a map to get things done through the day.

Now, I just need to find someone or some people to help me organize my house—to go through and get rid of stuff, lots of stuff. I felt so much better when I organized my little corner of work. Can you imagine how I would feel if my home was completely organized? Talk about happy. Honestly, if I don't do it soon, I'm going to drown in the house with all this stuff! Ugh!

On a fun note, this evening I attended an online seminar by the Boston Tea Party Ships and Museum. It was a seminar on Liberty Tea. I really enjoyed it, and I love that there are so many groups offering these types of education classes online so we can learn. I have two more classes to take from them in the next few months. I'm very excited about that.

Tonight, I came home and made some delicious chicken chili. I haven't made it in months and it tasted so good. So now I'm here at home, enjoying my chili, and watching a show on TV about the fire at Notre Dame in France. Having visited this beautiful historical landmark as a young person, it tore at me when it caught fire. It's a very interesting program. It's in French, but translated and they are talking with the firefighters. It was such a sad day, but out of such devastation comes beauty and I hope that someday I will have the chance to see it again.

I hope everyone is having a good week and that you are looking forward to the weekend! I know I am!

September 19, 2020

It's been a good couple of days. I'm not sure what has really changed but for some reason I just feel a little better.

It may be that for the first time since March, life feels like it's kind of going along now. Yea, it's different from March, but there's been a small sense of normalcy back and I can say it feels good.

My husband's mood has been more upbeat and the past two days and I have seen a childlike glow in his eyes. I know it has everything to do with him being able to reopen his establishment, and for that I am so grateful for him. The only downside is now we appear to be back on our 'never see each other' schedule. As I lie here ready for bed, at 12:52 a.m., he still is not home.

Call me selfish, but I really love the guy and I miss him when we aren't together. Granted there are times we are just in the same room, but we aren't talking, however he's there. So here I go, having to get back into the routine of my Thursday, Friday and Saturday nights alone. I know I can get used to it again, like I did before. I just really enjoyed not being used to it for a while.

Tomorrow is a crazy busy day in the tearoom. We are maxed out by current day 50% standards. I'm very happy about that, but these days also make me anxious. I always want everything to be so perfect. I know my amazing team of two will do it with me, but it still makes me anxious. If these Saturdays keep as busy as they have been I will need to find some help in our kitchen! Seriously!! Wish I had someone I knew who was looking for a weekend deal...it's time to get serious about looking!

Well, off to bed I go. I need to get some good rest to be on my A game tomorrow. Not only are we swamped but it's Bryan's birthday! It's going to be a great one!!

September 19, 2020

I want to wish a Happy Birthday to my amazing man. You are the love of my life, the calm to my crazy, and the hardest working man I know. I couldn't imagine my world without you and I'm glad you chose me to walk with you through our fun and completely blessed life. I look forward to celebrating you today and for many, many years ahead! I love you, Happy Birthday!

September 19, 2020

What a day, I'm beat! Well, actually I'm not, but I am a little tired. I'm glad I have a day to recover, but I will say that I hope I stay this busy for a while. It's so nice to move!

Our day started off just perfect. The tearoom was ready to go, tables were set, I had the Fall tea samplers done for in-store purchasing, and all was ready for our guests. It was just a matter of being able to handle the amount of guests on a limited team member day.

The 12 p.m. seating was our busiest and we had the most tables. All but two tables were used. It just seemed like it all melded together. Guests came in, we got them seated, got their teas, got their food and it all worked out. How perfect! I was able to stay in the kitchen and work and clean and visit guests in the tearoom. It gave me a lot of time to think about my business. It was all good thinking.

Our 2 p.m. teatime was a beautiful engagement tea. They had the most beautiful centerpieces that I had to take photos. It just made the tearoom even more beautiful, if that's possible…

The day kept me running and it felt good. Now it has me thinking about marketing and some goals I have for my business. I am putting my plan together now. So excited at my vision of what I want it to become. It's like falling in love with it again, majorly. I am just going to need some help with broad scale marketing, and upscale marketing. I can't wait!

Tonight I enjoyed a delicious dinner at Thai Bistro. I just love it there. Now I'm home relaxing. Well, not completely relaxing, I'm reading. I love reading and while Bryan is at the brewery later in the evenings I am not going to focus on TV, but instead on reading. For pleasure or business, it doesn't matter. I find I sleep better and relax better, and I don't feel as bad about wasted time.

I want to give a huge shout out to my niece Ava for making her Uncle Bryan the most awesome birthday bracelet ever. I know he loved it! And to our amazing friends John and Connie, thank you for bringing Bryan dinner for his birthday. We are so blessed to have friends like you!

BTW, a note about the new business...we are working on the background stuff now and hope to be moving forward in the unit in the next few weeks. I can't wait to get that up and running. Now, to find someone to help run it since I am going to be super busy with my tearoom too. Fun times ahead!!

I wish you a relaxing Sunday. I know I'm going to be taking it easy, using only my brain to make plans for an exciting future!

September 21, 2020

Today was a nice day. Bryan was brewing, so he had to be in early. I was able to relax and take my time getting around, which was nice.

I really didn't have any plans. My goal was to relax, not work too much, and just enjoy the day, which is a first for me for a long time. Usually everything is planned and I'm moving non-stop. So instead I decided to just see where thing went.

I decided to go do some grocery shopping. I haven't been to the grocery store in a while, so it was nice to plan some meals and get some good food for our house. While I was there I ran into quite a few people I know, including my friend Joanne! Jo and I must have stood in the produce section and talked for thirty minutes. It was so good to catch up with her! I have missed spending time with people and just visiting. Truly, it was nice. And I hope her homemade pizza came out yummy!

I spent the afternoon at the brewery. I don't know that I was much help, but I did get the pumpkin into the

That's Jacked Pumpkin Ale. At one point the entire brewery smelled like pumpkin pie. I also made the Apple Pie Sangria, since it had run out. While there, I got to visit with some of our amazing guests that I haven't seen in so long. Truly, the human connection is wonderful and something I have missed since March. It's been in limited quantity, but it seems people are starting to come out and be around more, even though cautiously, and it warms my heart.

Tonight I made my husband dinner, which is something we haven't done in a while. I knew he was working hard brewing, so I wanted to have dinner ready for him. I made some delicious boneless pork chops with BBQ Applewood rub and corn on the cob. I made both in the oven and it was delicious. I felt good that he had a good meal to eat when he got home.

Now on to tomorrow, it is back to work. I've got lots to do and lots of ideas for business and myself. It's a new dawn, a new day, and I'm feeling good!

Here's to a great week ahead!

September 21, 2020

Today was a great day, although any day is great because we are alive!

My day started by meeting with my amazing friend Valerie. Val gifted me with some beautiful tea pots for my shop and I can't wait to use some of them for photo shoots, too. I am truly so blessed!

I worked in my tearoom today. It was a nice day to get some computer work done. I needed to go through our online store for teas and make sure that everything is set up right. I also added our Fall teas and all I have left is to add the Fall sampler.

During the early afternoon, I took some time to go get a massage. I've been trying to make it a habit to go weekly to work on my neck muscles. Today my massage therapist and dear friend told me that my mobility in my neck this week was so much better than last week. She was able to get in there and do some deep tissue massaging. We don't know if it's because I was there last week or if it's because it wasn't the end of the day. Either way, it felt good and I'm looking forward to more work next week.

Tonight Bryan and I enjoyed a delicious culinary experience at one of our favorite restaurants, Thai Bistro. Au, the wonderful owner fixed us a homemade Thai meal, something that she makes for herself when she wants a traditional meal. We happen to have a conversation with her and her husband last week when we were there for dinner. Bryan had asked her about traditional Thai meals verses Americanized Thai meals. So tonight we made plans to try what she enjoys. We left the menu up to her, and it was something like we've never experienced.

For those of you who know me, I am a very picky eater. I don't do a lot of vegetables and the only seafood I do eat is snow crab. I knew this was going to be an adventure for me, but I was going in with an open mind.

I don't recall all the names of every dish we enjoyed but I can tell you, they love flavor and spice in their food. It's absolutely delicious the way the flavors explode in your mouth. There's just no experience like it.

We started with salmon salad. They marinate the salmon in lime and seasoning and serve it raw, in chunks on a salad with a delicious dressing of shallots, garlic and spices. Now, I was apprehensive of raw salmon, I don't even like cooked salmon, but oh my gosh! The salmon literally melted in my mouth, like a deliciously tender piece of steak. I was expecting it to be fishy, but with the marinade and dressing there was no fish taste at all.

Our second dish was a fruit salad with seasoning and juices of other fruits. The fruit on the plate absorbed the tart juices and it was so fresh and delicious. I especially liked the apples and strawberries.

The third dish was a sliced steak with the most flavorful dipping sauce. Again, the flavors were amazing and the heat melded so beautiful with the medium steak, making the flavors just explode in your mouth. It was slightly hot but in a good way. I especially liked this dish, not only because of the beef, but because of the spices and flavors that built on my palate. We actually brought home the sauce to use it as a marinade for some boneless ribs I'm making later this week.

Our fourth dish was a warm and lemony salmon soup. Now, if you didn't know it was salmon, you would have thought it was chicken. The broth cooked the salmon so it was moist and tender, but again no fishy taste. I especially loved the broth! In Thai food, they use a lot of lemongrass, and the addition of it in this soup makes it very fresh and light.

The final dish was a curry dish with vegetables and shrimp. Bryan enjoyed the shrimp and I enjoyed the sauces. It was served with jasmine rice, which was yummy.

Overall, this culinary experience was wonderful. I love that Au explained all the dishes, told us how she made them, named the ingredients, and shared her love of them. The flavors that they build in their traditional meals are absolutely delicious. Truly, it was an experience that you rarely get, but we have grown accustomed to as we frequent smaller 'mom and pop' restaurants. I will probably never visit Asia, but tonight I had a great appreciation for how they build flavors and enjoy using spices and foods we don't traditionally see. I can't wait to do another culinary experience with them in a few months. Until then, we will enjoy our regular Thai food because even that food has delicious flavors!

September 23, 2020

Today was a nice day for a day off that I worked. I got to sleep in a little, which always seems like a good idea while it's happening, but then it puts a wrench in the day and I always wake up a little groggy.

Today, instead of going to Tampa to visit a tearoom that is closing, and looking for furniture for the salt room, I decided to stay closer to home and get things done. For the past few days my neck has been giving me a little grief. Not so much pain, but just bobbly and unstable, so I didn't think it would be wise to take a long distance to Tampa right now.

No, instead I decided to tackle the tea closet. I know my team has been working to keep our inventory updated, but every now and then I get to the point where I need to look for certain teas and have a hard time finding them. So, for four hours this afternoon, my mom and I pulled every tea out of the closet and our cabinet, refilled, restocked, made inventory reports, and got it organized. It was a lot of back and forth and I walked a lot, according to my watch, but now it's done. Now I feel like I have a little more understanding about where we are and I feel really accomplished.

Tonight I had my Tea Mastermind meet up. There are only a few of us, but I get so much out of getting together with these ladies. As stressful as so many things are in business, there's something about conversing with your peers. Each time we get together the organizer asks us about our 'sparkles.' I love that part of our conversation because we can talk about things we are doing. It reminds me of the good things I am working towards and how far I've come in my business. Tonight, I talked about how our Halloween tea sold out in less than twenty-four hours and it's still thirty-five days away. I talked about our tea and cheese pairing, our partnership with Cabot Creamery to make that happen, and about the Riviera Room which will open soon. It's funny how in the day to day we often forget about the extraordinary things we are doing.

After my meet up I came home and had every intention on ordering dinner out, but I forgot I had bought ground chicken, so I made us homemade tacos. After all, it is taco Tuesday right? Bryan was at the brewery kegging the IPA, so I had time to get it ready before he got home. It wasn't a fancy dinner, but it was nice and home cooked. Tomorrow night I'm going to plan another meal. It is so much healthier and less expensive than eating out, for now.

I hope everyone has a great evening.

September 23, 2020

I'm just not sure how I ever got so blessed to have this life. Truly, I know not everything is perfect, but whose life is? Not even a celebrity or the wealthy have everything perfect all the time. My life is pretty close to as perfect as it can be.

Today I was able to take my time getting up and getting around for work. I knew what I was going to wear and what my morning had in store, for the most part. It did take me four tries to get my hair up, but if that's the worst of it, I'm lucky!

Everything at the shop ran well today. I had the pleasure of enjoying tea in the tearoom with my friend Nancy. We talked about business and how to transition it to be more viable in today's world, and to what we want it to be. In today's world it's been called a pivot. Businesses need to do it and there really is a science to it. I know she is going to continue to be successful and I'm glad I get to watch what she does!

I also had a visit from my most lovely friends David and Midge. Have I told you how much I love them? Truly, they kind of adopted me when I was just getting involved in our community and they have been amazingly supportive of me ever since. Today they brought me another adorable teapot for my collection. I am going to get them out this week and take photos so you can see them. They are tiny and oh so colorful. I wish I had about a hundred of them, so I could put them all over my Christmas tree. They are just so cute!

I didn't stay late at the tearoom today. For the last few days by neck has been giving me more spasms and the nerve on the left side of my neck is pinched. After holding my head up for a few hours at work it becomes more painful and more of a bobble head. Today it was quite intense so I decided to go home and rest once we closed. I'm glad I did.

Tonight Bryan and I enjoyed dinner at Sip on Grand with the moms. I enjoy going there because the food is delicious, the atmosphere is unique and modern, and there are great people there. Sean is doing an amazing job with the place and I am so happy for his success. Tonight we enjoyed several flatbreads, a charcuterie board, and a Panini. All were equally delicious and provided us a great variety for dinner.

A few weeks ago, while we were visiting one of our other favorite restaurants, we had a conversation with our bartender/waitress. She's gotten to know us pretty well over the past few months. In our conversation we started talking about what we enjoy doing. She told us that we seemed like people who really liked nice things, and like to try new things, like foodies who like really good and unique places to eat. Well, now looking back I think she was right. I really love looking for a great place that combines my love of a tremendous customer experience and beautiful atmosphere with good food and drinks. I'm sure you're all thinking... no kidding...LOL.

So, I figured since I share my day with you, including multiple facets, like dinner, I'm going to share my photos and impressions of places I visit too. It won't be all the time, but I will gladly continue to share them on my profile when they become part of my adventure.

We are in the homestretch of the week, my friends! Until tomorrow...

September 24, 2020

Today was an interesting day in our tearoom. We had a few tables, but it wasn't too crazy. One table definitely kept us on our toes and almost made Dawne jump off a ledge. Never have I had anyone carry their teapots out front to the gift shop to ask for refills, especially when our tea hostess was standing in the tearoom. It was a comedy of errors, a guest wanting to be VIP but not understanding tea etiquette. We have that from time to time but not frequently. We doted on them and gave them the best time they ever had, and while I'm not sure if they will visit us again, they were happy and singing our praises when they left. The party came from St. Pete and Palm Harbor and admitted they had never done anything like tea before. Dawne recovered beautifully and no one but us was the wiser.

Tonight I came home and had every intention of working on my house early. Truthfully, I was so tired that I sat down with an ice pack on my neck and dosed for two hours. I hate that because when I got up at 6:30 p.m., I had that dreaded groggy feeling.

I finally did get to work and got lots of laundry done. I got all of my dresses hung back in our mini-closet and even got a part of the kitchen cleaned. I still have a long way to go for just that one room, but I'm glad I got it started.

My goal is to make my house look like a model home by Christmas. You know the kind you see in magazines and go, "I want my house to look like that." I know I probably won't get the outside done, but I'm thinking I will be much happier if I can get the inside done. I mean, let's be honest, we are never here anyway. Why do we have so, so, so much stuff? I'm starting to make piles and just get rid of things. I want my house to be beautiful and simple and when people walk in I want them to be in awe, for it being so tiny.

Yes, Bryan and I have a tiny house. Well, not technically a tiny house. Did you know that to be classified as a tiny home you have to be five hundred square feet or less? In our defense, we are six hundred and fifty-seven square feet. If our house was a one bedroom instead of a two, we would technically be considered "tiny". Regardless, it's tiny by today's standards, but we live like we are in 1,200 square feet. So now you can see my hardship, and why I'm just done with all this stuff! Don't be surprised if I make a ton of piles to get rid of and my mom or Dawne decide to come over and have a sale with all of it. I've already told them they could keep the money, just get rid of it, LOL. So, that's my mission when I am home…create a beautiful model home that we barely live in but is pretty when we are here.

Before I start to work on the next space I will be sure to take pictures, so you can see the before and after. It's really amazing how much stuff you can accumulate!

Well, on that note, I'm turning into bed. Hopefully I'll rest well and tomorrow after work I can get a little more done!

September 25, 2020

My day was really good. There wasn't any one thing that made it stand out—just everything seemed to flow along for the most part.

The gift shop did decent today, but the tearoom was very slow. I think it was giving us a break before tomorrow, when we welcome over thirty-five guests for tea. What started at the beginning of the week as looking slow turned into a full day.

Since the announcement came down about being able to increase capacity, we are now able to accept a few more guests than before. While that makes me happy, I am also keeping staff and guest safety my top priority. It is not my goal to pack my tearoom, but merely welcome guests and put out as many tables as we can safely. We are not going to sit groups near each other, and we are going to do our best to continue to keep space between parties to keep them safe.

One thing we will be able to do is open our parlor area back up. I am excited about being able to accept walk-ins for happy hour and cream tea again. Yea! I plan to make that announcement to our guests next week.

This afternoon I had a few friends visit me in the tearoom. First was my friend Dawn who came for a visit. I am so excited for her upcoming adventures. She is a strong and courageous woman, and I truly love the time we get to spend together. She is a beautiful soul, always so happy, sweet and caring. I consider it a privilege to be able to call her a friend.

Later in the afternoon, my girl Melanie stopped by. Oh boy, get her and I together and things go to another level! Truly, I needed a girl's day today and did we have fun chatting! I know I'm around people every day and I talk to many friends, but sometimes I just need girl time and Mel is my girl.

I even ended up at dinner with her and her husband George, who is a good sport, and my mom. First we couldn't decide where to go and then after looking at Facebook and seeing Boris and Carrabba's chocolate cake dessert, that clinched the deal for us. It was off to Carrabba's for a nice dinner. Boris was there and it was so good to see him. He's always so nice to us and everyone there. I'm blessed to call him a friend.

Dinner was fabulous and we laughed and talked like old times— you know pre-COVID. It felt normal again— whatever that is. All I know is it felt good and is something

I truly missed. I know that it may take some time for things to get back to normal, if they ever will, but that's okay. As long as I can cautiously spend time with my friends in safe environments, then my heart will be full, because that's what I missed without knowing I was missing it.

I hope you all have a great Saturday!

September 27, 2020

It's been a nice two days, for the most part. The tearoom was really nice yesterday and it seems that we are really hitting our stride with a smaller staff. Working more efficiently has been really good for us. As we get busier we find that we are running out of room in our kitchen...that's a problem for another day.

I am not sure if I shared my revelation about my goal for my tearoom. Over the next few months I want to build us up so we become the "Ritz Carlton" of tearooms. I want our place to be the 'it' place in the Tampa Bay area. The goal is to be completely swamped and creating these beautiful gatherings and memories for our guests. I want to be the place that people have to bring guests when they visit, not just in our area but the entire region. I don't think it's too much to ask. It's going to take some time to build but that's what I'm working for. I want us to be so busy. Now it's time to get myself to work.

Today, I did my run to Restaurant Depot. I had to look at some things for our new evening venture, The Riviera Room. I was able to pick out some amazing desserts and other things to offer. This week we have our health inspector coming in to sign off on us having beer and wine. Then comes approvals from the city and state, so we can get our license and get open at night with wine! I'm so excited to add this new option to our existing business! I hope to open it in the next few weeks.

This afternoon and tonight I did a lot of relaxing and some reading. I hurt my back earlier today, I pulled it out at the hip bone area and it has been hard to do any walking or bending. Couple that with constant small muscle spasms in my neck, and today has been a fun day! I'm hoping a good night's sleep is all I need to function a little better tomorrow. I can't take being down for two days.

Here's hoping our week gets off to a good start!

September 28, 2020

Today was a very relaxing and comfy day for me. I took my time getting up and actually started my day by doing emailing and other work from bed. I know that probably sounds crazy, but when my body hurts, it feels so much better lying down. With my back hurting and my neck giving me issues, I thought it would be best to lie down while I could.

By the time I got up and around, I checked to see if I could go to my massage early. Thankfully she said 'yes.' I knew if I could just get there that I would start feeling better. Boy was I right! A little work on my lower back and I was as good as new. She also did some extensive work on my neck and the nerve isn't inflamed right now. Yea. Now, with the neck I know it won't last too long, but I'm glad for some relief.

Today I actually got several things done that I wanted to do. First was a trip to Bed, Bath, and Beyond to get some new rugs for the house. It wasn't until I was looking back at some old photos that I realized we have had some of these kitchen and bathroom rugs for ten years. Ten years! It was definitely time for new. Also, I had to grab some plates so I could get ready to take some photos of desserts for promo for the Riviera Room. The bonus was that we found a beautiful photo that we are going to use as our base for the salt room.

After that, I ran to Jo-Ann's to grab some cake supplies, and I ended up finding a cute fall mug for a tearoom photo, and two funny pairs of socks for my husband. Lately he's been into crazy socks, so I got him a t-rex trick or treating that says 'trick roar treat.' If you know my husband, he often says he's a t-rex because he has shorter arms, LOL. He can't ever reach the bill at a restaurant. The second pair was for Thanksgiving and they have a corn cob on them and say 'so corny.' LOL, I'm so glad he likes crazy socks and that he has a sense of humor! Overall, it turned out to be a good shopping day.

Tonight we ventured to Tarpon Springs to Johnny's Taphouse & Grill for dinner. Our favorite waitress, Molly, took good care of us like she always does.

Now, I have to share something really impressive with you. We thought we would stay and watch the first period of the Lightning game and we did. But something happened in that place as the game was getting ready to start. The announcers said they were going to sing the national anthem and the sound for the game was on all the speakers. When the woman started singing, everyone in the restaurant stopped, except one crying child whose father finally grabbed and told her to be quiet and listen to our song. I'm not kidding, I mean everyone. Staff stood still and people stopped talking…a surreal moment in a small bar and restaurant, in a world at each other's throats, and a year that has this far been pretty much something you would read in a sci-fi novel. It showed me that regardless of how far apart we are in political views, we all, or almost all, most love this country. It's unwavering and it's something we all need to remember. We all have the same goals and dreams. Yes, our paths may be different, but we have the same end in mind. For goodness sake, Bryan and I can never agree on the best path to our destination. Maybe if we remembered this, the word compromise wouldn't be such a hard pill to swallow—maybe we can all continue to stop when our national anthem is played, and show our love for the amazing place we live.

Ok, so now that I've said all that, I only have one more thing to say. I've been a Lightning fan since 1994. My brother and I were even on the front page of the then St Petersburg Times when the Lightning went to the playoffs for the first time in history. Bolts, we love you, we thank you for giving us hope in what has been a rather bleak year, and we want you to win for us just as much as you want to win for you. So, let's get this done!

September 29, 2020

Today was one of those days that, while I did a lot, most of the day was a disappointment—not all, there were some good moments. Therefore, I'm going to share my day with you but my momma taught me if I can't say something nice, not to say anything at all. Heeding that advice, I will not share names or places. So, here's my day…

I arrived at my tearoom about 10 a.m. I had the goal of doing a few errands around town before my mom and I headed out to Val's Home Decor near Tampa. We wanted to go there because we are working on ideas for our Halloween tea and instead of waiting until the last minute, we are starting now.

My mom is my driver these days since I can't go more than a few miles without neck pain or spasms. So we head out, get gas in the truck, stop at our jewelers, and run through the bank drive thru to do some deposits. Then we headed to Tampa.

Our first stop of the day was to a tearoom that is closing. It was the first tearoom I had ever visited, and the one that helped me fall in love with the act of afternoon tea. I remember it being everything I wanted my place to be—a gift shop, an elegant tearoom, an escape from the crazy world outside. So I don't know why I was so disappointed when I visited today. First off, they are only doing tea to go, so the tearoom is closed for good. As I looked around their shop, I was shocked at how much stuff they still had, merchandise that just doesn't move. Over the years I have really worked to carry merchandise that guests want. We tend to turn over inventory quite a bit, but so much of what was there is what I remember from years ago. I'm sad to see them go because I think we need all the tearooms we can get, but my rose-colored glasses were off when I went there today.

Our next stop was IKEA. We had two goals there. First was to look at some plates for the Riviera Room, which we found and I brought home to give them a try. Second was looking for chairs for the salt room. All the chairs we have found are extremely expensive, so I was hoping IKEA would have something we could use that would be comfortable for our guests. I was really wishing we would have some luck, but no. That was strike two. Now it's back to the drawing board since I really don't want to resort to those anti-gravity chairs.

After IKEA, we were starving so we ran over to a local brewery for lunch. I'm not much of a beer drinker, which is the understatement of the year, but I enjoyed their Purple Drink that was a sour. The only problem with sours for me is they tend to hit me later—as in the sourness hurts my jaw later. Of course, today was no exception, so as we were heading back home I could feel the sharpness on my jaw. It wasn't bad but a little uncomfortable.

While we were at the brewery, we ordered lunch. It was okay, but the server forgot to put our order for a pretzel in so we didn't say anything. The burger was so tiny that I had quite a bit of bread left over, and the fries were so crispy we couldn't eat most of them. I was disappointed because the last few times I was there for lunch, pre-COVID, it was so good and it's always been my go to when I'm down near IKEA.

In the way back we stopped at Val's, the original reason for our journey. We found a few things and then headed to another place to look for some more items for our centerpieces. We did much better at the second place, but by then it was pouring down rain and time to go home, so we didn't get to look around too much.

Tonight I had my weekly Tea Mastermind meet up. While the day didn't go as I had planned, knowing I was meeting up with my tea peeps online made the evening better. Tonight we tasted teas sourced from Vietnam and one of the group's members conducted the online tea tasting with us. It was so enjoyable and is one of the reasons that I look forward to Tuesday evenings.

Despite my disappointment in a place I used to look up to so much, stores not having what I'm looking for, and subpar lunch, the day is now a wrap.

Here's to a great day tomorrow, with great guests and delicious tea!

September 30, 2020

After yesterday being a disappointing and weird day, I wasn't sure what today would bring. You know how you get into a rut or something, and it seems to last for a few days...

My morning started off ok. I must have overdone it yesterday with my neck, so I had a hard time getting up today. It felt so good to lay and not have the pressure on my head, or my neck cranking in one direction. Getting around wasn't too bad, I just had to move a little slower. It wasn't until I went to drive that my neck issues started. I get really tense and my neck spasms when I try to look left. And I have to look left—I can't pull out into traffic and not look left, LOL. Unfortunately, at some point I have a feeling that I am going to need a driver, so that I don't put myself in harm's way or get to a point where I'm stuck and can't drive.

The tearoom was quite busy today. It's weird, but from the minute I got there I was busy. I helped in the kitchen, helped set up the tearoom, and did odds and ends. I didn't even get a chance to sit down until the 12 p.m. seating was almost over. Not that it's a problem, but it was just weird stuff all day—people in, conversations, helping guests, visiting with tearoom guests. Overall it was a great day, just weird.

Tonight Bryan and I enjoyed a nice dinner together. We talked and shared about our days. I told him how I really enjoyed that we weren't running around for a few nights. I think that's one of the reasons why I liked the brewery closed a few nights a week. I know it won't last but it was nice.

Tonight, when we came home, we opened up the house for the first time this Fall. It was so nice to have some fresh air, and have it be a little cool so I could use a blanket. It reminded me of being up in Tennessee. That reminds me, a month from now and we will be back up there. I can't wait!

Well, here's to tomorrow, another day where I hope the weirdo feeling is finally lessening.

October 2020

October 2, 2020

I felt like my day was run, run, run! From the moment I got into the shop it was go.

I had lots of things I had to get done today. I had to run to the bank, post office, and Mmmm Delicious Cupcakes, all for the shop. Then I had to do some general office stuff, like print more tea sampler packets. We have been selling a lot of our Fall samplers and I needed to get caught up. This afternoon we had a virtual meeting with our copyright attorney for the brewery. We've got to get our ducks in a row.

Honestly, it seems like these days I am never caught up. We are constantly chasing after it and are never getting a break. While I'm thankful for being so busy, I really just need a few days where we can get caught up again. I just don't know how to get to the point of being caught up. And honestly, I feel like I'm just treading water. It's exhausting.

While the tearoom wasn't too busy today, we did have quite a few tables, so that was good. Every day when we have guests in, it reminds me how special our place is, and how blessed we are to have such wonderful guests. It's a reminder about why we do what we do. Providing such a beautiful environment and experience and having our guests enjoy it gives me drive to keep going.

This afternoon we had the power turned on at our new location for the salt room. We had to go over and look at a few things and get the air turned on. Turns out I think the thermostat is bad and we need to get a new one.

Still, I ended up running Bryan back and forth between that location and the brewery to get more batteries to try. That was a big mistake—after the first trip my neck started having major spasms. It was so bad at one point that my head got stuck looking to the right and I couldn't move it. I haven't had spasms like that in a while. So I finally made it home and got an ice pack on it and tried to relax. The only time I ever get the muscle to truly relax is when I'm sleeping, so I took a nap. That helped and it finally started feeling better.

Tonight, my girl Lisa, and her beau, who is so nice, were at the brewery, so I decided to run up there and visit with them. Our friend Jean was there too. We didn't stay long, but it was nice to be out with friends. My husband even bought me two drinks! I have missed spending time with my gals and friends. One thing that I can say is I don't go hang out at the brewery because it's not in me to sit there. Also, my husband is working, so I don't want him to worry about me. However, when I find out some friends are there, it gives me people to hang out with, and I enjoy being there. I've missed that over the last six months and I'm so blessed I have friends I can meet up with.

Well, here's to a nice Saturday! Hoping you have a great start to a great weekend!

October 4, 2020

It was another normal day at the tearoom. Actually, the gift shop was quite busy today. We sold quite a bit of boba tea and our amazing William Dean Chocolates. I'm always pleasantly surprised when guests come for those items. It means we have made some really good decisions on additional items for our shop.

This afternoon I ran over to the brewery for a few minutes. Mostly it was to take some paperwork over, but it was good to visit with some of our guests there too. I'm so glad that the brewery was busy, safely busy, but I might add a bit crazy. After being closed so long it has been quite an adjustment to seeing people around. I know my husband loves it and so does his team, so that makes me happy.

Tonight was a quiet evening at home. I didn't bring any work home and I didn't do much except relax. I did watch a movie and I made my favorite cheap girl dinner—

ramen. I know, I bet your wondering how I can eat that, but I love ramen. I even get my special soup bowl and chop sticks out that I got from Epcot Japan and use it. It makes me feel a little more sophisticated when eating such an inexpensive meal. I actually thought about this and I'm sure if I had a dining room table to eat dinner at then I might actually fix dinner. But the truth is, in this little house we have snack trays and eat in the living room, so eating things like ramen seems perfectly acceptable. Also, my husband hates ramen, so I enjoy eating it on the nights he's at the brewery. So there you have it, my cheap dinner story, LOL.

Tomorrow I am attending the online conference for the US League of Tea Growers and I'm excited to see what is going on with tea growing in the US. Exciting times, I can't wait to share more with you.

Have a great Sunday!

October 5, 2020

What a good Sunday. Despite the rain and crummy weather, I still managed to get a lot done and feel good about what I can accomplish tomorrow.

My day started with breakfast at Rose's Bistro with my mom. Bryan couldn't join because he was brewing and gets started on that pretty early. He did reap the benefits of my leftovers though. Yum, yum!

Mom played my chauffeur again today and took me to Home Depot. I had to get a new thermostat for the salt room, so I picked that up along with a few other things. I was totally surprised to see that they had all their Christmas stuff out already. But then again, nothing should surprise me, it's 2020!!

This afternoon I attended the virtual conference of the US League of Tea Growers. It was our annual business meeting and it was great catching up with the league members. Angela is doing a great job moving the league forward and I look forward to helping her and the league in the future, however I can. I really feel it's vital for the US to have a strong tea farming community as getting commodities from foreign countries may prove more difficult in the future as demand grows. Very exciting times! Also while I was virtual, I was also able to get two hundred and fifty packages ready for stuffing to go out to our Sips By subscription service. Double tasking, go me!

After my conference, I stopped over to the brewery for a little bit. Bryan was brewing the blonde today and all went well thanks to some brewing help from Jeff. I'm glad the brewery is on track to keep taps full and keep our customers happy. That's so important.

While I was at the brewery, I chatted with my friend Michelle. You know, usually I'm running in and out of there, so I don't get to visit much. We chatted and she asked about the salt room. So I thought, what better time than now to give an update...we secured our unit in September, power is on, and the architect just got back to us with our plans and some minor changes. Once we get that finalized, hopefully this week, we can apply for grants and permits! I know I probably don't seem as excited as I should be and it's because I know the work ahead of me.

The pressure to keep two extremely positive and successful businesses going strong without losing quality, while developing an entirely new one seems like something only a lunatic would do at this point. Here I am—the lunatic. Not to mention, I have a lot of apprehension on how the salt room will be handled. It's no secret that the tearoom is demanding on me and my team and that leaves little to no time to run another business. So I'm going to have to put my trust in someone to do what I would do and that is very scary to me. Finding that person I can trust to treat my guests awesome is going to be hard. Does anyone have any suggestions? In all seriousness, I know it's going to be a success...it just scares me. I need to push through it...how is yet to be determined.

      Here's to a productive and prosperous week for all of us.

October 5, 2020

      Man, I must have really slept wrong last night because my neck was so, so, so sore this morning. In fact, moving to get around was difficult. Of course I managed to get around, but not without issues. I even debated if it was really worth leaving the house. Couple that with a screaming headache caused by outside pressure and sinus issues, and I was a sight for sore eyes today. Of course, I pulled myself together and pushed on.

      I had a massage scheduled and that was my saving grace today. I was able to get a little relief in the muscles in my neck. Truly it was perfect timing, like by body knew it was time. And while it helped, I felt like a bobble head and that I was off all day.

      That doesn't help when I have all these hopes and plans to get things done on my Mondays and Tuesdays. Once they come around, I'm usually so exhausted and don't get half of what I want done. It's a little disheartening and depressing. In fact, I can't really think of anything I got done that was productive. Ugh!

      I did get to my jewelers to pick up a ring that I had resized. It was my grandfather's wedding band and it means the absolute world to me to be able to wear it. He was the first man who ever loved me and I just loved him so much. I miss him every day. I've had the ring since he passed away and it was so big I couldn't do anything with it. I finally decided to get it sized and they were able to size it down to fit on my thumb. It fits perfect and looks so good next to the ring that I wear that was my grandmother's.

Tonight, we went over to the salt room. I purchased a new thermostat for the A/C unit and Bryan wanted to get it installed. Turns out it didn't work, and we think it's because there isn't power to the thermostat, as the old one was battery. We will have to get with the landlord and get the A/C company out to look at it. I'm excited about getting things started there so we can get it open. I'm hoping to have our website and Facebook up and running in the next two weeks and be able to start pre-selling packages for salt room service. I can't wait to get that done!

Other than that, I don't think I did anything worth mentioning. I have a lot on my plate tomorrow. I have to get a mailing out, take photos, and work on my newsletter. I know there's a lot more than that, but if I can get just a little bit done, it will have been a success. Hopefully I sleep better tonight and don't wake up tomorrow in pain like I did today. Here's praying!

October 6, 2020

I learned this morning that I can get quite a bit of work done from my bed and I'm not in nearly the amount of pain then when I'm up. That doesn't mean I can spend all day in bed, although some days I wish I could. Now I'm learning a little more about how I can deal with this neck thing. So, if I go to bed earlier, get good sleep, and then when I wake up I spend some time in bed before getting right up, the pain doesn't set in right away. It's the darn weight of my head that causes the bobble and ultimately the pain. I'm actually amazed how much I can get done when I'm not dealing with the pain.

This afternoon I attended a work session about our town's master plan. It was good to give my input, along with others, so we can work toward a common goal to keep making our town great. I'm very excited about the future.

After my meeting, I was able to get the mailing done that I wanted to get out. I got it all addressed and stamped and it's ready to go for tomorrow. Yea, there's one thing off the list.

Tonight, I finalized my tea and cheese pairing for tomorrow. Yum! I'm really looking forward to sharing what I have come up with and having our guests try the different pairings. It's actually self-guided after I go over some basics, so it will be a relaxing night. Hey, anything that combines my love of tea and my love of food makes me happy.

I also had my weekly tea mastermind meeting. I truly love those meetings. Tonight we talked about tea and origins and what's important when we present about tea. I love that part—I love being around my tea peeps because it helps me with my self-esteem and my confidence in my business and the tea world overall. There are days when I feel a little down and out about what I do, and need a little motivation. My tea group really helps keep me going and moving in the right direction, something invaluable.

Well, here's to the start of a good week in the tearoom—mid-week for most of you. Fingers crossed!

October 7, 2020

As if 2020 couldn't throw any more curve balls, here comes more...

I know you know about the issues with my neck. I keep working and praying that it gets better but I have days when just getting out of bed is chore enough. Added to that the hormone issues I've had for about ten years...like I haven't had any hormones. All of the sudden this week, for some unknown reason, I have a ton of hormones doing weird things. Hot flashes and so many other things...Bryan thinks it's kind of funny, but also feels my pain and has been really good about taking care of me not feeling 100%

because of it. Truly, I feel fine except hormone things, it's always something.

Today I dealt with sweating, being hot, and just overall being uncomfortable. Seriously, how does this happen at forty-two! After ten years of nothing. I used to think I was lucky my hormones stopped early. I was glad I didn't have to deal with this for the past ten years, it was my silver lining. Ugh!! Thank goodness I work with an understanding crew and they always help out extra when I'm not 100%. My team did a great job in the tearoom and gift shop. We were mildly busy during the day and we also had to get ready for our tea and cheese pairing event.

Tonight's event was on the smaller side, but I actually enjoyed that. It allows us to be a little more relaxed and personal with our guests. We get to talk and share more stories with smaller groups, more than when we have a full house. I was really pleased how it worked out and how nice the pairings were. Tea is truly so versatile and I'm glad I was able to share some new pairings with our guests. Yes, tea goes with more things than just tea sandwiches and scones! I'm looking forward to our next pairing event! And maybe in the meantime, I will write a blog or two for my tearoom website about pairings. That actually sounds fun!

Tonight, Bryan and our friend Travis fixed our gate out back at our house so we can stop parking in the front yard. It was kind of self-serving, why we wanted to stop parking out front. It's Halloween season and we have some awesome blowups that we can't put up when our cars are there. I'm also kind of hesitant to put them up because we will be downtown on Halloween and we won't be handing out candy at home. I guess we need to make sure we don't turn our displays on Halloween night.

Speaking of Halloween, we have a Halloween tea on Wednesday, October 28 and I'm trying to come up with some unique displays for outside the entrance of our tearoom so our guests can take pictures before they come for tea. If anyone has any ideas—old carriage, hearse, a display for photos, etc.—please let me know. I'm so excited about this year's tea and I want to make it awesome! I have a few things planned, but I want to add more to make this extremely fun!

Well, it's time to turn the brain off for now. I'm sure I'll have more ideas soon, but tonight I just need a little break. Hoping I stay cool and sleep well. Seriously, how do these women do it who don't have A/C? I'm so glad I live in this time! Looking forward to a good Thursday ahead!

October 8, 2020

Today I slept in late. Well, I was up early, but was still tired so I went back to bed and ended up hitting the snooze button for almost 2 hours! I was shocked, but apparently, I needed it.

With my day starting off so late, it was a little weird. I don't know if it's because I got going so late, but it was like I just couldn't get my day to click. I did some work, but it felt like I was in a haze. That's probably from all the snoozing, LOL.

This morning, I put a pork tenderloin into the crock pot. I actually started marinating it 2 days ago and we have been so busy that we haven't had time to grill it. Today I figured better get it cooked. Finally, a plan for dinner that we aren't trying to figure out at 8 p.m.! What a concept!

I did finally hit my stride at the tearoom around 2 p.m. and was able to get some social media stuff done for our two new ventures. I still need to get a few photos to beef up our presence, and I have to get our salt room website going. I hope to send the Facebook pages live in the next few days. Yea! Here we come—Riviera Room and Coastal Salt Room!

Tonight, I came home to a delicious dinner of seasoned pork tenderloin cooked in the crockpot, mashed potatoes, and gravy. It was fabulous and it was nice for Bryan and I to sit down and have dinner before he went to the brewery, as I wouldn't see him until really late tonight. Hey, I'll have dinner with him whenever I can as long as I'm not cooking at 9 p.m.! I don't mind being an early bird. LOL!

After Bryan headed out, I decided to get ambitious. While I seem to have lots of things together in my public life, my private life is far from it. Not that it's too bad, but it's just complete chaos and a mess, the house included. Because we don't spend a lot of time there, we tend to set stuff down and not take care of it, which can lead to lots of stuff we don't need and an abundance of accumulated junk. Like, it's a serious problem!! Think of the early stages of hoarding, completely packed but not dirty.

I had this vision of my home, simple and clean and comfortable, but most of all easy to maintain and relaxing to come home to. Right now, it's stressful when I come home. So tonight, I decided to tackle one project. I tackled our mud room/laundry room. I threw away two large garbage bags of stuff, including rugs and such. I purchased new rugs for the room a few weeks ago. I had already cleaned the cupboards in there a while ago, so I was ahead of the game for this project.

Man, I worked up a sweat! Sweat was dripping down my nose, which is probably not the best thing to do when having hormone issues, LOL! Well, now it looks really nice! And now that our back gate is fixed, we are going to start parking out back again, so this room is the first one I see when I get home. It's the cleanest room now. Maybe it will help me feel not so overwhelmed. The rest of the house is going to be much more difficult, so I'm not really looking forward to doing it, but I know I need to for my sanity. I'm truly thinking it's the reason why I don't feel good a lot of times, the stress is brutal.

Well, I have to do some more laundry before I go to bed. Here's hoping your Friday is awesome!!

October 9, 2020

For some reason, I was able to get up at a decent hour this morning. What I mean by that is I was up in the eight o'clock hour and was at my shop by 9:15 a.m. I'll pause for you to get over the shock!

I was able to get some general work done and start working on some other projects by the time my team came in and opened the shop.

I had tea lunch today with my friend Diane. I always love it when she comes to visit me. We talk and laugh and before we know it, hours have passed! Like 3-1/2 hours! I don't even know how we have so much to talk about, but we just get going and the time flies. I mean, it probably helps that I think she's awesome and we have great conversations. I'm so glad she's in my life. I can't wait to try the gorgeous blueberry lemon cookie she brought me from a bakery in Lecanto. I swear I am going to that blueberry farm for lunch with her soon!

I had lots of great visitors today...Jacob stopped in and visited for a little bit. Man, he is running around town constantly and is amazing! And John from Heros came in, too. He was working on a spread that includes the use of our pepper jelly. I guess the reaction to the new spread has been a hit and I can't wait to try it myself.

During my visits today, our state inspector came in and inspected our kitchen. I called him to come and sign our application to allow us to serve beer and wine, which he did when he did our general inspection. Now I need the city and the Florida Department of Revenue approvals, and I will be ready to submit our application. The Riviera Room will be open in just a few weeks. I am excited and can't wait!

Tomorrow I am sampling a few more desserts. It's a tough job but someone's got to do it.

Tonight, I had dinner with a good friend I haven't seen for a few months. I always enjoy our time together! We had Thai and it was delicious as always. So good and consistent! That's so important to me in business.

Well, I had every ambition earlier in the evening to work on my kitchen. I mean, after cleaning up my laundry room, I'm so in love with how nice and pretty it is that I want to do more. But by the time I got home and did some laundry, I was too tired to do any more work. Here's to a new day tomorrow, when I can work on the house after my day at the tearoom. I'm looking forward to getting another space done.

So, Tuesday is wine dinner at Carrabba's. I've heard from a few of my girls that are planning on going. Sorry guys, gals only.

October 10, 2020

Today I managed to sleep in a little with my husband. Honestly, of all the days of the week, Saturday is the one day that he doesn't have to get up early, so today I decided that I should sleep in a little too.

I got to the tearoom just as it was opening. It was going to be a slower day, mainly because this weekend for the past ten years has been the Cotee River Bike Fest, and our tearoom was closed. In fact, looking back we tended to have a slow week this week every year. Then of course we didn't have tea on the weekend, so despite it being slower we had guests in the tearoom, which was good.

Today I worked on getting more tea packaged up for the subscription service. We are really behind, so I thought I would work on it when I had some down time. I was able to stuff 150 bags in my spare time. Tomorrow I am going to try to stuff another 200 so I can get the next batch out. I'm determined to get caught up. Ugh! I have a long way to go!

Tonight, I went to dinner with my mom and her friend Linda. I was craving Carrabba's and even though I will be back there on Tuesday evening for wine dinner, I wanted something different then what we will he having that night. It was good and we had a nice time. Good company always helps! Linda cleaned her China cabinet today, so after I got home, she sent me some photos of her China. Her China sets are beautiful, and one set is Limoges from France. So cool!

The rest of my evening I spent folding laundry and relaxing. I have to go to Largo to our restaurant supplier tomorrow, so I need to rest up. That trip tends to take a lot out of me, and I have a few other things I want to do tomorrow, so I'm hoping I can keep pushing forward.

Here's to a nice Sunday for all of us!

October 12, 2020

Today was quite a good day for getting things done.

My day started with breakfast with my mom at Rose's Bistro. I'm such a creature of habit that I always order the same thing. I do that mostly because I know that when I order it, I know exactly what I'll get.

Then it was on to Restaurant Depot. We didn't have a lot to get, but they were having some sales that I wanted to take advantage of. I was able to pick up what we need for the tearoom for a few more weeks so that was good.

When we got back, my mom and I worked on stuffing bags of tea to send out for the subscription service we are a part of. Within about 40 minutes we had two hundred bags of tea done. Tomorrow I am mailing them out. Then I will only have another five hundred of this tea to package before it's done, and I can start on the next season.

This afternoon, I enjoyed lunch at the brewery. It was brew day so we ordered from Cristiano's pizza, across the street from the brewery. The brew today was the River's Bend Irish Red. That means the Blackwater and Little Italy Stouts came out yesterday and next weekend it will be the Blueberry and Biker Blondes. How exciting! Our taps will be full again! I think Bryan and his team are doing good keeping things up right now. Yea!

After lunch I returned to the tearoom. I had to try out one of our new desserts for the Riviera Room. All I can say is, oh my, a chocolate torte cake. It has a cookie crust on the bottom, and layers of mousse and chocolate cake. It looks like it would be really rich, but it was so nice and light—just what I was looking for to offer. I'm so excited that I am working toward our evening opening.

One of the reasons I have been putting this new evening venture off is because I have been trying to figure out the logistics of making it happen. This is adding a lot of new options to what we do, and I have been struggling to figure out how to do it efficiently. Today, riding back from Restaurant Depot, talking to my mom, I think we figured it out. Now I'm going to explore and research whether my idea will work.

Tonight, I took some downtime for me. Bryan finished brewing and came home around 10:30 p.m. While unwinding we decided to watch the first of a series that was recommended to us. It's called Prohibition by Ken Burns. Oh man, just watching this, it's so similar to what we are going through right now. Especially as they debate people's rights and how far they extend. Yes, they are talking about prohibition, but those same ideals can be applied to today. Crazy! It's funny how the years go by, but the fight only changes slightly. I'm looking forward to the rest of the episodes.

Well, another start to a week is upon us. I hope your week starts out great!

October 12, 2020

What a nice day. I don't often say that, but today it just seemed like a calm and easy flowing day for me. Maybe it's because I was so happy when I went to sleep last night—I'm not sure. Bryan and I had a nice night together—we talked, cuddled, laughed, and spent some quality time together. I felt content when I went to sleep, and I slept really soundly. In fact, I didn't even hear his alarm go off this morning.

Imagine my surprise when I was lying in bed and Bryan comes in and tells me he decided to take the day off to get some things done around the house. I was pleasantly surprised.

We had breakfast at Herschel's and then he helped me get my scanner working so I can scan some documents. Then he went his way, and I went mine. I stayed in my office, did some accounting, worked on a few things, and then spent the afternoon attending the virtual summit for World Tea. It was great and I have so much to share!

On his way, he stopped at Walgreens and picked up meds and bought me my perfume. My grandparents used to buy it for me for my birthday and Christmas and I ran out a few weeks ago. I'm so excited that I get to wear it tomorrow. He also fixed our back gate, so we can park our cars in the backyard. Thanks to our friend Travis for helping. I also mentioned how I wish we had the hot tub cleaned so we could start using it. Can you believe he cleaned the cover off, emptied it, refilled it, and shocked it tonight! Now we will be able to use it tomorrow. I am just so excited! I don't think we have used it in a year or two. We've been too busy. So, I am vowing that we are going to use it to relax now.

After the summit ended, Bryan and I went to dinner at Longhorn. I was craving a steak. I just love it when we have this time to ourselves. Not that I don't love being around people, but we have such good conversations, and we enjoy spending time together. Then we came back and did a few little things around the house.

Tomorrow, I have a few things to do for our beer and wine license, and then a meeting and day two of my summit, followed by wine dinner. It's been two great days in a row. I am vowing to make these great few days continue to be a great week.

October 13, 2020

Well, ever have those days that you feel like you move all day long, but you never really get anything done? That was my day today.

This morning started with a nice massage. I was feeling good this morning, so the massage was just icing on the cake. I find that I have more flexibility in my neck these days, but I'm still dealing with the occasional pinched nerve. It wasn't bad this morning, but it got worse as the day went on. Probably because I had to do some driving and any time I'm behind the wheel of a car, I find that my neck just tenses. I truly wish I could afford a chauffeur.

After my massage, I went to my shop and got another 500 teas bagged up and dropped at UPS. After shipping them off, I grabbed lunch and headed back to my shop.

At 2 p.m., I met my friends from Florida's Sports Coast over at the Richey Suncoast Theatre to introduce them to Melissa, the theatre's awesome director. With the history of the theatre and the amenities it offers, in addition to the amazing new things she is doing there, I can see a great relationship between those two organizations. It has been a long time coming and I'm so happy that, after having a conversation years ago about a partnership with the theatre, others are seeing the value of this great place. I am truly so happy!

This afternoon I also attended the World Tea Virtual Summit. I enjoy watching and learning about industry changes. I just wish we were able to meet in person. It's not the same and while it's nice to learn stuff, there's just something about being able to connect in person.

Tonight was our first wine dinner since spring. Eight of us ladies converged on Carrabba's. It was so good spending time with my mom, Linda, Tara, Ashley, Jillian, Bernice and Elaine. We were missing a few gals for this dinner but look forward to the rest of our gals joining us next time! Thank goodness Boris and his team are such good sports. We had so much fun!!! We laughed, shared stories, drank wine, and enjoyed good food. Truly, while I enjoy the food so much, it's about the time we can spend together, connecting and laughing, that I love the most. I can't wait to enjoy it again. I have missed the human connection.

Now I'm at home, relaxing, and working on labels for more tea. I don't know if I will ever get caught up, but I am sure trying.

Tomorrow is going to be a busy day at the tearoom. We have a full house at our noon seating! It will be the first time in a long time that we are this full. I'm ready for the work! And I am ready to welcome our guests and to start the week off great!

October 14, 2020

Today was one of those days that I dread and look forward to at the same time.

I was at my shop before 9:30 a.m. because it's the first day of the week for us and we were going to have a busy day. Our first seating had twenty-two guests in three different parties. Now, I love days like this, but I want everything to be perfect so it's a little stressful at the same time. Of course, I know our team is awesome, but I also know the more you have going on the more opportunities for mistakes or issues.

The team worked beautifully together, and it seemed like everything just fell into place. Our parties showed up staggered, which allowed us to get them seated and situated before running to the next party. I love it when their timing works out like that.

This afternoon was slower in the tearoom, but I was busy on the virtual conference with World Tea. Today they announced the winners of their annual awards, and I am so excited that some of my friends won in their categories. The tea industry is continuing to evolve, and I am so happy for those who are continuing to move us all forward.

Later this afternoon I had to do some running around. I have an opportunity to design some hot tea cocktails for the winter months. I had to get some glasses with handles to use that would allow for some photos, and I had to get some little props. It's kind of a fun project for me as I love creating and pairing things. It's kind of like what they do with coffee, but with tea instead. Kind of like when you order an after-dinner coffee with some liqueur. The first drink was an Earl Grey and gin hot toddy with fresh orange. I tried it and it was really good. Bryan loved it and drank it quickly.

When I got home tonight, I had a very large delivery sitting in my front yard. It's the first four chairs for the salt room. Now, if we can just get things moving there, we can open quickly. I can't wait to get the chairs put together and try them out! We took them over to the salt room, so that's step one. Also, the plans for the salt room will be signed and ready by Friday. How exciting!

Tonight we enjoyed dinner at Boulevard Beef & Ale. We hadn't been there in a while and thought tonight would be a good time to visit them. We enjoyed their delicious mashed potato appetizer. Bryan enjoyed their pork chop, and I really enjoyed the meatloaf. I totally love mashed potatoes and gravy, so it was a win for me! Thank you, Boulevard Beef & Ale, for the delicious dinner!

Well, off to make some more winter hot drinks! I'm super excited to get these down and have a full tasting tomorrow!!

October 16, 2020

Today ended up going in a different order than what I thought when I got out of bed.

The plan was to work at the tearoom all day, do some errands, and after work, then head to Largo and pick up food and chocolates for the tearoom. Well, I ended up reversing my whole day and it worked out well.

Since the tearoom was slower today, I decided to take the day to get my errands done. I took my mom with me as my chauffer. I had to go to Largo to check on some items for our kitchen. When I was there this weekend, they were out of one of my major food items. They were supposed to get them in yesterday, but they didn't. Now I am left scrambling to figure out a replacement and that's just time consuming. Tomorrow that will be my mission.

Then we ran over to William Dean Chocolates to pick up chocolates for our shop. While there, I chatted with Marsha for a few minutes about desserts as we are still having trouble finding gorgeous show stopping desserts for our dessert room. I also thought, since my day was different, that I would enjoy some of their delicious gelato. Oh my!! I had raspberry cheesecake, and it was amazing! I wish we had a gelato place near us—one that makes it like they do. It was so good.

When we got back to the tearoom, my real work began. I was asked to design a warm cocktail, so I decided to design a few. I felt it was good to have my staff help me because if I had to drink them all, I would be in trouble! I mean, it's one thing to have a drink, but when you are designing a beverage like this, you have to do a lot of sampling to get the right blend. Good thing for me, with my sommelier background, I have learned a lot about flavors and building them together. I didn't have to remake any of the cocktails! My team was wonderful about tasting and talking about the drinks. We also photographed them, so we have a record. I wish we had a way to make these for our guests.

After all that testing, I attended the annual meeting for New Port Richey Main Street that was held at the Richey Suncoast Theatre. It was nice to see what they have done in the past and what they are planning for the future. With the new businesses and all that is going on around us in the city, it's nice to see the organization gaining some momentum.

That was really it for my night. After the meeting, Bryan and I grabbed dinner and then I came home to write up all the recipes I developed. It took a few hours to get that done, so now I'm tired and heading to bed. I'll be ready to tackle another day tomorrow.

Have a great Friday!

October 17, 2020

Oh boy, my day, my day...truly an uneventful one.

So, one thing I realized over the last several weeks is how well my business runs without me there—not every day, but most days I'm not even needed anymore. I don't know if that is something I should be happy or sad about. I mean, I'm happy I have an amazing team, but really, they do what they need to do and rarely need my support to make things run smoothly.

Take today for example. I don't think I really did anything that benefited the team at all. Sure, I ran to the city to get our beer and wine permit signed. Yes, I sat and watched some of the great programs from the World Tea virtual conference to keep up to date on industry happenings. Yes, I scheduled some social media. And yes, I stopped and visited with some guests. Other than that, I've done nothing constructive. I don't know if that makes me happy or sad.

There are so many things I want to do for my business, so many ideas, but I never get to them. So many things I think of doing, to market, to further my influence and contributions to my industry. How do I set myself up to do these great things? I know I'm sure I could really do some great things, but I struggle with taking the time to do them. I'm so good at directing everyone and everything else except myself. Help!

This evening we enjoyed some delicious food at Thai Bistro with some great friends John and Connie. I love going there and tonight it was much needed. I've been stressed out lately and it was nice to just sit and relax and chat. I'm so truly blessed to be surrounded by some great people.

Tomorrow is a busy day in the tearoom. Both seating times are pretty full. We are still under capacity to keep our guests safe, and we continue to be conscious of social distancing, but it's exciting to be seeing so many guests. I'm looking forward to a fun day!

Wishing you a great weekend!

October 18, 2020

Do you ever have those mornings where you wake up and just can't go back to sleep? Yea, so that was me at 6:45 a.m.! Ok, pause for shock because I know I did as I laid in bed wide awake that early. My mind started wandering because I'm still looking for desserts for the Riviera Room. I've been looking everywhere, then it hit me, and the lightbulb went off. I was so excited to get online to see if I had found my solution, but I didn't want to wake Bryan up with my bright phone, so I just stayed in bed staring at the ceiling. After about ten minutes my neck muscles started spasming and my head just shook back and forth. Well, after a few minutes of that I figured I might as well get up and ready for my day.

I couldn't believe it; I got ready, folded laundry and was at my shop by 8:20 a.m., before any of my team—only by a minute. As I was parking, Dawne pulled in. I felt good being there and getting a few things done this morning. We had a busy day on tap and the last thing I wanted was for any of us to start the day stressed out. By being there early and helping, we started the day stress free.

It was a nice day in the tearoom. The hardest part continues to be changing over the room when it's full at noon, and to be ready for the second seating. With the extra cleaning, it's a tight transition. Today I was sweating working to get it done. I think I even drank 1/2 gallon of water. It was all worth it though. As busy as it was, it felt great to be moving and seeing our guests again. Not that it's normal, but it's feeling ever so slightly like that. I just hope it keeps up.

My friend Michelle from Chocolates by Michelle came into the shop today to drop off replenishment chocolates to sell, and a flourless cake for us to try. It smelled and looked amazing, and I can't wait to try it tomorrow. Of course I will take photos. I love that she brought it for me to try! I'm so glad we work together in business. This week I'm also going to try the meals she makes. Hey, anything to get me out of cooking!

Tonight, my mom and I ran to Tarpon Springs for a quick research errand. We didn't stay long, just long enough to get what we needed. Tomorrow the research continues as we look to build our Riviera Room menu. I'm so excited! Truly not just because it's getting closer to opening, but because I have been searching and praying to find what I need to make it spectacular and I'm getting closer.

After our running, I decided to call it an early night. I came home, boiled some chicken, and made my delicious chicken stroganoff. It's like beef stroganoff, but with chicken and a chicken gravy base that I make. I always serve it over pasta. Well, I made a big batch tonight and I know some people who are going to be really happy because they are getting some. It came out delicious and I ate way too much of it. I definitely got my fill, so now I will share it. I also got some laundry and reading done. Though I miss Bryan because he's working at the brewery, I do love that I get a few things done around the house when I'm alone.

Well, tomorrow is taste-testing day—lots of samplings of desserts. I really hope my sugar is low in the morning otherwise it's going to be a rough day. Maybe, if this goes well, I will have to invite some friends to help me sample again in the near future, so I can make my final decisions.

I hope you all have a great and relaxing Sunday!

October 18, 2020

Last night was not a good night for sleeping for me.

Today started off with me waking up at 3:15 a.m. to an empty bed. I called for Bryan, and he didn't answer, so I called his phone and he answered from the living room. I fell back asleep only to be woken up with a cramp in my shin at 5:45 a.m. That caused me to get up and get a hot pack to try to make it go away. Then I finally got up around 8:30 a.m. I'm hoping tonight I get a full night's sleep; I miss those.

I had a nice breakfast with my mom at Herschel's. Then, I was so tired that I went back home and relaxed and took a nap. It was nice to have some downtime midday. I really needed it.

This afternoon I went to the brewery and enjoyed lunch with the crew there. Then I brought over desserts and had some help sampling about a dozen potential offerings for the Riviera Room. Thank you so much to Bryan, Mom, Elaine, Tara and Jeff. I know it was a spur of the moment and it was difficult trying all those desserts, but I do appreciate the feedback in helping me make some decisions. I am really happy about the direction I am going with for this nighttime venture. A little more work and it will be ready to go. I can't wait until November to get the Riviera Room open!

Tonight, Bryan and I got to enjoy the hot tub for the first time in years. I was so good to just sit and relax. I am looking forward to making that a part of our Sunday evening routine to relax before we start the week.

Hope you have a great Monday!

October 19, 2020

What a great day! It wasn't my typical Monday. Normally I am working around my shop getting little odds and ends done. Not today.

Today we had the opportunity to host a TV program in our tearoom for taping. It was an opportunity to share all the great things that are happening in our cool town. It was me and Lisa from Lis's Pieces Artisan Boutique. Since we both were voted Best of the Best, we were tasked with helping to promote our downtown and share why New Port Richey is up and coming. I couldn't think of anyone more perfect to have next to me as we both work together to change our town's image. I think we both did great, and I can't wait to see how the segment turns out. I want to give a huge shout out to Jacob for the opportunity to represent my community!

I also want to give a huge shout out to my amazing team. Dawne came in early and prepared scones and made us the workings of an entire Afternoon Tea. She also helped with setting up the tearoom and getting us tea. My mom also came in and was there to make sure we were taken care of if we needed anything. I felt so good, and we really showed unity and how we all work together. I have had some great opportunities to show off our beautiful place, but it wouldn't be possible without my team. I hope they know how much I appreciate them and what their support does to help keep me pushing us forward. Onward to more great things!

That shoot took up much of the day, and then it rained so I didn't get much else done. That's okay though because I have tomorrow to finish up any loose ends. The tearoom looks like it's going to have a good crowd this week, so I have to get on the ball.

Tonight Bryan and I enjoyed a quiet dinner at Boulevard Beef & Ale. It was delicious and now I'm full, so I'm going to relax for the rest of the night and read some of my tea books. I've really been trying to spend at least thirty minutes reading a day and I love it.

Hoping you are having a good start to the week and that it continues tomorrow.

October 21, 2020

My morning started off relaxing and calm. My neck was giving me a little pain this morning. There is a nerve in my neck that is pinched and any time I lift my head the muscle pulls on the neck, and it creates this pressure and ache that goes through my head. I find it's at its worst in the morning and at night. Once I get used to it during the day, I tend to adjust my movements to limit the pain.

Today I laid in bed until 9:30 a.m. It was nice to doze in and out of sleep, but I always feel bad later when I didn't get up right away and I wasted that time. I'm always torn between getting up and having my neck muscle get more rest. Today, the neck won.

I had a lovely massage today. Phyllis has been my lifesaver through all of this. She keeps me moving, my body functioning, and my neck mobility possible. Today she even did some reflexology on me. I really love that because I can feel certain parts of my body being triggered as if there was sensitivity or blockage. Today she hit the right spot, and I felt my left kidney twinge. There must have been a little issue there because throughout the day I was feeling the same twinge. Nothing strong, just a little pinch and then it was gone.

Today I got a bit of running around done. Well, actually my mom drove, and I was the passenger. We went to the bank and our storage unit to get a bigger unit for the brewery and tearoom to share. I am going to need some help moving things, so, friends beware.

Afterwards, we went to Home Goods where we got some pillows to take to the camper in Tennessee. It will be nice not taking things back and forth for a while. I also found the most adorable unicorn overnight bag for my lovely niece Ava. I met her this afternoon to treat her to Vampire Penguin, since she had a great first day at school, so I gave her the bag. She absolutely loved it, and it made me so happy! It was a really cute bag.

Tonight I attended my Tea Mastermind gathering. I absolutely love that hour of my week. We learned about business etiquette and then talked about our week and discussed our business issues. It was great and I look forward to next week. I have so many things I want to accomplish in my tea world, and I just have to make a start. I also need to figure out where that start is.

One of the first things I have to do is get myself organized. I need to move a ton of books to my upstairs office. Do I have any strong friends that might be able to help me next week on Monday evening? It's just too heavy for me. With my neck I'm not supposed to lift a lot of things. I have a ton of tea books at my home office that I need to have in my work office. I also need some more help moving furniture upstairs. I hate asking for help, but I really need it these days. Gotta get my stuff together!

Tomorrow is a pretty good day in the tearoom and I'm excited about a great week ahead. I hope your week is going well too!

October 21, 2020

This morning, I got up early for me and got into work at a decent time. I knew we had a few tables and a few 'to go' teas today, so I wanted to be prepared and ready.

The tearoom had a good day. It was nice to be busy on a Wednesday. We had other guests stop in, 'to go' teas, and lots of people calling for reservations.

In addition to regular tearoom activities, the team and I got menus set for our Halloween tea on Wednesday, set up a Halloween Day tea event, finished our VIP tea and shopping menu, discussed revamping our tearoom and parlor brochure, and got our tea 'to go' menu updated. I sent projects to the printer and even got my register updated with changes. It was nice getting things done. I'm trying to get prepared for our season, hoping it's going to get back to being a little more regular, like it was before the shutdown.

I'm also trying to get set with some new things at the tearoom. The Riviera Room is coming together, and we have to work on some regulation things for the tearoom. Fun stuff. Not really, it's a lot of work, but it's all for moving our companies forward. I'm not sure how things are going to work out or what our final decisions will be, but it's important to look at all aspects and come up with a solid plan. That's what I'm working through now.

Tonight, Bryan and I enjoyed dinner at Sip on Grand. I enjoyed the ambiance there and we had such a nice time. We even ran into friends who were enjoying their night, too. It's always so relaxing and I'm glad that Bryan and I had some time to ourselves. I know these days will become more limited, so I am enjoying them as much as I can right now.

We are in the home stretch for the week. Let's finish it strong.

October 23, 2020

It was a slow-moving morning, but once I got going, I was good. Today wasn't too eventful, just a normal day doing normal things.

The tearoom was busy today, especially at our 12 p.m. seating. We had all but two tables filled with reservations, and we had tables for happy hour that came in just after 1 p.m. I washed dishes today and I have come to not mind the job. I figure if I'm washing dishes, we must be busy and that's a good thing.

This afternoon I worked on a few little projects that I keep putting off. I had to update our brochures and menus and do a lot of emailing back and forth with people. I still have a crazy list, but I'm slowly working through it. I'm also working on our long-range plan. We are coming up on our five-year anniversary which means my five-year plan is just about up. We accomplished so much on the list, but it's also time to re-evaluate and work on the future.

After work I did some running around. We are getting a system to play music through the tearooms and gift shop.

Instead of having different music in the gift shop and tearoom, it will be the same from room to room. It's something I've wanted to do for a while and now that we are picking up a little more, it's time to do it.

Tonight, I had a low-key evening at home. I did some laundry, but I didn't do much else. I had planned on doing some work, but I really enjoyed just hanging out. I didn't even make dinner...thank goodness for takeout and delivery!

Tomorrow is going to be a great day. Hoping I can keep working through my list and progressing forward. Onward and upward, toward the weekend!

October 23, 2020

Today was an overall good day. I woke up at a decent time and actually made it to work by my goal of 9:30 a.m. It was my hope to head right out to Largo to pick up boxes from William Dean Chocolates for our chocolate case. Well, the best laid plans...we didn't leave until after 11 a.m.

It's no secret that things have been rough for businesses since March. So many of us were on track to have a record year until the rug was pulled out from under us and the doors were locked. Since reopening, we have been very blessed that our guests are slowly coming back. Still, it hasn't been enough to make up for the month we missed, which was in our busy season, so I have been trying to figure out ways to get creative to keep going. At times it has been daunting and downright aggravating. And we still push on.

A little over a week ago I decided to talk to someone I look up to and respect about all that is going on in my business—my concerns, my needs, and my hopes for the future. Today I received some much-needed support and guidance. While I can't say who or what, all I can say is that

I am very excited about some things I can do to create a unique additional dining experience, how we will go about doing that, how we are going to be able to expand what we do in the tearoom, and what capacity we can handle. Sometimes it gets tight in the kitchen with having a full tearoom and it's hard. For the first time in probably six months, I feel like there is hope and excitement for the future, not that I haven't been happy or excited, but this is something I have needed. I can't wait to share as we start to make some small adjustments. After that visit and conversation, I was able to head to get our boxes and pick up a few things at our supply store.

The rest of my day was very nice. I worked on a few little things around the shop and rearranged my dessert case. I even had a visit from my amazing niece who, after her first week back at school, was given a star student award. I am so proud of her and honored that she came to show me her award.

Tonight, I spent a little bit of time at the brewery. I'm not usually there, but I was meeting up with a friend. I just love when I get to spend some time with Diane! Being women in business, we know the struggles we face and it's so nice to have someone to talk to.

After that, I went back to my shop to work a little more. My mom went to dinner with her friend and Bryan was working at the brewery, so I was on my own. Not that I mind, but it's nights like tonight when I realize how lonely it can be to be in key positions. I have friends, there's no doubt, but not many that I hang out with or go out and do things with, even dinner. It does make it lonely sometimes.

So, I came home and warmed up pizza from last night and watched a show on the PBS channel we subscribe to, called *10 Homes that Changed America*. It was cool, and I'm always into educational stuff. But then I wanted something fun to watch. I found one of my all-time favorites, *Hello Dolly* from 1969. I have loved the music and costumes since I was a child. It's so uplifting. That's something I really needed. I may or may not agree with the views of the actors in it, especially today, but they did a great job in the movie and I'm so glad I watched it tonight. I especially loved singing along with the songs. Songs like: 'Before the Parade Passes By' and 'Put on Your Sunday Clothes' are all about picking yourself up and making yourself feel better. It's something I really needed. How about you, do you have a movie that lifts you up?

I hope you have a great Saturday! Be sure to have an adventure!

October 25, 2020

I don't know what it is about most Saturdays, but I usually find it hard to wake up and get going. Maybe it's because it's one of the few mornings my husband isn't out of bed and gone before I get up…it's kind of nice waking up next to someone.

Today the tearoom wasn't overly booked. We did have reservations, but it wasn't at capacity like last weekend. The gift shop stayed busy though and that's the cool part. When one is slower the other is busier. I love how that works.

I also took some time to run with Bryan to Lowe's to get some bistro lights to hang from our awnings in front of our shop. Our neighbors at Lis's Pieces Artisan Boutique put them up and they look so nice, so I talked to Lisa, who was gracious enough to take a few minute out of her crazy busy moving day to explain how they did theirs so we can make ours look nice too. I really think it's going to make our place look nice, and I think it will look even nicer when we get ready to put up bistro lights in our alley. I truly am so excited about the alley and back of our building and how we are going to utilize it. It's going to be so great! Providing outside dining has been a dream of mine and now I'm working toward making that happen.

We planned on getting the lights up today but didn't get to it as the brewery got slammed. Thanks so much to our awesome guests for making that happen! I imagine we will do it on Monday evening.

I did get a few things accomplished today at my place. I got the linens and China on the tables in the main tearoom for Halloween. It looks so amazing! My mom made these adorable centerpieces with black roses and spiders, and I draped black netting material over the chandeliers. I can't wait to keep decorating and make it look amazing for our guests on Wednesday evening at our annual Witch's Tea.

I also hooked up our new speaker system. I got so tired of having different music in the gift shop than in the tearoom, so now we have a system that plays throughout. It's so nice going from room to room with the same music continuing. It reminds me of being on a ride at Disney and as you travel through it the music just continues…it's pretty cool. I know it's a little thing, but these improvements just make it better for the guest experience and that's what I strive for.

Tonight my mom and I had a nice dinner at Thai Bistro. It was a quiet night and after working on things at the tearoom; it was just what the doctor ordered. The food was delicious and the team there is wonderful. I love that they know us and that we are regulars.

After dinner, I stopped by the brewery to drop food to Bryan and then headed home. I got some laundry done and finished a book about having tea at The Ritz. It was an older book, kind of small, that my friend George found in one of the storage lockers he bought—think storage wars. I've been trying to read each night and I've made my way through three tea books in the last two to three weeks. My goal is to read a little each night to reinforce what I know about my industry and to pick up any little interesting tidbits I can.

So now it's time for bed. I have an exciting and busy day tomorrow and I have to be up early.

Have a "Beau-tea-ful" Sunday!

October 26, 2020

It's not often that I get a real day off. Like, the kind of day that I don't go to the tearoom and Bryan doesn't go to the brewery. What? You say.... Yes, I kid you not. So, what did we do?? We braved the heat and spent the day at Disney's Magic Kingdom.

I wasn't sure how I would feel about being at Disney during all the craziness we have experienced lately. Honestly, I was pleasantly surprised at how Disney is working really hard to keep us safe. In fact, I dare say that it almost felt like it did many, many, many years ago when you felt like it was a more personal experience.

Bryan, my mom, Bernice, and I arrived on property around 11 a.m. and hopped the monorail to Magic Kingdom. Of course, we hopped the resort monorail so we didn't have to wait in the line for the monorail that runs directly to Magic Kingdom. They have put up separators in each cab to keep guests safe. We sat in our own part of the cab, and it was very nice.

Once inside the park, I was very impressed at how the guests were spaced out. I have not been able to walk down Main Street without people bumping into me left and right, probably since I was a kid. We walked along, slowly, taking in the beauty and calmness of the park. Usually, people are running around trying to get to this ride or that restaurant. Today, it just seemed like everyone was just kind of going with the flow.

We started in Adventure Land and walked the Swiss Family Robinson House. I want to say that the last time I did that I was a kid, maybe ten years old. I'm sure back then I thought it was primitive...today I thought I would love to get stranded on an island and relax in a house like that. It's funny how you change!

We enjoyed Pirates, Splash Mountain, Under the Sea, Haunted Mansion, Small World and Seven Dwarfs Mine Rollercoaster. It was the most rides we've done in one day in a long time, and all without Fast Passes. The wait times were nowhere as long as they used to be. While lines seemed long, with the spacing between guests the lines moved almost continuously and before we knew it, we were on the ride. Thanks Leah, for telling us about the posted wait times verses actual times. I've also decided that I want to work for Disney and go to their parks as a guest and do things as a guest and then report back to them about things that aren't right or don't have their 'Magic.' For example, in just a quick look going through Small World I found ten quick things that, if fixed, would lead to more of that magic feeling they used to have. I wonder if there's such a job as a 'secret guest'—like stores with secret shoppers. Maybe I could suggest that to Bob Iger.

I also enjoyed the fact that they had floats go through the park one at a time. Instead of having guests sit ten deep waiting for a parade, every now and then, the music would change, and a float would come through. It was actually a great idea and I hope they look to keep that format in the future. It would be nice to just stop for a few minutes and watch a float go by. Then you can catch as it goes by without having to stop your entire day.

What was the best part of our day?? It was having a late lunch in the castle at Cinderella's Table. It was just amazing to go inside part of the castle. It's absolutely gorgeous, just as beautiful inside as it is outside. Our server was very nice and kept bringing me hot water and more teabags! I love that the place isn't that big. It made it so much more personal. The one thing that has changed is that the princess, in our case Cinderella, didn't come to the tables, but she did make several appearances and talked to guests from afar. The food was fabulous and honestly, I don't know how we will ever eat anywhere else again when we visit!

All in all, it was great to get away for the day. Well, mostly away. I still checked the business social media and wrote my Sunday tearoom post while waiting in line at Pirates. I wish we didn't have to wear masks. That really was brutal and caused me to overheat. By the end of the day, you could tell everyone was over it! Other than that, it was pretty perfect. Thank you, Diane, for taking care of the brewery while we were gone. We really needed the break and appreciate you very much.

October 26, 2020

It's funny that I never learn that a full day of fun leaves me in pain the next day. Of course it was all worth it, but I need to remember that when I have those full days, I need the next day to recover. Today was recovery way.

Today was one of those days where I kind of wished I would have stayed in bed…I mean it wasn't a bad day but more of a struggle physically.

This morning, I got up at a decent hour and went for a massage at 11 a.m. It was much needed because after yesterday walking around and my head pulling my, neck muscle was in pain, and I was pretty much stuck looking right. The massage helped to loosen things up, which I needed.

After my massage I had to go to Office Depot, so I also stopped at the party store. I was looking for some window clings but didn't find any I liked. Then I decided to treat myself to lunch at Olive Garden. I just wanted some soup and breadsticks. It was nice to sit and relax and conduct a little business while enjoying my meal.

After lunch I ran into JoAnn Fabrics to check out any last-minute Halloween items and then I came home. By this point my body was saying no more and my neck was stuck to the right. I tried so hard to relax my muscles, but it just wouldn't work so I got some ice packs and laid down on the couch and fell asleep. I slept for an hour before Bryan got home. Honestly, I probably wouldn't have gotten off the couch if we didn't have things to do. Still, I got moving again.

We went downtown and enjoyed a nice dinner at Boulevard Beef & Ale. Our friends Michelle and Travis joined us with their daughter Emilee. We had a really nice time; it was unplanned, but perfect. That's why I totally love our town!

After dinner, we discussed some plans for the alley way next to my building that Travis is going to help with. I am very excited about the plans to make the area look nice.

Then we decided to try to tackle the bistro lights on the front of our building. Well, it didn't go as planned at all. First, the outlet we were going to use outside wasn't working. We ran home and got an extension cord to use the outlet further down for now. Then we started to hang the lights and we got to the second awning and realized we couldn't hook 2 strands together. That was it! We took them all down, put them back in the box and I'm taking them back to Lowe's tomorrow. What a waste of time for my poor husband. He's such a good sport, but I was totally over it. Truly, after my day and not feeling great and getting up and trying to do something, I was just done. And he's so calm and cool and acting like it's no big deal. I don't know what I ever did to deserve him.

I came home disappointed, folded some laundry, filled out my voting ballot so I can drop it off tomorrow, and went to bed. My neck is still having spasms here, so I'm hoping I can get to sleep soon and that tomorrow will be a better day! It has to be better! Why, you ask? Because tomorrow the segment about New Port Richey airs on

Daytime, a Tampa based midday talk show. I just hope my neck cooperates enough for me to enjoy it.

Have a great Tuesday!

P.S. Thank you to all my amazing friends who have liked my page: Coastline Salt Room. I'm so excited to bring this to our amazing town and I thank you for your support as we work to get it open. I promise it's going to be a beautiful place!

October 28, 2020

Last night, I slept on my side and this morning when I woke up, I could barely move. The muscle must have stretched during the night because every time I moved my neck the muscle spasmed and pulled on the nerve. It made getting around early this morning quite difficult.

I was up nice and early and was into the brewery by 9:30 a.m. so that we could open to watch the Daytime TV Show where New Port Richey was featured. It was so nice to see our friends and watch the segment together. I really appreciate everyone who came: Chris, Bonnie, Bernice, John, Tara, Debra, Lisa, Jacob and Shery! It was so nice to share that amazing experience with you all. Now, we are going to have a watch party at the brewery any time they feature our downtown.

Today was a busy day. So busy that I actually made a list last night before I went to bed so I could make sure I didn't miss something. I had some errands, which made it hard with my neck. I was very careful to take my time, but it was a struggle.

Once my errands were done, I worked in the tearoom, finishing up decorating for the upcoming Halloween tea tomorrow. I also got some additional tasks done. I managed to get a lot of things off my list, but I still have more...

Tonight, I attended my Tea Mastermind group. It was really nice chatting and talking about our businesses. I also gave a tour of my tearoom to the group. It was nice to share my space with them.

After that, Bryan and I ran down to Dented Keg Ale Works. They opened tonight with guest taps, and it was really nice. I'm so glad they are open. I know it has been a long road for Rick and Sheila, but now that they are open, there are good things ahead.

When I got home, I cleaned out the guest room so I could get Ava's bed back up. She will be staying with us a few nights a week so we can take her to school. The last time we had her was March and I miss her. I'm looking forward to spending time with my munchkin! Oh, and I also started cleaning the bathroom. I think the last time it was cleaned well was six months ago. It's one of the benefits of never being home. It looks nice now and the only thing I have left to do in there is clean the shower and scrub the floors. All in due time!

Well, off to bed. Tonight, I'm sleeping on my back, so I won't have any issues with my neck pulling. I'm looking forward to tomorrow. It's going to be a fun day.

October 28, 2020

Today was a great day, but boy am I wiped!

I didn't get to my shop too much before we opened. I knew it was going to be a labor-intensive day. Today was our Witch's Halloween Tea that sold out back in September. We had eleven tables with guests. We only have twelve tables total, and one was saved for goodie bags and take-home surprises for our guests. Tonight's twenty-eight guests were greeted with a cute Halloween backdrop to take photos at, and then a nice tea meal. We even had some amazing actors from the Richey Suncoast Theatre that came over and interacted with our guests. That was pretty cool! We also had a really nice photographer, Phil, who came and took pictures of the event so we would have a record of the good time we had.

Today I spent most of my day in the kitchen of the tearoom. I worked with Dawne to get things ready for tonight. My goal was to get us set, so we only had a few things to do quickly before guests arrived. We worked through the menu and knocked everything off the list. It went smoothly and it was nice to be ready. I don't think I've spent so much time in my kitchen in a long time! It makes me want to get in the kitchen more and experiment and have some fun with food.

I've discovered over the last few months that I am totally a foodie. I enjoy creating flavors and pairings. I like it when people can truly enjoy what I create. I love it when they find what I created to be delicious. It's become something I'm very proud of and that I strive to achieve. I hope to create more pairings in the future, as well as more flavorful food for people to enjoy.

Tonight was great. I didn't get to interact with my guests to much because I was in the kitchen, but I'm so glad the way it turned out. The tearoom was beautiful, we did a great job decorating and making it look pretty. I hope everyone enjoyed it! I can't wait to do more special events. Our guests really like it, and it helps me be creative and keeps me moving forward.

Now it's time for a hot shower, my body hurts, then to bed. Here's hoping the rest of the week is great!

October 29, 2020

Man, who knew little kids get up so early! It's been almost seven months since we last had Ava over to spend the night so I can take her to school. The last time she was here I practically had to pull her out of bed. Not this morning...she was checking on us at 7 a.m.! Ok, so for those of you that know me well, that's super early! I yawned almost the whole day! But there's nothing I wouldn't do for that girl...

Despite being tired, I did manage to drag by butt out of bed early. I got some laundry done. The highlight of my day was a child's laughter while she was playing with our cat, Sam. It's amazing how a child's laugh can put a smile on your face, no matter how tired you are!

Today was a rough day. I would say, like the days when you party too much the night before, but I didn't party. I was just exhausted at the intensity of Wednesday night's event and how much it really took out of me. I wouldn't trade it for anything, but man, am I glad it was a slower day today!

We got the tearoom all set back up and we are now ready for our Halloween tea on Saturday afternoon. I'm looking forward to that, it's a much smaller event but will still be fun!

Tomorrow is scheduled to be a slower day in the tearoom too. I'm hoping we have some good gift shop traffic. And I'm looking forward to checking a lot of things off my 'to do' list tomorrow that I didn't get to today.

Here's to finishing the week strong! Have a great Friday.

October 30, 2020

Today is a rough day, that's all I can say...some very hard business decisions to make. If I wasn't on Paxil, I might have even teared up a little.

Tea room, brewery, and salt room will be ok, just worried about my tea brand. Some really tough decisions that will impact the brand are on the horizon and it makes me sad.

October 30, 2020

For the most part my day was okay. I was awakened by a cheery little girl whose laugh is completely infectious and puts a smile on my face, even if it's 7 a.m.! Then, I got up to help her get ready for school and she wore her Halloween costume. So today, I got to drop off Wonder Woman at school. It was absolutely adorable.

Then I had breakfast with my mom. We haven't done that in a while, so I thought since we didn't have to rush in today, why not. Breakfast at Grandma Sally's Restaurant was perfect as usual!

The tearoom was ok today. We had great guests and I'm so lucky I get to say that every day. It wasn't busy, but I will take quality over quantity any day.

This afternoon I chatted with a colleague of mine in the tea world. As we get busier with our tea side, we need to buckle down on regulations. Not that we don't keep things super safe right now, but as we grow there is more regulation. I just want to be sure we are doing what is right, but man, going to the next step is going to be brutal both financially and physically. I'm just not sure how we are going to do it, especially since we were hit so hard this year with closures. Thank you to all my friends who reached out to me about wanting to help or having ideas. It means so much to me. Sometimes in business you just feel lost.

Tonight was relaxing. Ava and I ordered pizza for dinner; she colored and watched a movie. I did laundry and relaxed. Now it's time for bed. We have some guests for tea tomorrow and a fun little Halloween tea in the afternoon. I have to get up early and pack since we leave for Tennessee tomorrow night. I can't wait to get away to cooler weather and to relax. I need a few days away with downtime to really think about my future and make some plans.

Wishing you all a great Saturday!

October 31, 2020

Today was a good day. I woke up early and was feeling good, so I did some laundry, grabbed a few things for my shop, and headed to work.

My team was already hard at work and had everything ready for the day even though it was only 9:45 a.m.! We had a few tables at noon and today we decided to have a paired down version of our Halloween Tea at our 2 p.m. seating. We had four tables attend and it was really nice. We knew all our guests, so it makes it extra special because they are like our family.

I actually got a lot done today. I had some things for the businesses that I had to handle before we left for Tennessee, and I actually got them done. Things like quarterly taxes, yuck! Checking on our beer and wine license, a video will (in case anything should happen to me while traveling, but don't worry, when I get back, I am going to make a formal written one), saw my niece Ava for Halloween, and finished up some odds and ends. I think today I was more productive then I have been all week, LOL. Maybe I should plan to go away more often!

Bryan and I headed out about 6 p.m. to our second home. It still feels so weird to say that, and even more weird to realize that we really have our own place in our second favorite state. This time we are leaving more things in our camper, like pillows, linens, hair dryer...now you know it's getting real!

This trip is a little get away for just me and Bryan. No, the moms didn't come this time, so we won't have any funny stories about them to share...but I'm sure Bryan and I will keep you entertained over the next few days.

We had to get away now to celebrate our ten-year anniversary. It will be ten years on November 13th. I can't believe how fast the time has flown. I guess it's true what they say about time flying when you're having fun. So, we will celebrate this week at the place Bryan asked me to marry him, the place we honeymooned, and where we spend our time when not in Florida.

We will only be here a few days. Then I have to get back to attend an online tea conference that I am very excited about. I have some great sessions I'm attending. Also, we have to get the shop ready for the holiday season. I can't believe it's almost that time...I love the holidays and I'm excited about what we have planned for the tearoom.

This week while I'm away, relaxing, I'm going to take some time to get things set for when we get back. Some exciting things to get ready for! And, I have some things to think about—really relax and meditate on.

I hope you had a great Halloween and that you have a really nice Sunday!

November 2020

November 1, 2020

Last night we made it to Macon, Georgia, and stopped to stay overnight. When I woke up this morning I went to take my morning pill for my diabetes, and guess what??? I left it at home! I managed to grab all of my other meds, but because that pill comes in a larger package it's kept in a separate part of my cabinet. I had to come up with a plan, and fast because we were not driving back to Florida. *Note—I also forgot my bags with my photography and teacup props to shoot more promo photos.

I quickly found a Walgreens near our place in Tennessee and submitted a request for a prescription refill. Of course, because I had it filled eighteen days ago, insurance said no. So, on our way through town, we stopped and told Walgreens what happened, and they got it filled for me. Yea! I can get back to normal tomorrow.

While we were in Maryville, we decided to go downtown. I had found a brewery nearby just in case I had to wait a while for the prescription to be filled. We only waited ten minutes, so we headed downtown afterwards so that Bryan could enjoy his vacation by visiting a brewery. I have never been downtown, so I was looking forward to checking it out. The brewery was cute, and Bryan liked their beer. We plan on going back downtown on our trip to check out some restaurants and check out downtown to see if we can get any new ideas for our town.

By the time we got to the camper it was 4:00 p.m. and almost dark (ugh!). It was cool, but the wind kicked up and that made it much colder. We planned on cooking hotdogs on the fire but with the wind, we decided to go grab dinner at one of our favorite little restaurants. They were busy and that's good.

The rest of the night we hung out in the camper—what we call our home. The heat is on, and we are wrapped up. It's supposed to get down to twenty-eight degrees tonight!

Bryan gave me the most beautiful ruby heart ring for our ten-year anniversary, and I gave him my grandfather's four diamond wedding band. I wanted him to have it because my grandpa meant so much to me and I miss him every day.

Tomorrow, we don't have any plans. I'm looking forward to that.

Wishing you all a great start to the week.

November 3, 2020

Our morning started off with near freezing temperatures. The field next to our camper was absolutely beautiful with frost covering it. It was a site to see and enjoy, until Bryan tried to use the sink and realized our water hose froze in the middle of the night. The night before, we had been sure to make the faucet drip all night, so it didn't freeze, but it wasn't supposed to be as cold last night. Oops!

We got around and went to breakfast at a new place because ours was so busy. It was okay but nowhere near as good as what we were used to.

After breakfast we went out to Cades Cove to drive to loop. We had a mission to find one of the hidden gems of the Smoky Mountains—the Pearl Harbor tree. The tree was planted by a man on the day of Pearl Harbor as a memorial. He placed an old rim of an automobile around the sapling to protect it. Over time the tree grew around the rim and is still there today. We have tried to find it for years, but recently one of the hiking sites explained the directions to the tree a little better. That was all we needed. We hiked into the woods with no trail—a huge no-no in the mountains—and finally saw the tree. After a very steep climb, we were face to face with it. People still visit it today and leave flags with current military personnel.

Instead of taking the main road home this afternoon, we decided to use Rich Mountain Road, a one-way unimproved road out of Cades Cove. It was a beautiful ride and took us way out into the woods, far away from people. I just love roads like that where you can't get lost, but you feel like you could.

On our way back into town we received a call about the incident downtown. We are shocked and saddened, and saying prayers for anyone who may have been impacted. I know it was an isolated incident and we all need to pull together and be downtown strong. We worked so hard to revamp our businesses and offerings downtown, making some amazing strides and you have my word that we will not let this deter our hard work. If nothing else, it makes us only want to work harder. And that's just what I'm going to do. Tomorrow it's time to sit down and brainstorm so I come back with a plan.

This afternoon we went to Smoky Mountain Brewery. This time we checked out their place in Maryville. Bryan had a flight, and we had some appetizers. It was nice, but it's a little more commercial than we usually like. Unfortunately, all the other smaller local breweries have modified hours right now and don't open until Thursday.

When we came back home, we had a fire outside. It was a beautiful night for a fire, definitely not as cold as it was last night! We also enjoyed some homemade chicken chili that I made in the crock pot earlier in the day. I mean, what goes better with cool weather than chili? And white chicken chili is my favorite. It was delicious and hit the spot.

I'm sure many of you are tied to the TV watching the election results. For us, we handed in our mail-in ballots over a week ago. We checked a few days ago and they were accepted and counted, that's why I don't mind being away right now. I resolved weeks ago that whatever the outcome, I am still going to do what I do. I'm still going to work as hard as I can and build my business. Sure, I have my opinions and desire of whom I want to represent me, but I am not giving in to the fight. My success is dependent on my work, so tomorrow is another day where we will continue to work toward our future.

Tonight, we are not watching anything about the election, but instead watching some of our favorite shows, like Storage Wars. I hope your night is as stressless as ours.

November 4, 2020

This morning, we got up and headed toward the national park. On our way, we stopped at one of our favorite breakfast restaurants, Elvira's, for some food. It was awesome as usual—I love their hash brown casserole! Then we stopped in Harper Brothers to grab a chai latte and headed out.

Our mission today was to find the troll bridge in Elkmont. We parked and headed up Little River Trail. I had a teacup in hand because I didn't want miss an opportunity to take a promo photo. The directions weren't very clear, but about 150 feet up the trail we found a little foot path off to the right of the main trail, just like the directions said, so we took it. Now, one thing they say about hiking in the Smokies is to never leave the trail. Still, knowing the area well, I made a note of some significant landmarks, and made sure I could always hear the river. We were about forty yards up the trail when we came across an old homestead where an old fireplace still stood. Just beyond that, a bigger trail led up to the main trail again and...the bridge!

Our time at the bridge led to a little photoshoot for my teacup and for me. I rarely take photos or let Bryan take my photo, but today, teacup in hand, we took some photos I hope show my love of tea that also can be used to promote my new blog—when I get it up and running.

After spending some time in Elkmont, we made our way to Gatlinburg Brewing Company, to their Gatlinburg location. There, we met up with our friend Chris from home. He is up here traveling, hiking, biking and finding some peace and solace. We enjoyed lunch and a few beers. It was truly a highlight of our trip getting to spend some time with a friend from home.

On our way back home to the camper, we stopped at The Island and Bryan enjoyed a beer at YeeHaw Brewing. We also made another stop at the Beef Jerky Outlet and Paula Deen's shop. It's funny, tonight was a work session for the city about Railroad Square so as I was walking around, I had my earpiece in, listening. I'm glad I did…they have some great plans, but I am definitely feeling very strongly about keeping access to our parking lot that is owned by our building. I can't talk much about it here since I am working on a letter about it. It was just a very interesting conversation. I'm sure everyone at The Island thought I was crazy talking to Bryan and telling him what was happening. Still, thank goodness for technology, so I can stay connected while away.

Tonight, we hung out at our camper, had no fire, and just watched TV. We enjoyed our leftover chicken chili and some downtime. Tomorrow, we head into Pigeon Forge for a buying show. I'm not sure I'll buy anything, but I'm excited about meeting with some vendors!

Hoping you are having a great week. And remember, don't let the stress get you down…life is wonderful, and we are so blessed!

November 5, 2020

Today is our last full day in Tennessee. Today was one day that we actually had plans. So, we got up and around and went on our way.

On our way out of our campground we stopped in the office and scheduled our next year's visits up here. The campground owners, a really nice family, put up a happy ten-year anniversary wish on their sign. How amazing they are that they care that much about their guests. I am so excited to have a place up here that we are planning on using quite a bit. I'm so looking forward to that too, because while we didn't have a big agenda for this trip, it was so nice to be able to just relax and be in our favorite place. I know we are a ways from retiring and being able to be here more, but I look forward to working hard so that we can make that happen. I can see myself here for longer periods of time, writing, doing some photography, and taking some time to just slow down. It gives me something to work towards and look forward to in the future.

This morning, we visited a little coffee shop in town. While we don't drink coffee, we were looking for some pastries to take in the car on our way to Pigeon Forge. They had some delicious apple fritters and Bryan enjoyed a chocolate, chocolate chip muffin. They did have tea bags available, but we made our own tea before leaving the campground, so we were set. This morning's choice was my own blend, Lavender Vanilla White tea. I forget how much I love that tea!

Our mission today was to visit the gift and souvenir show in town. I wasn't sure what to expect, but it was more souvenir based. We visited one of our vendors that handles our New Port Richey merchandise. We are going to do a redesign of our merchandise, so that we align better with the vision of our city, while also keeping our signature style. I'm looking forward to that.

After the show, we decided to head over to the gift show in Gatlinburg. There we saw our sea glass jewelry company. I was able to get some of their items ordered, so we will get them in for guests to purchase for the holiday season. I am so excited! Their products are beautiful, and our guests love them.

Between the two shows, we were only there for a few hours, so we grabbed lunch at a new BBQ place in town just off the main street. They had amazing food, and I loved their pulled pork sandwich. They are not a chain, which I love, so I can't wait to take the moms there when we come up next year.

On our way out of town, we drove through Roaring Fork Motor Nature Trail. I really enjoyed that ride through the woods.

Afterwards, we came back to the camper and got some things cleaned up so that packing up tomorrow is easier. Then Bryan had a fire and roasted hotdogs. Now we are just relaxing and enjoying the last of our down time. Tomorrow, we head back and my head is already starting to spin with all that I need to do. I'm not going to think about it now though. No, I am looking forward to getting home and getting revved back up, but for now I'm taking these last moments to just relax and breathe.

Here's to a great Friday and the weekend being so close we can feel it!

November 6, 2020

This morning is always the hardest to wake up to every time we are away. It's time to pack things up and leave our beautiful place behind. I always love our time there, but I also love coming home. Now we won't be back until March, unless we decide to take a quick few day's trip up before then, which is always a possibility.

On our way home we had to make a stop at a place I have passed for the past twenty years, every time we make this trip. A guest at the brewery told Bryan about the best place for bacon anywhere—Benton's Country Ham. Funny we always drive by it, so today on our way out of town we stopped. The place has been there for decades and even Mr.

Benton was there. One of the customers was talking with him. It was so cool to see this small-town interaction. Truly that's what our country is...a man who has had his business for decades, making a living, employing people and being a good person. It's so refreshing. Bryan grabbed a couple pounds of bacon, and I got some prosciutto. I can't wait to try it. If it's good it will become our stop every time we come home, since they are closed on Sundays when we come into town.

Traffic coming home wasn't too bad. Heading into Atlanta was a crawl. I'm really glad it was because there is an Air Force base near there. As we were crawling on the interstate, we saw one of their four prop cargo planes go overhead in front of us and drop six to eight parachutes out. I'm not sure if they were cargo or people—I would guess cargo—and they must have been doing some drills. The plane circled around two more times, so we got to see that too. It was pretty neat. Every time we come through that area, we always see something. Last time we saw military helicopters. I'm sure people on that street see it every day, but we don't so I just love it!

Other than that, the trip home was uneventful, unless you count us trying to get dinner and at a drive thru. Wouldn't you know, just as we got to the pick-up window the power in the whole area went out. It was only for a few seconds, but just long enough to reset their computers. Thank goodness they had given us our receipt so we could show them what we ordered, LOL.

We are now home and unpacked. Laundry is in the washer, and I am in bed. Tomorrow, I will go back to my shop and meet with my team over some tea to talk strategy. I'm also attending a great virtual tea conference for the next two days. I'm very excited about that.

Here's hoping my Saturday is productive and educational, and that yours is relaxing!!

November 7, 2020

It was so nice sleeping in my own bed last night. I must have been out good, because I vaguely remember Bryan waking me up late saying I was sawing logs so loud. I have the best bed at home, a beauty rest, and the best pillow. While my bed in the camper is comfy, thanks to my mother-in-law getting us a memory foam cover for our anniversary, it will never compare to my amazing bed at home.

I arrived at work this morning just before 10 a.m. I had asked my team to be there to meet and talk about some things about our future. I planned on having tea, but Bryan wanted breakfast, so we all went down to Rose's to enjoy breakfast together before starting our day. Our chat was more about plans we have and things we need to do to keep going. I can't say this year was easy, it's been beyond difficult, but my team is resilient.

That brings me to the most important part of my post tonight...I know that it has been a heck of a year. That no matter how creative our minds may have been in January, we could never have predicted how this year would play out. That includes up to and through this past week. I know some people are happy and some people are mad. I don't have an answer about how to make everyone happy. The only thing I know that makes everyone happy is tea, LOL.

Our focus has been all over the place for so long, and with so much going on, it's been understandable. But here's what I need now...I need everyone to find peace with the way things are today and figure a way to move forward that is healthy and uplifting. The reality is that so many of us have struggled with one issue or another or many, but it's time to take care of each other and build the area where we want to live. Our town has been doing an amazing job rising from ashes, so to speak, and we are becoming the beautiful Phoenix. But that will only continue with your support. Small businesses are suffering today, and my biggest concern is not about the presidency, but the survival of my town. I do not want to see all that we have worked for come undone.

So, as happy or sad or mad as you are about the current situation in your life, let's pick ourselves up, brush each other off, and go support those who keep us all going—those who support our local way of life. For the best way we can have positive impact on each other, and our community is to care about it.

My biggest fear over the past six months or more hasn't been who will be elected locally, statewide, or even nationally. It has been that when all of this is over and decided, guests will still be afraid and won't come back. That people won't come and eat at our restaurants or shop in our shops and at some point, we won't be here for you to come back to. So please, don't let your feelings about world or national happens change the support you have for your local community and small businesses. Now more than ever we need you. Please don't let my fear become reality. We are all in this—every resident, every business owner—together. So, let's make our community the best it can be by working together.

I ask you to please encourage your friends and family to support local small businesses. Don't be afraid to come out, but exercise safety first. Don't stop spending because you are afraid of the future. Our future is now and every business in our town needs you.

I hope you agree, but if you feel differently, I understand that too. The beauty of our town is we can agree to disagree and still respect each other. I respect each and every business owner, resident, family member, friend and stranger. Despite different views, we can all work together to keep our town strong and I thank each one of you who has and continues to this day to support my business and my dream.

November 9, 2020

    Today, despite being my day off, I was up at 8 a.m. I dislike getting up that early when I don't have to be some place or have any definite plans. I mean, I had things to do, but not that early. Because I was up so early (for me), I texted my mom and we met for breakfast at Herschel's downtown. It was great, as usual.

    From breakfast we went to our shop storage unit to start getting Christmas stuff out. I never realize how much holiday stuff we have until we start to unpack it every year. We filled my entire bed and inside of my truck and my mom's car with just bins of decorations and merchandise. Then we had to make a second trip back to get the six Christmas trees.

    After we got the trees, we decided to do a little rearranging in the gift shop to help focus on some areas that have struggled a little. Then we decided we had to get a few more things from storage, so off we went again. Third time's the charm, right? Not so much. We thought we were done running to storage on the second trip, so when we pulled in for the third time, we realized we forgot the keys. Oh yes, they were hanging in my office back at the tearoom. So back we go to the tearoom to get the keys to make a fourth trip to storage! Oh, the joy of it all, LOL.

    We were able to get some rearranging done in the gift shop and came up with a plan for decorating. I know it sounds kind of glamorous, planning a beautiful shop set, but it's so much work. I don't mind doing it, but I put so much pressure on myself to make it beautiful. I am hoping I can pull it off again this year. If things turn out the way I'm thinking, it's going to be really nice and inviting.

    This afternoon Bryan ordered pizza and we went over to the brewery to enjoy it. Our friend Jillian and her family stopped by while they were having photos taken downtown, and we spent a few minutes visiting. We haven't had much time to visit lately, so I really enjoyed time with them. The brewery also got a little busy, so I had to jump in and help

Bryan. It wasn't crazy so I was able to handle it. It was also nice to visit with some friends and chat about all we have going on. I absolutely loved unwinding with my friends Sean, John, and Michelle! We had a great conversation.

I stayed to help Bryan clean up the brewery a little bit after we closed, and then stopped by my shop quickly, and then went home. I'm tired after my day, so I'm heading to bed that way I can get up in the morning and start all over again. I have a feeling I'm going to be at it all day tomorrow. I'm excited to get my shop done and see what else I need before the buying season. Hoping to have some major accomplishments tomorrow!

Wishing you a great start to the week. Hopefully it won't rain us out too bad!

November 26, 2020

Well, after waiting for over two weeks for a response from Facebook, and being blocked for creating another account, today I decided to try making a new account again. So far, I'm still here and it's been a few hours, so that's good. We will see if it sticks.

One thing I have learned about this whole process is that you really are a number. While many things we may do rely on our ability to access accounts here, there is no urgency from the other side. It doesn't matter if you send your ID thirty times (yes, I did that) to prove who you are, the fact that there's no acknowledgement should say so much to each of us. I know it has to me, and it's sad. Yet, I continue on with daily posts and advertising for my businesses. Crazy, isn't it?

So, enough about that...on to my day!

Today was a great day! My beautiful niece spent the night last night, so I could take her to Place (a before and after care program at the schools in our area) today while her mom worked. There's something about waking up and having a six-year-old in the house awake and happy. It brings energy to the day. It's a good thing because I needed it.

I don't know what it was about today that gave me a different feeling. It was a busy day in the tearoom. Maybe because it was our Monday and then we have tomorrow off, I'm not sure.

Silly things happened and it just made me feel off a little bit. So much so, that when Dawne pulled the extra bottles of champagne out of the fridge to make room for all the food, I reopened the bottle that had already been opened, and I poured myself a big ole glass. Halfway through the day I had actually had two glasses! I never do that, but for some reason today it just seemed like an okay thing to do. Of course, I didn't drink more and stopped early because I'm responsible and had to drive later in the evening.

The day was really good...double what we did in gift shop and tearoom from last year. I am so grateful for that because we are trying to make up a lot of lost ground from earlier this year.

Tonight, I picked up Ava from Place and she was a ball of energy. Oh my, I wonder where it continuously comes from. Still, her energy gives me energy.

We came home and waited for Uncle Bryan to get home before going to dinner at Herschel's. We are really enjoying that place and I'm so glad they are open. We eat there several times a week. Tonight, they had a band playing and we were the only table—it was our own little concert! After the band finished playing, we gave Ava some money to put in their tip jar. They were so appreciative and gave Ava their tambourine. They told her to shake it really loud when her parents were asleep. LOL, so I sent it home with her when Deidra picked her up!! It was so nice of them though. And she just loved it. What kind people! See, we can be nice and care for each other.

So, that's what I'm leaving you with today. It's the little gestures that go the longest way.

I wish you all a beautiful night and a fulfilling turkey day tomorrow.

November 26, 2020

Happy Thanksgiving!

What a wonderful day! Not just because I was off from my shop and had some downtime, but because the day was relaxing, and I got to spend it with some of my favorite people.

Our day didn't start early by any means...the brewery was so packed last night that Bryan didn't get home until mid-morning. That is kind of typical of the evening before Thanksgiving in the bar world. So needless to say, we slept in this morning, and it felt good.

Instead of going out to breakfast this morning, I made my homemade sausage gravy and biscuits. I have wanted to make it for a while, so I'm glad I had the chance this morning. I also had to make the stuffing for our dinner, so I was definitely having some fun in the kitchen.

Today for dinner we went to my mom's house. We didn't do anything fancy, which is just like us. We had honey baked ham, turkey breast and all the fixings. It was delicious and there was not a lot of fuss, so it was perfect. After dinner my friend Elisa and her husband came by for tea and dessert and Bryan had a fire in the fire pit outside. Even Wendy came out and cooked a few marshmallows with him.

Bryan played outside a lot with Ava today. She wanted to play hide and seek and throw a ball and he was more than happy to do that with her. She was so happy, and it was so fun to see. In fact, tonight after we got home, I was doing laundry, and I could hear her talking to him in the living room and they were laughing. It made my heart smile. See, we don't have any children and I am completely okay with that, but every now and then I think about what an amazing father he would have been. I just hope he doesn't ever regret not having a child. Unfortunately, I won't ever regret it, but it does make my heart smile when I see how much she loves him and how much he loves her.

So, another Thanksgiving is done. I'm so thankful for everyone in my life and my life in general. I am thankful most for my husband, who is always taking care of me and doing all he can for us, I am truly blessed!

The next two days will be busy at the gift shop and tearoom, and I couldn't be more excited! I love this time of year both at my shop and home. Here's to an amazing holiday season for all of us, a great way to finish a mediocre and crazy year!

November 27, 2020

I always forget how crazy this particular week is every year. Being open in our tearoom and gift shop for one day and then being closed for a day really throws me off as far as what day of the week it actually is. All day today I thought it was Saturday.

It was a fairly good day at our shop and tearoom. Compared to last year's numbers we were up in sales, and up with the number of guests we had in the tearoom. At this point in this crazy year, I'm happy to be close to what we did in previous years, but actually beating those years really says something about our community and our resilience in our town.

Today, Ava helped me in the gift shop. She is such a good little helper. For being six years old, I think she only complained about being bored two or three times. I just love that she can come with me, and I can teach her things like how to make pyramid tea sachets, LOL. Honestly, she is so good and so helpful, and I'm truly blessed that on the days that she doesn't have school, I can take her to the shop, and she fits right in. She even got her own name tag today, even though she complained that it bugged her being on her dress, LOL. Oh, and we made Tara a name tag today, too.

Tonight, we enjoyed a nice night at Herschel's in downtown, across from the brewery. We find that we like to go there every couple of days because their food is really good, and Bryan feels comfortable leaving the brewery for a little while, but still keeping an eye on it. They had a great musician outside and it was nice to sit out there and relax after a long day.

Ava and I returned home this evening and watched The Polar Express. I love that movie during the holidays, and she never saw it. We got almost two-thirds of the way through it before her mom came and she had to go home. After she left, I went back to my shop to get more things ready before tomorrow's big Small Business Saturday. I was able to get some more tea sachets made, got all of our free tote bags ready, and updated our sidewalk sign for the front of the store. I had hoped to accomplish more, but it was getting late, and I knew I needed to get some rest before tomorrow.

Tomorrow looks like it's going to be a great day. The tearoom is booked with fifteen more guests this year than last year. And we opened up our happy hour time all day tomorrow, so that way guests can stop in and enjoy some tea sandwiches and tea without reservations. We usually only do this Wednesday through Friday, but I thought it might be a good opportunity for Small Business Saturday as well. Now that I'm home, it's midnight, I'm going to bed to get my rest so that I can be ready for an awesome day downtown tomorrow.

If you're around, stop by and see us. We rely on your support to continue making our downtown vibrant and we appreciate all that you have done to keep us going thus far in this crazy year.

Here's to a great Saturday!

November 28, 2020

Small Business Saturday!

This morning came too quickly. Staying so late at my shop last night, I felt like I didn't get much rest. When I got up and looked in the mirror, I actually had dark spots under my eyes. It's been a long time since I've had that. Still, I push forward. Today was going to be a day to be reckoned with!

I got to my shop at 9 a.m. and helped a little in the kitchen. I didn't have to do much because reinforcements came pretty quickly in the morning. So instead, I spent some time getting out a ton of online orders that we had received and finishing up a few things from my list that I missed the night before.

At 11 a.m., we opened the doors and had a few guests come in to start our day. It wasn't until 12 p.m. when the tea seatings we're getting started that our guests came in to shop for Small Business Saturday. From that point on the tearoom and gift shop were nice and busy with guests coming in and out, and we did our best to keep socially distanced and everyone safe. We knew today was going to be a busy day, but our goal was to ensure our guests' safety at the same time. I think we accomplished that between both the tearoom and the gift shop.

My team was amazing today too. Everyone gave 110% and we all came together to make it a great day. Even as tired as we all got, we all pushed on. I am so proud of my team today and every day. Thank you to Debra, Dawne, Tara, and Carol!

Small Business Saturday has always been a great day for our shop. It's an opportunity to kick off the holiday season with guests shopping in local establishments and supporting locally owned small businesses. I remember our first year of Small Business Saturday, when we bought the shop, and was surprised how many guests participated by coming downtown.

Today was no different and I know the other shops and business owners and I felt the love from our community. To say it has been a difficult year in general is an understatement, but today helped reassure us that the American spirit is alive and well and wanting to support us.

If today is any indication of the holiday season that we will have, I consider myself blessed and fortunate to be able to do what I do every day in my town, and that people appreciate and love us. I am looking forward to a great holiday season and I can't thank all my friends and family enough for their continued love and support.

It is true that the middle of the year was difficult, the business is currently down by over thirty percent for the year, but today's show of support helped us to bridge the gap slightly and know that we have made the right choices to stay in business and continue on. There were times when I questioned what was best for both me and my business, and I even contemplated making changes to what I do. Today and so far this holiday season, we have seen that making the decision to stay open and continue on was definitely the right one.

After working all day, wearing a mask for six and a half hours straight, and just being 'on,' when we finally locked the door, I was exhausted and ready for a break. So tonight, we ran to Herschel's for dinner with our friends

John and Connie and their family. It was the perfect end to a busy, but perfect day in downtown and in the tea shop. I can't wait to see what the rest of the holiday season holds for us as I feel like people need to get out in small safe spaces and that's something we can provide.

Tonight, I planned on coming home and working at my house. Last year we did not put up a Christmas tree at home and this year I would really like to. But after today and all my hard work, I have decided to take a respite, enjoy a nice cup of Cinnamon Cha Cha rooibos tea from my tea brand (Driftwood Tea Company) with some French vanilla creamer (I call it my Cinnamon Bun Latte), and watch one of my favorite Christmas movies—Elf. It was the perfect end to the perfect day, and enough rest to be able to get up and start tomorrow with renewed energy as I prepare for the coming busy week in our shop.

I hope you all had a beautiful Thanksgiving weekend, and to my fellow business owners, I hope that Small Business Saturday was just as great for you not only in sales, but connections and being with our guests as it was for me.

Here's to a relaxing and productive Sunday.

November 29, 2020

There's no rest for the weary, especially during the holiday season... in retail...and having a restaurant.

This morning, I was up before my husband. In our house that is an anomaly because I love my sleep and he often has to get up and get ready for work long before I ever think of getting out of bed.

Today I had a goal of getting several things done including some shopping at our restaurant supply store and working on either cataloging all of my tea books in my office upstairs or cleaning our living room which hasn't been cleaned in probably five years. Now for those of you who know me and know how I like things a certain way, that may be the case in my shop, but at my home it kind of has the feeling that anything goes. I like clean and neat, but I spend so little time at home that it rarely matters what our place looks like. But I do know that when I come home to relax, the more cluttered and crazier it is here, the harder it is for me to actually feel relaxed.

My reason for getting up so early was to be able to get to our restaurant supply store before the mad rush happens at midday. Usually, we get there when there are tons of people. It's chaos, hard to navigate the isles, and takes a while to check out. Today, when we got there the parking lot was only a quarter of the way full. Score! Project number one is getting checked off the list all before noon. We were back, unloaded and ready to go onto the next project before lunchtime.

My afternoon consisted of working around the house. I had thought about cataloging my books in my office, but I decided I would feel better if I was able to come home to a clean and organized home, especially the living room, which is the first thing I see when I walk in the door.

I started going through stuff around 2 p.m. this afternoon and it took me until 9 p.m. tonight to be completely done. That includes sorting bills, books, magazines and all kinds of stuff that made its way into the corners and nooks and crannies of our tiny little living room. I dusted, moved tables and furniture, and worked hard to throw a lot of things away. At this point in life there's no reason to move things from one place to another. If you're not going to use them, it's better just to get rid of it now then to move it ten times before getting rid of it a year from now. Especially in a house of our size where we have only 650 sq. ft. to live, I have come to realize that less is so much more in our space.

I did take a break this afternoon while working in the living room, to take a trip to Home Depot. I really want to put a Christmas tree up this year in our home, as we didn't put one up last year. Even though I currently have seven Christmas trees between my shop and tearoom, there is still something nice about coming home to a beautifully decorated tree. I really missed that last year and felt like I didn't get the full experience of the holiday season. So today I decided I definitely want to have a tree and went looking for a new one. I found a few that I liked but wasn't sure what size tree would fit best since we have limited space. Now I have some ideas and I can't wait to get my tree up and decorated so my home will start to feel like the holidays as well.

    I hope you all have a wonderful, relaxing and productive holiday weekend. I had one of the best, most productive, and gratifying weekends between my tearoom, gift shop and home. I'm looking forward to a great and busy holiday season ahead and I hope that yours is filled with love.

Wishing you a great Monday and a great week ahead!

December 2020

December 1, 2020

Note to self...when you decide to clean your living room after three plus years—use a mask. The dander from the cat and the buildup of dust is going to kill your allergies for several days. Trust me, I'm learning from experience.

For the past few days I have been using a new pillow, hoping it would help my neck while I sleep. It actually did the opposite. This morning, I woke up and could hardly move. It's a good thing I had a massage scheduled for today. Needless to say, that pillow is now gone.

After my massage, I went to my shop and worked on our cyber-Monday sales and some other social media for the first part of the week. I didn't stay long, but I got quite a bit done.

My mom and I spent some time in Tarpon Springs today. We enjoyed a nice lunch at Johnny's Tap House. Then we wandered down to the sponge docks to go to the flag store she likes. I wanted to get a holiday flag for the front of my shop and a flag for my house. I was in luck and found the perfect flags!

Then it was on to Home Depot. I have been debating about buying a new Christmas tree this year. We haven't put up a tree in several years and I just felt like it was time for something nice. I found the tree I liked a few days ago, but just couldn't pull the trigger. Today, after cleaning the living room and making room for a tree, I decided today was the day to get it. I did and I put up when I got home. It looks perfect.

This afternoon, after all my running, I was finally relaxing at home when my phone rang about the brewery. Apparently, the unit behind us had water coming in from the wall that separates us. I hoped in the car and went running down there. Luckily for us, there was very little water in our unit. There was nothing leaking or running either, which tells me it must be coming from inside the wall. I hope it gets figured out so that it doesn't happen again. I feel bad for the guys behind us; their water was ten times worse than ours.

Tonight, I finally got all my books up to my office. There were eight bags total and I'm so glad they are out of my house. Tomorrow I am looking forward to starting to catalog them so I will finally know what I have.

Here's hoping my allergy issue subsides tomorrow. Between the dust and the changing weather, it's bound to wreak havoc on me. Great, just what I need.

Here's hoping the week continues good and quickly for us all.

December 3, 2020

Monday evening I was able to finally get our Christmas tree up. I was so excited to be able to have a tree this year and to have a clean living room with a spot to put it. I wasn't going to wait another day to get my tree up. The best part was that in the evening when it was so cold, we lit the fireplace and I got to enjoy my tree and a fire together. My husband is such a good sport because the fireplace makes the house quite warm, so he switched seats with me in the living room so that I can get nice and toasty.

Tuesday, I spent most of my day in my upstairs office. I had the opportunity to purchase a large collection of tea and industry books that were delivered to my home several months ago. They have been floating around my house in big boxes and bags since they got delivered, and I figured it was finally time to get them to my office and get them cataloged. I spent part of the day logging all of the books into the computer, so I know what I have and I don't continue to buy duplicates. I also spent time doing some bookkeeping and general business stuff that I have been putting off for quite a while.

Yesterday was a great day. The tearoom was quite busy during the day for general reservations, and the evening 'Tea After Dark' with our Victorian Carolers was a success. This year we decided to have several caroler events at the tearoom so that we could help spread the holiday cheer. At our first one, guests completely loved and felt like they were able to get into the holiday spirit. Yea!

Today was the first day I slept in a little bit compared to the rest of the week. After last evening's event, I was so tired that it took a while to try to get out of bed. And when I did, I found that my neck wanted to spasm constantly. It is something that I fought all day and only got worse as the day went on. Tonight, my head is turned to one side and if I try to move it the other way it just shakes back-and-forth. I guess if someone asked me a question and I wanted to tell them no, my head shaking would be perfect, LOL. The pain isn't bad tonight, but I notice it more than I usually do. I think that's just from being busy and running constantly, and that's something I'm still not used to.

The tearoom and gift shop stayed steady today. It is a nice welcome change from the precious season, when things were slower. I love seeing all our guests come back and new guests visiting us for tea and shopping. It makes the day go so much quicker when we stay busy, and I love it. I have also been able to schedule some additional events for us and started planning our activities for national hot tea month in January. It feels good to be working toward getting our press together for that special month.

The salt room is continuing to move forward, and I am very happy about that. I have the applications for our grants almost done and anticipate turning those in on Monday morning. Our permit is ready for pick up, but we can't start the work until the grant is approved. Once that happens, I anticipate things will start to move quickly. Hopefully before then, my Facebook page will be figured out and I will have access back to my page for the salt room. Now that I have a contact at Facebook, I am hoping the situation gets resolved rather quickly. For now, I will continue using my new page to keep you all updated.

One thing I have learned over the past few weeks is that you all enjoy reading about my day and that makes me feel so honored. I will continue to write about my days for as long as I can, sharing my ins and outs and all the rounds with you as long as you enjoy and continue reading.

Wishing you all a fabulous Friday and a great start to the weekend ahead.

December 4, 2020

Nothing wakes you up faster at 4:30 in the morning then a 6-year-old yelling at your cat for being in her room. I still haven't figured out how Sam even got in there with the door closed. Maybe it was all a dream for her, but our early-morning adventure consisted of me finding Sam and making sure she wasn't in Ava's room. From there we moved onto her nightlight not being charged, and then her not being able to sleep. I don't know if I'm a good or a bad aunt because I told her to grab her pillows, lie on the couch, and try to fall back asleep since she couldn't fall asleep in her bed. She eventually fell back to sleep and woke up at her regular time. No matter how many nights I have her, I still have not gotten used to being woken up in the middle of the night by a child. I don't ever mind, but it does come as a shock when it's something you're not used to.

Today was a great day in our gift shop. The gift shop continues to outperform the records from last year on a daily basis, and I don't know how we are doing it. My mom works so hard in there to make sure everybody finds the gifts that they want and need. And the tearoom did well today, too. We had several guests in at 12 p.m. and some 'to go's' as well. I don't really have any expectations for this year, so the fact that we are having lots of people in and lots of sales far exceeds anything that I could've imagined at this point.

I also had some time today to work on my tea blog. If you haven't checked it out yet, check out my previous post for a link to my www.myteajourney.com which is where I put my blog when I write it. I wish I had more time to write more often, and I'm making an effort to do so. Hopefully they're fun to read as well, maybe not as much as my daily posts here, but still interesting and fun at the same time.

Tonight, I came home and relaxed for a little bit before meeting Bryan for dinner downtown. Then I ran back to the brewery and got to visit with our former brewery team member, Lisa. I am so glad she's back in town for a few weeks to visit and it was so nice chatting with her, David and Chloe for a few minutes before I headed back home.

Now, I'm taking it easy at home, trying to prepare myself for a very busy day at the shop tomorrow. There's always so much added pressure when you're extremely busy to continue to make sure that everything is just perfect for each guest. Our first two seatings have large parties tomorrow and we added a private gathering at 4 p.m., as well. All hands are on deck tomorrow as the gift shop will also be busy with Christmas shopping. I love this time of year, but it does get exhausting. I try to get as much rest as I can in between days, so that I'm at the top of my game for each of our guests that visit.

It really doesn't help that my neck spasms tend to get worse under stress and pressure. I have noticed when I come home that I am able to do very little other than sit with an ice pack or heat pack and rest. It's not like me to not be running and doing constantly, so I feel like I'm falling down on my job and not being able to do all that I can. I'm hoping that as I push myself a little more this holiday season that it won't continue to get worse, but instead I'll find a better way to cope with it.

I still enjoying coming home in the evenings and relaxing in my nice and clean living room. My allergy and sinus attacks are almost completely gone from all the furniture being moved and cleaned. I am feeling so much better that I can really enjoy the space now. I still have not decorated the Christmas tree yet, but I'm looking forward to doing some of that this coming week. One thing I did learn is that I live with a person who loves colored tree lights on the Christmas tree. I have always enjoyed the simplicity of white lights, so having bright colors on my tree is an adjustment. Thank goodness the tree has different settings. I can see me changing it to white when I'm home and Bryan changing it to color when he's home. Our poor tree will be so confused by the time this season is over.

Here's hoping your holiday season is starting off great and that you have a wonderful weekend ahead.

December 5, 2020

Today was a great day. Except for the fact that I got up later than normal, probably because I was wide awake at 1:30 a.m. when I realized that my husband was still not home from the brewery. While I know they are usually safe and nothing major goes on, there is something about waking up at 1:30 a.m. to an empty house that is a little concerning.

I got into the tearoom by about 9:15 a.m. this morning. Surprisingly enough, my team in the kitchen had just about everything done. I arrived early, so that I could help if they needed anything since today was such a big day. Turns out they were good, so I went about my business to get all of our online orders shipped out. We seem to get most of our orders early in the week, so I work on them to get them out by Saturday.

The tearoom was steady all day today. Our 12 p.m. and 2 p.m. teatimes were filled with large groups, and we added a 4 p.m. teatime for a third group. I am glad that it's so busy; it helps get us in a little bit better position than we were just a few months ago.

Tonight, after such a long day at the tearoom, I just came home and relaxed. I ordered out dinner and watched the movie I had wanted to see for a while. Overall, it was a productive day while I was out and not so productive when I was home. I wish that I could just keep going, but sometimes my neck just says no. Here's hoping I can have a productive day tomorrow and a little less stress and pain on my neck to actually get some things done.

I hope you have a great Sunday!

December 7, 2020

Today, despite it being rainy, it turned out to be a pretty good day. Of course, I don't know how it could get any better than getting up and getting a massage first thing in the morning. I have found that my once-a-week massage appointments help calm me down for the rest of the week, and also help my neck ever so slightly. The deep tissue massage always feels so wonderful and for a few days afterwards, even though I'm a little sore, I actually feel better.

I spent very little time at my tearoom today. It's not that I didn't have a ton of work to do, but I decided to get some other things done that I needed instead. Our health insurance changed for the year, so I had to go to Walgreens and let them know and get all of that settled. It's something I've been putting off for a while but got done today. Then I had a guest who purchased tea that I needed to deliver, so off I went toward Trinity. While out there, since Chick-fil-A wasn't open yet, my mom and I had a nice lunch at Chili's. I always love their chicken enchilada soup and cool days.

We made a run to Home Depot, so I could look at a few things as well. I didn't end up buying much, just an extension cord, so I have a good one for putting up the Christmas decorations outside. I'm hoping that we get that tackled in the next few days.

That little bit of travel and activity was really about all my neck could handle today. I have learned that I definitely have limits when it comes to how much activity I can do in one day. Although I will say that when I am in motion, I always feel so much better than when I take time to sit down or stop.

Tonight, Bryan is working on getting the IPA into the bright tank, so that it can start carbonating. That meant not much work or anything getting done at home, but we did go out to a nice dinner at Boulevard Beef & Ale

I always enjoy talking with Lou. She is such an awesome person. I don't usually have a lot of people to talk to and just chit chat with, so tonight I spent almost an hour just catching up with her. It's nice to have somebody to talk to, because in the business world you find that you don't necessarily have a lot of friends that you can chat with about business and life in general. I am glad that she is next door.

Now I'm home, relaxing on the couch and watching *Santa Clause 2*. I don't know why, but these movies never get old to me. I'm hoping tomorrow is a great day, as I have quite a few things to get done. I hope your week is off to a great start, too!

December 8, 2020

Today was a great day. It started off around normal time for me, which is about 8:30 or 9 a.m. I know all you early birds must be rolling your eyes at me, but you're also probably not up till 1 or 2 a.m. either. Ha ha, LOL.

My first project this morning was to get some Christmas lights on my house. I can't thank all of you enough who offered to come and help. Had I been better prepared, or let's be realistic...had everything been put away in the same place from the last time we used them, I could've probably found all our decorations. I am still not sure where they are. I searched both sheds and the front porch, I had no luck other than one big strand of lights and one blow up that blows up but doesn't light. Needless to say, I did take a quick trip to Home Depot to try to get some more decorations and ended up with another little blowup for our front yard. I hung the lights as best as I could and actually feel pretty good about how they look. Any other year, I would have wanted the house fully decorated on the outside, lining the trees and the house. But these days I'll take what I can get and leave that adventure for another year.

After lights were hung, I quickly ran to my shop and then decided to take the trip to Trinity to enjoy the newly reopened Chick-fil-A. The new place looks nice and the drive-thru runs much smoother, though I don't know how that's possible because it was pretty smooth already. Of course, I got my favorite chicken sandwich, and it was absolutely delicious and worth the drive.

After that, I made a quick trip to the bank and then home to work on a few projects.

One thing I have noticed over the past several weeks, for me at least, is that I have become a lot more selfish with "my time". Normally on days that I'm off, I would have no problem spending eight to ten hours in my shop catching up on work. I'm not sure if it's the holiday season or what has changed, but for the last few weeks I have really wanted to do things at home and be at home instead of being at my shop. Now that doesn't mean that when it's open, I mind being there, I love my shop. But I have found that I need that break away just a little bit and I have been enjoying getting things done at home. So today, I had a little selfish day as well and worked on getting some laundry done and making sure the house was picked up. I'm actually thinking next week I may take my Monday or Tuesday and bake cookies! I know—crazy right?

Tonight, I had my weekly Tea Mastermind meet up. Talk about invigorating! Our assignment last week was to create a video that we can post on our social media and our website. Usually, I don't take the time to do the projects, but this time I thought I would make an effort. I spent some time this afternoon going through photos and thinking of a message I would like to send to my guests for their support for this year. I made a video like I always do and sent it off to my tea friends. I was shocked at the response as most of them sat in silence afterwards, one almost in tears. It wasn't my goal or desire to make anyone feel heartfelt and warm and wanting to shed a tear, but that's exactly what I did. It was really nice message to our guests of the tearoom, and I can't wait to share it with them this holiday season. Now I'm really glad that I took the time to see the project through and I will probably take time to do the other projects from now on, knowing the benefit for me and for the group.

It's time to wind down and get ready for bed. I feel like today, even though I didn't run constantly, I accomplished so many things for me and my business. It was a perfect compromise and a perfect balance, and I hope that I can get this to continue because, for the first time in a long time, I actually feel at peace.

Hope you're making it a great week so far and that it continues to be great for you.

December 9, 2020

I knew today was going to be a very busy day. I had planned for it in my mind several days ago. And of course, it did not disappoint, but everything worked out perfectly.

The tearoom was on the slower side this morning, but the gift shop picked up in the early afternoon. That was actually okay because we had a full house for "Tea After Dark" tonight, so it gave us a chance to prepare for the evening activities during the day and not rush around.

One thing I was able to get accomplished was proofing our newsletter for the tearoom and gift shop. I used to design it all myself and just have it printed, but since we started working with Minuteman Press, Tricia has developed some beautiful marketing items for us to use. I wanted to keep everything going in the same direction for appearance and consistency, so I had her design our newsletter. Oh my gosh—it is beautiful! Today, I went through some changes with her and hopefully we will have a final proof and it can be printed tomorrow. I cannot wait for my guests to see this newsletter!

This afternoon I had a visit from two of my favorite people in the whole world—Midge and David. They had a small collection of little tea pots, that were a couple inches tall, that they have been gifting me over the past several weeks. I absolutely love them because they are so adorable—the teapots and Midge and David. I think they have gifted me five or six already, and I have a shelf to go up in my gift shop behind my register to show them off. Today they brought me a beautiful collectible mini teapot that Midge had for over 20 years. It had a painting of a Renoir on it, and it is absolutely stunning. I plan on adding it to my private collection that I can keep and enjoy for years to come. I'm always so grateful that they think of me and want me to have these items that meant a lot to them.

This evening, we had our second of five Victorian caroling events. It was a wonderful time with so many guests that we know and call family. We are really working hard to social distance and keep everyone safe, and I hope that our guests saw that again tonight.

Well, I'm going to bed early tonight. The next three days in the tearoom can only be what some would equate to finals week in college—lots of things going on, lots of things that have to be done, and for us, lots of guests coming in. I am so grateful that this holiday season is going so well and that our guests are coming back to be with us. I can truly feel the love from them.

Here's hoping the rest of your week finishes up well and that the holiday spirit is starting to grow, so that you can really enjoy the coming season.

December 10, 2020

Last night I slept so well. It probably had to do with the fact that I snuggled up with my hubby. It's not that we don't do that often, but we don't cuddle long before he puts on his c-pap machine. Last night we both fell asleep, and he forgot his machine and I forgot my mouth guard. Yes, we have weird things in our life. I think it was about 3:30 a.m. before we both woke up and realized he needed to put his machine on.

Ava was up at 7:15 a.m. At least she's considerate when she gets up, as she comes and closes our bedroom door, so we don't hear the TV. Then Bryan got up about 7:30 a.m. to get ready for work. When I finally woke up around 8 a.m., I must've looked at him strangely because he asked if something was wrong with his clothes. I asked him why he was wearing jeans today and he said because he wears jeans every Friday. I had to inform him that it was only Thursday, and he still has one more day to go before the weekend. He was running a day ahead of schedule and had to change. LOL. This is the story of our lives.

Day 2 of finals week went well. I think we are finally getting in our groove for our busiest season and focusing on keeping our guests safe. It has been so nice to have everyone in since this year was so hard, and we missed our guests. The current strain on our business is our tea side. We are getting so many orders online and so many people coming in for tea that we are having a hard time keeping up. In fact, we're pretty much underwater. I may have to find somebody just to come one or two days a week for a few hours to bag tea for us. If anybody has any suggestions, please let me know. It's not a lot of hours or money, but it would be a tremendous help and a little spending cash for someone. My current team is already so extended trying to keep up.

Tonight, we went to dinner at Herschel's, then Ava and I came home to relax with some downtime and to get ready for bed. I have found that because my house is a little more under control, I stay busier in the evening instead of being depressed and sitting on the couch. I know it's hard to believe, but that's something that I actually used to do a few short weeks ago because being home was so stressful with things not being together. Tonight, I'm finishing up linens and other laundry, and working on a few other things from my office for tomorrow. I'm trying to get a little ahead of schedule. It feels so good to have things coming together, especially right before the holidays.

Tomorrow, we submit our grant applications to the city for the salt room. I am really excited to get that project going as well. It seems like a lot on my plate, but there are some small adjustments coming for me and my role in the tearoom that will allow me to focus on the public relations and guest side, versus physically being in the tearoom to help. I will always be there during the day to meet and greet the guests, but my focus will be to help drive in more traffic. With that also comes in element and execution of our latest venture at the salt room. I am looking forward to getting that going, especially since I've been having allergy issues the past week and a half. If I had my salt room open, I could've gone there and sat for an hour and all my sinus problems would have been gone within a day. This is all the more reason to get the salt room up and running.

Here's to rounding out the week with success. I hope y'all have a great Friday!

December 12, 2020

If ever there was a day that I could have cried before 10 a.m., it was this morning. For those of you who know me, that says a lot since I'm on medication to help prevent emotions.

Last night Ava was up several times which caused me not to have a good night's sleep. It's okay for me, but I felt bad for her because this morning she was still a little tired. On our way to school I got a call from our plumber about the drainage issue we were having with our toilets at the tearoom. They needed to remove the toilet and run the machine through the entire line. The worst part about things like this is after Covid, trying to rebuild, and then having unexpected issues come up—it cost money that we don't have. It stinks as we try to get things back on track. I think that was the reason why I was emotional over everything today. Having to call a professional to come out and do something when we just don't have the money, it's so hard.

I got to the shop by 9:30 a.m. and ended up running out to Trinity to find wheat bread for the tearoom. By the time I got back the plumbers had augured the lines into my neighbor's unit and we're still not able to find the blockage. After about twenty minutes a city truck pulled up and told us that there was a problem with the building across the street and they were going to be working on blowing out the lines. Within about fifteen minutes everything was cleared, and we were back up and running. I was so worried they wouldn't find it, we would have to cancel our reservations today, and that it would cost me a fortune to fix. It was a busy day, and I just cannot afford to lose more revenue.

The rest of the day went well, and I got a lot of projects done. I even took an hour or so out in the early evening to rest a little bit before going back to work and finishing up some bigger projects. Perhaps the highlight of my day was getting my new newsletter printed. I was like a kid at Christmas because it was so beautiful, and I was so excited to pick it up. I can't wait to get it in the mail tomorrow. I'm so excited that I spent the last four hours stuffing, folding, sealing, labeling and stamping them so that my guests can get them by Monday.

Tomorrow's another busy day on the table with full seatings at 12, 2 and 4 p.m. It's very exciting, but I'm looking forward to a break for a few days after we close.

Hope you have a great weekend and it's filled with lots of fun things for the holiday spirit.

December 16, 2020

I know it has been a few days since I've written. I have had a lot going on, and so many things that I think to write about, but by the time the evening comes I am so exhausted and usually either fall asleep on the couch or head to bed before I get the chance to write anything.

Sunday, I worked on some teas in the tearoom and then opened my shop for a few hours so people could wander in while they waited for the golf cart parade to start. It was a lovely afternoon; we sold quite a few of our new lattes. I really love them, and I can't wait to be able to offer them full time. I think they are a great way to showcase what tea can do as a latte and mixer.

Monday, I went for a massage. I actually go for a massage every Monday to help try and calm the muscles in my neck and back, so that I am not in so much pain. It usually feels really good and provides some relief, but relief doesn't last long because the stress returns, and my muscles tighten quickly.

Monday afternoon we braved the crowds and headed out to Chick-fil-A in Trinity. I am so glad they're open again because I really missed their chicken sandwich. It was good as always, and for as many cars as they get through there, they do a good job getting everyone in and out quickly.

I spent some time at my shop in the afternoon, working on a few small projects. Even though it's the holidays and we are super busy, I have been trying to give myself at least a few hours break from my shop when we aren't open. So, I spent the afternoon at home working on a few things around the house.

Tuesday morning, I dropped Ava off at school, and then my mom and I headed out to Restaurant Depot. When we got there it was a madhouse, with the staff running the forklifts all over the place. I wonder if Tuesday is when they get their deliveries. We found a lot of things that we needed for the restaurant because it's going to be a very busy week. When we went to check out, they normally just go around the cart with their scanner, but not today. No, they moved everything off of our cart onto another cart. All of my perfectly placed items were removed, and they actually put the chicken on top of my water bottles, which made me freak out. Ultimately, I had my cart stacked so that I could very easily load it into my truck, and they messed the whole entire thing up. That was the start of my aggravation for the day. And once that starts, I find every little nitpicky thing wrong, and it just adds to my aggravation.

After getting back, I spent some time in my tearoom kitchen. Yes, it's great to have a team that handles things on a day-to-day basis, but there are things that they miss because they are working so much. I scraped the oven clean and put the kitchen back together after the weekend so that when my team came in today, they didn't have to worry about putting things back, and could get right to work. Then I worked on cleaning and setting up the tearoom for today, since I knew it was going to be a busy day. I also re-signed a new lease for my space in the tearoom. So, for my friends who ask how things are going and how we are doing, rest assured that as long as business continues to be decent, I don't plan on going anywhere. That makes me feel really good and I hope we can keep up all of our hard work.

Yesterday afternoon my friends at Florida Sports Coast contacted me to tell me that one of my tea hot toddies made it into an article about fourteen unique drinks to enjoy in the winter. It's on the website www.islands.com. When looking at the other drinks that were in the article, we are in there with some pretty big bars and restaurants in large hotels, like a casino in Las Vegas and several Westin and Ritz Carlton locations around the country, in addition to the country of Belize. What a great honor that our drink is among these other amazing establishments. I cannot wait to share with our guests so be on the lookout on our socials for the shares.

This morning is one of those mornings that I could've just gone back to bed. Do you ever have those days that, when you get up in the morning, you just know it's off? Today was that day. Not that anything was completely wrong, but it just seems like everything was a struggle. There are so many things that business owners deal with that people have no clue, they just seem to think it is all easy, fun and games.

This morning, I received an email from someone claiming I stole their photos to put on my website. I know it's a scam because the document it contains came from a Google account. When they filled in the information from our contact form on our website, they did not put their name or phone number, instead they put a gibberish bunch of letters. Still, it required some investigation to ensure that I hadn't done anything wrong. It took only a few minutes, but the reality is I have taken every photograph on my page. So, ha ha—jokes on them. But again, it's time out of my day that I needed to be doing other more productive things. It just never ends.

The tearoom and gift shop were both busy all day and again tonight for "Tea After Dark". Tomorrow night is our last "Tea After Dark", and I'm actually excited that these events will be done and that our special events this season have all been successful.

Tonight, I am home on the couch relaxing. My neck has been so bad over the past few days that I'm just not sure what to do anymore—between the spasms that move my head almost constantly and a nerve that is pinched to the point that if I turn one way or the other it sends pain down my arm and up my head. I don't have a solution, but I do know that as the day goes on, it gets much worse. When I lay down it feels great because there's no pressure on my head and my neck to keep my head still. However, I cannot lie in bed forever. As much as I wish I could, I think I would go crazy in the first day or two. So, I have to learn to manage my time and manage my movement. I know I can do it, but it's just such a struggle.

I'm hoping to lie on the couch and relax for a while, then to get a good night's sleep later tonight, so that maybe I will feel better in the morning. It's such a daily struggle, you can't even imagine unless you were going through it. I don't know what else to do and with working these long days. My tolerance seems to be less, and the pain is sometimes more intense. I will not stop living or moving because of the pain, but I can't even remember what it felt like before this disease. Still, I push on and will continue to do so until I can't do it anymore.

Here's to finishing out the week strong and getting ready to celebrate Christmas in a little over a week. I hope you are ready and have plans to have a really nice holiday this year.

December 23, 2020

The past week has been so busy that I have not been doing very well with keeping up with my posts. For those of you that have been missing me, I am sure now that the holidays are winding down for me, I will be able to keep up a little better.

Last week ended really strong at the tearoom and gift shop. I have been so overwhelmed by how many of our guests are visiting us and making sure that we are doing okay. It's also been amazing how many guests that visit are making it a point to shop small this year. We hear it every day, they want to put their money into our community and make it stronger. If nothing, 2020 has been positive in refocusing on spending money locally. I have seen it firsthand, and I have done it firsthand. It's a wonderful feeling to know that we contribute to keeping our local community strong and so many people support our community by shopping and eating with us.

Friends are also taking care of us—from Edie bringing us butterscotch candy, Fran's amazing Rum Cake, and so many Christmas cards. It truly warms my heart! I am so completely blessed.

On Sunday, Bryan, my mom, and my mother-in-law, and I put our Disney Annual passes to good use at the Magic Kingdom. We weren't in a rush, so we went later in the day, we rode a few rides, and then enjoyed dinner at Be Our Guest. The food was fabulous, and the restaurant is beautiful. It's a little loud in there, with tiled floors and high ceilings, but it was still very nice. I would definitely consider dining their again.

We spent the night at the Hilton by Disney Springs, as we have stayed there before. I have to say, while it was nice visiting the park, I was looking forward to the hotel stay the most. Not for any other reason, except it is so nice being able to relax and not be at home. Although, I love my house since most of the rooms have been decluttered.

Monday, we spent time at Hollywood Studios. We didn't have a plan that day, other than to try and get on Rise of the Resistance. Of course, that didn't happen because ten thousand other people in the park were trying to do the same thing. We enjoyed a meal at the 50's restaurant in the park. It was that good old-fashioned cooking...pot roast, meatloaf, fried chicken, and you get the drift. Our cast member/waiter was awesome and made the experience wonderful. I will definitely go back there again.

Overall, the trip was great. We laughed and relaxed—something we needed as we go through this holiday season.

One thing I have noticed over our last few trips to Disney is that I truly only go there to experience their culinary mastery. I have found that during the last few years I have become a foodie. I don't necessarily do a lot of eating, but I love blending flavors and creating dishes, and I truly enjoy good food. Building on flavors to make a delicious dish is something I look for when I go places. I find that I enjoy experiences when I can try new things, within reason as I'm still a very picky eater. It also makes me excited to come home and try making new things, putting food pairings together. So much so that I have recently thought about starting a food blog where I talk about my dining experiences—to highlight great food, showcase great combinations and share recipes. I am not for sure about it, but hey, why can't I be the next Paula Deen or Pioneer Woman? I think I could. So, my goal for the New Year: foodie blog that has me writing and doing videos. Before I do anything, I will plan it out, but it's an idea for now, and one that I'm going to explore in the New Year.

Now, I need to spend some time getting caught up on my shop. It has been utterly destroyed this season; we have been selling so many gifts. We also sold so much tea. I need to spend a few days just trying to get caught up on tea. Yesterday my team came in on a day we are closed and spent a few hours making tea bags and restocking the shelves. Today, they are virtually empty again...I really hope I can get a handle on it. That's one of my goals for the New Year...to be able to be better organized, so that our tea production runs more smoothly. Here's hoping!

Today was a very busy day in the tearoom. We had a full house, by today's standards. We were sure to space everyone and leave tables between guests. With our overflow area, we have done well to be able to keep the same number of guests, just over a larger footprint. In addition to the tearoom, the gift shop stayed busy, and Ava spent the day with me. Mostly, she stayed in my office and watched movies, except when we had a nice little tea lunch together. Yes, I cut her turkey and cheese sandwiches into a crown and tea pot, what aunt wouldn't? It was nice to sit down and have a pot of tea, too. Though I feel bad because my team works so hard, and they never get to take a break.

Well, it's time to get heading to bed. We have a busy day tomorrow and I still have to get some gifts ready. I am looking forward to relaxing after tomorrow, even if it's only for a day. My neck has been really hurting since the holiday season started. The stress and running around a lot hasn't given me much downtime to let the muscle calm down. Today, for a few hours, I was left staring at the ceiling, as the muscle was contracting constantly. I am looking forward to a few days after Christmas, when I can just relax and let the muscles in my body relax. I haven't wanted to rush the holidays, but now I'm ready for a little break.

I hope your time leading up to Christmas has been nice, that you have had a fun time gathering gifts for loved ones and have spent some time just enjoying the season. I know I have!

Here's to finishing the season strong and to me getting back on track with my daily posts, LOL. Have a great evening!

December 25, 2020

What a wonderful few days! Christmas Eve was pretty busy at our gift shop, and we had quite a few reservations as well. It made the time go by much faster than normal, and we were up a little bit over Christmas Eve last year. Hey, at this rate, anything even or up, I am just excited about. It's truly the little wins this year.

My amazing team took such good care of me. They signed a really nice card and gave me a gift. I know it's been a tough year for them too and it really made me feel good. Sometimes it's hard to know, as the boss, if you are making good or bad decisions and how you could improve them for your team and your business. I was just so humbled.

On Christmas Eve, we enjoyed a nice dinner at Longhorn. Bryan was looking forward to a good 'old fashioned' and a nice steak. To be honest, it was a really good night. The restaurant wasn't too packed, the staff was good, the food was good, and all around it was a great decision. I'm just still surprised that we were able to get our businesses closed and go to dinner together before the restaurant closed. It was a win-win for the night.

This morning, we woke up and enjoyed a nice breakfast with Ava and Deidra. We were able to give Ava her gifts and she loved them. She also gave us this beautiful canvas photo of her that was taken for her birthday earlier this year. It was just so beautiful, and it almost made Uncle Bryan tear up. I can't wait to hang it in our home. She and Deidra are such a blessing to us, and I just love our gift.

After breakfast we packed up the moms and headed out to Epcot. We decided on Epcot because we love their holiday kitchens and restaurants. It's also a park that's not as packed, so that's a plus. We arrived around 1:30 p.m. and started with a few drinks and some holiday treats. Some of the food and drinks were really unique. My favorite was the peppermint chocolate shake. It was more like a frosty, but with whipped vodka! So delicious and I was able to get the recipe, so I can't wait to recreate that one at home.

Tonight's special Christmas dinner was at Via Napoli, in Italy. It was delicious. Everything tonight seemed to be right on. I equate it to the fact that they don't take as many reservations and the restaurant is only half full, which means they can really concentrate on good service and even better food. Don't get me wrong—the last time we ate there it was good, but this time it was just close to perfect. I haven't been to a restaurant in years (I don't remember the last time) when my husband asked how something was made, and the server went to ask the chef how it was made so he could tell us. It was above and beyond, something that Disney used to be known for, but I felt was lacking in recent years. It was refreshing and made for a great evening and a great meal even better.

The last few years we have spent holiday time at Disney. During the past two years we have actually spent Christmas day at one of the parks. I've really enjoyed it because of how well they decorate and celebrate the holidays. But this year, while I enjoyed it, I almost wished we were having our annual brunch that we used to do. I love preparing the food and having friends and family over to our house. I am not sure if next year I want to stay home or not...I guess it depends on how the year goes. Or maybe I can do a brunch at home in the spring. Hmm...it's something to think about in the future.

I hope all of you had a great Christmas!

December 26, 2020

I'm so excited!! I just received the best Christmas gift ever! Facebook emailed me and gave me access back to my original page. I can't tell you how happy that makes me, because now I can access all my business pages. The only page that isn't coming up is The White Heron Tea & Gifts, which is my primary page. So, it looks like I'm going to have to access it through Bryan's page until they get that figured out.

At least I can restart my daily posts on here now. Yea!!

December 27, 2020

It's after the Christmas holiday and life is continuing to go on. I am so happy to be back on here, on my original page. It was a long process, but getting an email from Facebook with the code I needed to re-access my account was the absolute best Christmas gift I could have ever received.

The day after Christmas, our tearoom and gift shop were open. It was on the slower side, but we had already anticipated that. We had a few reservations, which was the whole reason we decided to open. I'm glad we did because, even though it was slower, we still had guests in for shopping, too. We were only open until 4 p.m., so it was just the perfect amount of time for us. I admit it was hard to get up and go to work on the day after Christmas, but we did it.

After we closed the shop, I came home and got to work on laundry. We were so busy during the holiday season that I had a hard time keeping up with all the linens. I managed to get two big loads of laundry done and two more loads in the machines. I love being busy, but getting caught up is rough. I also spent some time reading and doing some housework, definitely nothing glamorous.

For the past few weeks, I have been reading the book Be Our Guest from the Disney Institute. What an amazing book. It talks about their model of customer service and environment. One of the reasons I love going to Disney so much is because of all the thought that went into each aspect of their parks and environment. Yes, I like the rides and the fun stuff, but when I go to the parks, I really enjoy looking at all these different places and seeing how they planned them, and why. I finished the book on Sunday morning and now I am ready to look for another book. I just love reading!

Sunday was a relaxing day. I woke up and got back to work on the rest of the laundry. I had to get the tearoom linens done because Bryan informed me that he needed laundry done. LOL. The house laundry gets put on the back burner when it comes to getting the tearoom linen done. I got in a routine and was able to get whites in the dryer before I headed out for the day.

I headed over to the brewery to get some BBQ to eat. Bryan was brewing today and I have tried to get in the habit of going over to the brewery and eating lunch with him while he has some downtime. It was nice to enjoy lunch with him,

Jeff and Tara. I brought my work with me, so I managed to stay until Bryan and Jeff were done brewing and then headed home. I never stay that long, but I actually had fun visiting with our guests that are also my friends. I usually don't hang out there but with so many people I know coming in, it was nice to catch up with them.

Tonight, now that I'm home, my neck is giving me some real trouble. As I type this, my head is in a back position and if I sit back in my chair I will be staring at the ceiling. I can't get my neck to relax at all and the muscles are so tight. It's strange because I'm not stressed out at all, so I don't know what my head is being pulled backwards. I'm hoping that Bryan can help me by using one of my massagers to get the muscles to release. You can be sure I am going to be calling my awesome massage therapist tomorrow.

This week is going to be an odd week. I still have two more days off even though I will be working on the side. The tearoom opens for two days, and then we close for the New Year's holiday. It will be a total of five days off after New Year's Eve and I don't really know what I'm going to do with myself, LOL. The last time I had five days off, we were in Tennessee. This will be the first time in years that I will be home for such a long time at once. Wish me luck that I don't go crazy! LOL.

Here's hoping you have a great start to the last week of 2020.

December 29, 2020

Today was unlike any Monday I have experienced over the past few months. It was actually really nice. There was none of the crazy Monday stuff. I don't know, maybe the holidays and knowing 2020 is coming to an end is making my life a little more—Zen!?!

I woke up at my normal time this morning, but instead of getting up and moving, I decided to roll over and close my eyes. Usually I feel guilty doing that, like I should be up working, but not today. This morning, I actually didn't feel bad at all. In fact, I actually woke up feeling better and more rested. My neck was still bothering me, but I have learned this is a daily struggle that I am going to have to learn to deal with. This morning and all day, my head is still pulling back and to the right, sometimes the muscle gets so tight that my head really shakes.

After getting up and around, I decided to run to Publix and get some things I needed. It was a quick trip, and the store was pretty empty. While I don't mind going out, I am always careful, and I really like it when places aren't busy. I've been known to leave a place because it's too busy. After shopping, I came back home and decided to do some work from the comfort of my living room.

While I always have every intention of doing work from home, I rarely do it. Not today! Today I actually sat down and did some emailing, worked on info for some PR items, and got a few things on my list checked off. Granted it wasn't much, but I did it. I also managed to fold laundry, start more laundry, and empty the dishwasher. I really do enjoy being home, especially now that it has been mostly decluttered. It truly makes me feel so much better, and it makes me want to keep it this way. I can feel more cleaning coming over the next few weeks. Knowing how good I feel with what I have already done, I'm actually excited to be working on getting my life more organized.

Tonight, Bryan and I had a nice dinner out and then we stopped by my mom's house to grab a few things. We stood in the kitchen and chatted for about thirty minutes. It reminded me of old times. For the first time in a long time, I feel like we are starting to get back to a little bit of normalcy, although I know things will never be normal, just having a good feeling was nice.

Tomorrow, even though we are closed at both businesses, I have to get back to work. I am going to spend some time at my shop. I really have some cleaning up to do and I can't put it off anymore. We are also going to have a sale this week, so I need to get some things ready for that. I vowed to get myself organized (my records, etc.), so that next year will be much better. I also need to be able to focus on growing our two businesses and getting our third one off to the best start.

It's no secret that I have been battling lack of motivation because of how unorganized I have become—call it COVID-19 lack of motivation, basically I stopped doing everything when Covid hit in March. It's something that I have needed to do for months and it's definitely something I am not looking forward to, but I need to do that. Are any of you feeling that way? Like things just stopped in March and you just went through the motions? Well, I'm going to try to kick myself out of that and I need to soon.

Here's hoping your week is good and quick, and that you only have a few more days until you can have some downtime and enjoy the extended holiday weekend.

December 29, 2020

Today was another one of those days...the ones where I don't get up early...where I actually relax and get up when I'm ready. It felt really good and I'm sad that it's the last day I can do that until the end of the week.

I really didn't do too much today. I got the deposits done for the tearoom and gift shop and mom and I went out to Trinity to the bank and enjoyed Chick-fil-A for lunch. Well, let me tell you, that place is completely crazy. The traffic was lined up down State Road 54. Needless to say, we decided to come back downtown and have lunch at Rose's Bistro.

This afternoon, I worked on reconciling the books for the tearoom and the brewery. I only had to do two months' worth, so it wasn't too bad. It's just something I can't seem to keep up with, so it was good to take some time out today to get that done.

I also had my Tea Mastermind meeting tonight. I can't tell you how much I love that group and how motivated they keep me. Tonight, because of the holidays, it was just a time for us to catch up and chat. We talked about all kinds of things, and I realized a few things that I need to do. We were talking about goals for the New Year, and I realized that I need to sit down and redo my one-year, three-year and five-year goals for the tearoom. I did it when we originally opened and we have stayed pretty much on track, even this year. But now it's time to take it to the next level. Good thing I have a few days to come up with the plan...

Tonight, Bryan and I enjoyed a nice dinner at Boulevard Beef & Ale. He had to transfer his pale ale into the carbonation tank, so he had some time for dinner. I'll tell you; he works so hard. Not only does he have to deal with me and my crazy neck and not being able to do a lot of things, but he also keeps his brewery running and holds down a full-time job. People look at me and say they don't know how I do it...well I don't know how he does it. He is truly my blessing.

Now it's time to wind down for the night. I am reading the Time Magazine about Walt Disney and totally loving it. I just finished Be Our Guest from the Walt Disney Institute and found it just fascinating. People ask me why I like to go to Disney so much...it's not for the rides...it's for the genius that is Disney. I find the whole story fascinating, so I am so excited that my team got me the magazine about him. I am looking forward to continuing to read it and see what other kinds of ideas I can pick up for my business.

Hoping your week is going good so far!

December 30, 2020

I wasn't really sure what to expect today. For some reason when I look at my tearoom calendar and see it very full, I'm always a little panicked about how we'll be able to handle it. It's not that we can't, but it's that I want everybody's experience to be so perfect that I put a lot of pressure on us to make sure that everything is right. Of course, today was no exception and everything went fine, even though I do stress out about it.

The tearoom was quite full today though we continue to maintain social distancing standards. I am so glad that we are able to have a little extra space to lay out our room to offer tea for so many guests at one time. I am so truly blessed that this holiday season has been so wonderful in our tearoom. I am excited about with the New Year has to offer.

Tonight Bryan and I went to dinner with our friends Connie and John. It has been months since we have been down to BackDraughts in Tarpon Springs for pizza. I think I was missing their wings most of all. Of course, it did not disappoint and everything was delicious. It was nice to get out on a weeknight and have dinner with friends. It's something we rarely take time to do, but I plan to do more of this next year.

On our way back home, coming down Main Street, Bryan was going to drop me off at home before heading to the brewery. But as we approached the brewery, there was a firetruck and ambulance in front of the building. Of course we didn't go home, we ended up parking in going to see what was going on. Apparently, somebody started celebrating New Year's way too early and had way too much to drink, then decided to drive. She attempted to pull into a parallel parking spot before she passed out at the wheel, got sick, and went to the bathroom all over herself. Good thing she didn't seriously hit anybody. Rather, she hit a friend's car in the back end. There wasn't any damage and no one was hurt, so that was good, but I'm sure she's going to be feeling it when she wakes up in jail in the morning, LOL.

In other news, tomorrow is the last day the tearoom and gift shop will be open for 2020. It has been a long time coming. While this year had some very unusual and unpredictable ups and downs, it still feels like the longest year ever. I am looking forward to recouping over the next few days and getting us set up for the New Year. There are some very exciting things ahead for us and I can't wait to see what 2021 has in store. I will also be working on our one-year, three-year and five-year plans for the tearoom and I can't wait to see what I come up with.

I hope the last day of the current year is a good one for you. I can't wait to see you next year!

Final Thoughts

Looking back on it, I doubt any of us could have imagined a year like 2020. And while there was a time when things seemed to be 'touch and go', I think that everyone did the best they could with what they had.

I, for one, had no idea how my businesses would survive, or how to make sure that I, and those around me had what we needed to come out of the year as unscathed as possible. It was a lonely time in history. To this day, people still talk about how alone they felt being separated from loved ones, not being able to be social.

I don't think it was possible not to be changed by 2020. I know that I was. In addition to managing my daily interactions and dealings, I lost some amazing people along the way. Still, four years later, not a day goes by that I don't think of them and miss them tremendously.

Today we press on, living a life that is almost back to the normal that we knew before 2020. It's a time to celebrate joy and human connection, to be encouraging and respectful, to look out for those around us, and to help each other when we can.

I hope you have enjoyed reading what I wrote during 2020. It served as a glimmer of hope to my friends and family, and now hopefully it is that to you. You see, no matter where we are, no matter what we do, we can always be a glimmer, a glimpse, a bright light in the darkness of someone's life. That, my friends, is the true meaning behind what I wrote.

With Much Love,

Kelly

PS. At the request and encouragement of several friends and family members, I continued writing nearly daily posts through 2023. Be on the look out for my future adventures in upcoming books, and follow me online.

Kelly's Top Picks of 2020

Throughout my book, I mention quite a few that I visited or worked with. While it's nearly impossible to list them all, here are the ones that I mentioned the most. If I mentioned a place in my book that you are interested in, a quick online search should pull them up. *At the time of printing, all businesses were open and thriving.

BackDraughts: www.backdraughts.com

Boulevard Beef and Ale: www.boulevardbeef.com

Chocolates by Michelle: www.chocolatesbymichelle.com

Gatlinburg Brewing Company:

    www.gatlinburgbrewing.com

Heros Downtown Subs and Salads:

    www.herosdowntownsubs.com

Herschel's Scratch Kitchen:

    www.herschelsscratchkitchen.com

MMMM Delicious Cupcakes: www.mdcupcakes.com

Sip on Grand: www.sipongrand.com

Thai Bistro: www.thai-bistro.com

William Dean Chocolates: www.williamdeanchocolates.com

Kelly's Businesses:

Coastline Salt Room: www.coastlinesaltroom.com

Cotee River Brewing Company: www.coteeriverbrewing.com

Driftwood Tea Company: www.driftwoodteacompany.com

The White Heron Tea & Gifts: www.thewhiteheronfl.com

The End
(of 2020)